ALSO BY ANNA JOHNSON

Handbags: The Power of the Purse
Three Black Skirts: All You Need to Survive

The Yummy Mummy Manifesto

BALLANTINE BOOKS | NEW YORK

THE YUMMY MUMMY
MANIFESTO

Baby, Beauty,
Balance, and Bliss

Anna Johnson

A Ballantine Books Trade Paperback Original

Copyright © 2008 by Anna Johnson
Illustrations copyright © 2008 by Anna Johnson
Illustration design development by Maree Oaten

Published in the United States by Ballantine Books,
an imprint of The Random House Publishing Group,
a division of Random House, Inc., New York.

BALLANTINE and colophon are registered
trademarks of Random House, Inc.

LIBRARY OF CONGRESS CATALOGING-IN-PUBLICATION DATA
Johnson, Anna.
The yummy mummy manifesto: baby, beauty, balance, and bliss / Anna
Johnson.
p. cm.
Includes index.
ISBN 978-0-8129-7582-6 (pbk.)
1. Motherhood. 2. Pregnancy. I. Title.
HQ759.J617 2008   306.874'3—dc22   2007041797

Printed in the United States of America

www.ballantinebooks.com

9 8 7 6 5 4 3 2 1

Book design by Dana Leigh Blanchette

For my mother, whose love, generosity, and deeply creative spirit helped my father, my brother, and me blossom in every way. Thank you for teaching me the power of family.

PREFACE

Say It Loud: I'm a Yummy Mummy and I'm Proud

Osho, the Indian mystic, once wrote that when a child is born, a mother is born too. A woman, in essence, that never existed before. I feel this experience is true of all mothers. Most of us are astonished at the compromises we make, the creative solutions we concoct, and the accomplishments we manage to achieve, given, quite often, impossible circumstances. I began this book at three months pregnant and finished it on my son's second birthday. To mother and write at home, I had to completely reinvent time. The notion of an ordinary workday was inverted; after I spent all day with my son, Marcello, I sat down to write at nine o'clock at night, worked for five hours, slept for five hours, and began all over again at seven in the morning. As the hiding places from my curious toddler diminished, I found myself taking phone meetings on the silent bathroom floor and learning to compress the needs of a day into the solid gold of his nap times, which shrank minute by minute, day by day. On this journey, everything needless fell away, and resources and pleasures I once took for granted shifted in importance.

Like all new mothers, I got a taste of balance one minute and a crushing sense of inadequacy the next. Anyone who has not had a baby or raised a child has yet to learn "the dance," the moves for which are a combination of crazy kicks (distracting and amusing husband and child), swift dodges (evasion is our art), and violent swan dives (flying across a room when needed). As my breasts gently drooped, my son slowly blossomed and, blissfully, my soul stretched to accommodate it all. I felt bigger, in a good way.

The title *The Yummy Mummy Manifesto* was always meant to be tongue in chic. It began as a book about style and retaining the self and became, by necessity and learned experience, something much broader. In my own way, I have tried to bridge the gaps that I kept tripping over. Regarding pregnancy, I could find very little (in books, websites, or magazines) that moved beyond generic maternity style or explored the real nuances of dressing a lumpy little bump and a huge, water-heavy belly, and everything in between. I also discovered that there is virtually nothing for the pregnant bride. I couldn't find much about pregnant sexuality or desire, either. I could find even less about joy—the real joy in carrying a baby or birthing one, and the joy in the privilege of raising them up, day by day. In retrospect, I see the arc of maternal pleasure beginning with the mystical moment of conception, blossoming with the bold act of birth, and steadily building every year. A wise mother always looks for ways to find creative release for her children while factoring a few sneaky, selfish pleasures for herself. It is this tango, between moments of selfless, loving care and moments of deeply personal respite, that makes mothering and family living fun and emotionally rich.

Easygoing, sensual, colorful, individual, creative, and relaxed mothering is not the easiest path to take, perhaps in part because it is not supported by the popular view. Reading many books and websites about parenting, I sense a controlling perfectionism and apprehensive obsession with details and milestones (sleep! solids! poo!) that miss the whole. The desire for a sense of mastery is possibly the worst place to start in enjoying life with a child, or connecting with them. But go tell that to the alpha moms! The mania and pace that plague modern motherhood begin with our hysterically monitored pregnancies and continue into every stage of a child's early years. Underscoring it all is a nagging sense of competition among mothers: Who can ice the prettier cupcake! Whose kid can count to ten by age two! Who can look glam at the school gates! But who among us is ready to stop and question the source of such standards? And, more pressingly, what really constitutes being a "good mother"? Is it baking, floor polishing, booking toddler Gymboree classes, and buying educational toys every quarter? Or is it something as simple as being present and in the moment with deep love and respect for your child? If we all slow down and realize that the false velocity and perfectionism of modern intensive mothering are commercially driven, and are at best a crude marketing ruse playing on our deepest vulnerabilities, we might have a chance of really enjoying our motherhood in a far more personal way.

Mothers need to be able to dream on the job, pursue their own notions of bliss, and impart way more joy into the complex grind of getting kids raised. When we find the space to reflect, even for a few commercial-free minutes a day, we usually find the answers and the deeply buried instincts that were there all along.

Modern mothers need to come together despite the fact the media love to tear us apart, imposing disparate prototypes of mothering styles all neatly designed to war against one another: working mother versus at-home mother, yummy mummy versus slummy mummy, soccer mum versus slacker mum, alpha versus beta, perfectionist versus good-enough, lactivist versus formula mum, home birther versus hospital birther, single mum versus married mum, and younger versus older.

These highly entertaining polarities only succeed in turning us all into cartoons. But do we have to choose? Can you not have a shoe in each camp; kitten heel on one foot, Birkenstock on the other? Given

how complex life is, you will probably occupy any number of these personae. I was shocked at the diversity of my own experience while writing my own mad mama book: In less than two years, I lived three and a half months as essentially a single mother, traveled first class with my son and also hitchhiked with him on a country road, fed him organic veggie burgers and street-vendor hot dogs, sleep-trained him for one night and went to him for the other six hundred nights. I shared him with five different carers and never spent a night apart from him, I loved his father passionately and fought him just as vehemently, I dressed up for work and let the skinny jeans go, forever. I was more broke than I have ever been in my life and happier than I have ever known. I tried to make wild rice pilaf but fell in love with frozen pizza. I saw a personal trainer but ate all my son's leftovers. I remain to this day a simultaneous failure and a raving success.

Given all of these contradictions, I am happy to rescue the mantle of the Yummy Mummy from cynical disdain and even overkill. I loved this phrase when I first heard it nearly a decade ago, and I love it still; it hints at delight and suggests desire and a touch of mayhem. Being yummy does not mean being ridiculously posh. I am definitely not referring to the $300 blow-out mamas who lunch on wilted arugula with a squad of nannies in the wings. Nor am I trying to concoct or uphold yet another "type" of mother, designed to be unleashed on her opposites or imposed as a gold standard. Nor do I believe that lipstick and red stilettos will save your marriage, though they might rescue your sense of humor. No. When I say *yummy,* I mean joyous, naughty, delicious, creative, intrepid, and sensually alive.

Deep down, there is something subversively, rebelliously, naturally yummy in us all, and to abnegate that for a taupe sweater is a crime. I am not preaching a decadent disconnect à la celebrity moms, though there are certainly many choice moments to drink pink champagne in the bath. There will also be just as many moments to strip off heels and makeup and dance naked in the rain, utterly primal and uncontrived. A pagan priestess unleashed in suburbia.

And, there may also come a time when all you've sacrificed and learned will serve a higher cause, and your newfound strength might actually be the seeds of substantial social change. The revolutionary Yummy Mummy—why not? More militant books than mine have suggested that mothers have the power (and responsibility) to transform the world and must start with demanding their own rights and their children's first.

Garnering this hard-earned empathy and personal power, and acting upon it, is the best gift you could give a child, in an apron, in a little black dress, or with two bare feet planted firmly on the ground. Go forth and dare to be disruptive.

Deliciously so.

MY RED HOT MAMA

Motherhood Made More Delicious

How do you remember your mother, and how do you wish to be remembered as a mother? It's a simple question with a vast web of intimate associations. My mother was very young, just twenty, when I was born, and it seemed natural for her to wear childish denim miniskirts and corky heels to match mine. In 1972 mother-and-daughter fashion in New York City was at its most irreverent. We swanned into the supermarket in sequined berets, donned deco vintage fox capes at Halloween, and strutted silk velvet flapper dresses in broad daylight. My mother didn't iron, wear face powder, or a bra. She wore floral silk kimonos and her black hair in two thick black braids to her hips. She never left the house without black kohl eyeliner and mascara. She never had a proper makeup mirror or a proper ladylike handbag that snapped shut. Nothing she wore snapped shut. She loved

French perfume that smelled like burned vanilla and honeysuckle, and patted simple Nivea Creme on her pale, pale skin. She was yummy.

Thinking of your mother as a woman takes the distance of decades. The realization might happen when you're flipping through a book of old photographs or wearing a dress she once owned. That strange moment when you are precisely her age with children of your own, when you feel a stab of remorse for not seeing her as she might have seen herself: thrifty, extravagant, vain, self-sacrificing, dreamy, making do, or secretly splurging. All those small details you missed while wanting her to be the stable heart of your world.

As time passed, my mother dressed more quietly, in increasingly subtle and somber shapes and colors. Her concession to glamour remained a massive aquamarine ring, cherry red lipstick, and the black eyeliner—which was never abandoned. Age doesn't just steal youth; it also dilutes its radical essence and one's will to experiment, rebel, and provoke. Perhaps children also help rob that spirit by embodying it so fiercely themselves. And perhaps many mothers simply shift their focus away from the self, only to regain it in fragments.

My ideal is to remain as passionate as my offspring and not to abandon polka dots, vintage Stones albums, or black lace half-cup bras under the dull weight of practicality and sheer exhaustion. You can blame a lot of personal changes on parenting, but there is no excuse for beige, or elastic waistbands, or tortoiseshell Alice bands, or buffed brown pumps. The slide into dreary good taste is a thoroughly adult choice. Like buying a Volvo instead of a Jeep.

Unwittingly or not, we all dress by consensus. Fashion (and even antifashion) is communicated by group values. It happens in college, it happens in offices, it happens in the playground. Some social cliques prize plissé Hermès print scarves and skinny alligator belts, and some breed angora sweaters and ballet flats like rabbits. Yet no matter which unspoken uniform prevails, the temptation to conform rather than dress for your own soul holds powerful sway. Mothers seem especially prone to peer group pressure in the effort to fit in. My girlfriend Rosanna has the hottest, longest, brownest legs at playgroup and wears miniskirts and platform clogs. She's also forty-three. I have heard the sound of hissing followed by a sudden hush when she enters a room full of conservative mothers. And no matter how trendy, sensual, confident, or free you feel as a mother, this sort of social censorship is powerful.

There are many ways to silence your sense of self as the years pass. Clothing, perhaps, is the obvious signpost: blander colors, higher necklines, fuzzier textures, and an emphasis on comfort. Flip through any department store Mother's Day catalog, and you'll clearly see what I mean; "Mom" clothes have always been set at a lower voltage than high fashion. Movie mums often have their clavicles concealed with bits of lace poking out from collar and cuff. TV moms wear canary yellow and way too much pale blue. Words like *cozy, soft, homey,* and *comfortable* are associated with the clothes of motherhood, and, frankly, they make my blood run cold. I do not want to dress like an apple pie in human form or blend in with my collection of 1940s prairie quilts. I don't want people to describe me as a "small floral print" kind of woman or, worse still, see me as a watercolor study rather than a portrait in oils. I am happy to risk the future embarrassment of my child. To suffocate him in a cloud of L'Heure Bleue as I reach into his bed with long black satin opera-gloved arms on a Friday night, or as I walk him to preschool in a vintage kimono and hot-pink espadrilles.

The desire to keep yourself vivid and delicious *with* children is not just a matter of spicy contrivance, such as donning silk pajamas to clean the house. Nor is it as simple as baking jam tarts in a tight red sweater like lovely Nigella Lawson. Diana Vreeland was not famous for earthy glamour or even a trace of mumsy style, yet she had some remarkable ideas about creativity and children. She's the one who urged parents to plaster vast maps on the nursery wall to broaden a child's world view, to embroider a baby's pillowcase with a miniature galaxy of stars, and to get a kid to wear a tiny green Tyrolean hat. "The smaller the child, the longer the feather," she wrote in her famous *Harper's Bazaar* column "Why Don't You?" Not bad for 1937. Role

models for the ideal Yummy Mummy often come to me from artists, from eccentrics, and from women who never had children at all. I love to imagine how Frida Kahlo would have painted her nursery or to picture Katharine Hepburn teaching toddlers how to yell at the ocean or throw tiny snowballs at picket fences. Picture Gertrude Stein teaching the alphabet for the first time or Marilyn Monroe showing her teenage daughter how to enter a crowded room. I invoke all of those spirits when I think about my son, hoping he'll understand why I need thirty minutes in the bath alone with Mahler, why I play tigers on the Persian carpet with Daddy, and why the television is hidden away with the good china for disasters and special occasions.

Sure, there are bound to be times when a woman doesn't feel the will to be blazingly original, sexy, particularly chic, or even present to the endless demands of domestic life. When existence is a perpetual balancing act, routine and regiment seem a lot easier than constant reinvention. But for every full freezer and well-planned playdate, there is a random, refreshing alternative. A brief burst of light where you shock yourself out of well-worn habits. The night you let everyone eat breakfast cereal for dinner and play the radio full blast. The day you wear your college jeans and an outrageous pair of satin heels to the game with your husband. The rainy afternoon when you decide to paint the living room blueberry, "just because."

Becoming yummier doesn't have to be such a radical departure from normality. It could be as simple as being a little more yourself. Of course, this involves a very different sort of sacrifice: namely, a healthy dose of selfish ritual. Composing lists that have nothing to do with the family and everything to do with your secret inner life. Putting serious time into a disciplined passion that only you enjoy, be it tennis or salsa. Giving yourself a simple pocket of ten minutes every day where no one can reach you. Meeting your husband like a lover at the cinema on a Monday afternoon. Or finally buying the red dress you've wanted for a decade and actually wearing it. Damn the torpedoes.

Five years ago, my mother came to New York City and bought a floor-length silk and velvet hand-embroidered coat from Bergdorf

Goodman. The price of a business ticket to Paris or four refrigerators. Right at the precipice of purchase, she had a wave of panic and trepidation. "What is the occasion? When will I wear it and where on earth…?" We both stood there staring at the absurd luxury in a gleaming full-length mirror. Growing up, she had always told me to make the moment. She promised me that theatrical people always found the circus somewhere in town. And that there would always be someone who objected to the sun shining too brightly or roses smelling too sweet. "Mum," I said squarely, "*you* are the occasion, and, to quote Tallulah Bankhead, it *is* always cocktail hour *somewhere* in the world." We laughed all the way down Fifth Avenue and felt decadently, defiantly, and very blatantly . . . yummy.

Contents

PART 1
THE GODDESS EXPECTING

PART 2
STYLE SURVIVAL FROM YEAR ZERO

PART 3
TODDLERS, TIARAS, AND
EVERYDAY TRANSGRESSIONS

Part 1

THE GODDESS EXPECTING

1. MORNING SICK IN MANOLOS

Finding Your Feet and Holding Your Ground

Standing on an Upper Manhattan sidewalk in early spring, I saw a pregnant woman bounding toward me in three-inch heels. At first I was appalled, thinking immediately of her spine, the stress on her lower back and hips. But my knee-jerk shock swiftly melted into a smile. The lady was zigzagging through a traffic jam in that madly determined way that only New Yorkers know. She looked like a missile with a bump. On the very same day in the West Village, I crossed a woman on the street who was cradling her swollen belly with two splayed hands, her eyes half shut and her mouth half open. It was as if she had begun to yawn, or sigh, or moan, and simply left her mouth ajar, ready for the next wave of awesome emotion to engulf her face. She looked almost as if she were in early labor. She might have been. To the naked eye, she was uncouth, so openly vulnerable

and unwieldy in a city that jealously guards its space and conceals its frailties.

If you don't have a child, it is all too easy to make snap judgments about the way a pregnant woman should be. In public. In private. In bed. At the office. Overdressed, underdressed, lethargic, overweight, or ungroomed. Fashion and society at large have applied static standards of style, diet, and deportment to the gravid woman, as if there is a tidy, correct, or polite way to be pregnant! The social neurosis about the aesthetics of pregnancy manifests most clearly in the coverage of celebrities. The movie star who carries her twins in overalls is branded "lazy," the rock star who wears a message T-shirt and a mini with her bundle is "tacky," and those who gain too much weight (and don't shed it fast enough afterward) are simply "out of control." The constant policing of the fashion choices and weight fluctuations of the famous might seem like harmless fun in the context of a gossip magazine, but the ramifications for all mothers run deeper. If we're willing to judge the heavy pregnant body of a movie star mum so damningly or to celebrate her radical (and probably unnatural and unhealthy) postpartum weight loss, then how are we looking at ourselves?

The words *pregnancy style* too often contradict the very personal style of each woman's pregnancy. Mainstream fashions are repeatedly grafted onto very different bodies in very different contexts. In the corporate world, it is common practice for an employee to conceal her pregnancy for up to four months (as much for office politics as for health and discretion) and then to continue her term dressing as if in deeply conservative denial. In offices we are praised for carrying small, carrying neat, and, implicitly, performing with the same vigor as non-pregnant coworkers. Never mind that we might want to slam the door shut and lie down on the floor, or wear desert boots instead of pumps that pinch a swollen foot. When I look at career gear in maternity stores, it always strikes me as a uniform of dreary concealment with a heavy emphasis on business shirts. Worn, one presumes, to assert the fact that a woman loaded up with hormones can still mean business. It's not easy to fit in with a structure of manic efficiency when you are carrying a child, since work, by its very nature, is an environment of criticism, competition, and scrutiny. To survive the gap that grows between the private journey of your body and the grind of your public duties, I suggest work clothes that feel like shelter: soft shawls, wraps, and shrugs that make you feel cozy and protected under the glare of office lights. Generous, flattering swing jackets, karate-style pants, 1960s A-line trapeze dresses, a bright trench coat in the best fabric you can afford, and boots in a soft, stretchy suede that expand with you. Competence comes with confidence, so planning a strong work wardrobe for your entire term is not a matter of whim. On really tough days, you might just need the armor of a little black dress that is not so little.

The trick with feeling solid and proud in all your changes is to see yourself as growing, not merely getting bigger. In a world that fears and loathes *fat,* the expanding belly and natural abundance of flesh that comes with the territory fly in the face of chic. How many women truly revel in their fecund forms for the whole nine yards and almost ten months? How many cases of postpartum depression are anxiously wed to body issues and not to hormones at all? The pressure to fit in confronts the pregnant woman at every turn. Yet this ought to be the one moment in life when you can truly be outrageously, unapologetically, perhaps shockingly yourself. I love to imagine that the gusto, abundance, and unpredictable volatility of being pregnant alters a woman and stays with her forever.

I couldn't wear anything terribly trendy when I carried my son. Tight jeans, zip-up knee-high boots, short skirts, and anything bare or backless was off-limits, and yet it was my sexiest style experience to date. In the place of explicit clothes, I found pieces rich in sensuality. I was and will probably remain the plus-size sex kitten, and *no one* will make me trade these breasts for a narrow set of hips and knobby set of knees. If my body can't conform to the straight lines of pencil skirts, cinch-waist belts, and tight tailored sleeves, then my hands and feet

can still face Madison Avenue. I was one of those fashion-damaged pregnant chicks with a thing for accessories. I was morning sick in Manolos. But when my body bloomed and stayed blossomed a full three dress sizes larger, I didn't freak. I migrated.

Forced into a tight corner by a body that had been Botticelli and was now speeding toward Rubens, I took to theatrics: a fabulous skirt from Rajasthan worn low on the hip with a lime green camisole, a shrunken denim jacket and many bracelets, capelets and crocheted shawls to lend height, and a total banishment of anything resembling a trouser leg. Trawling eBay for any $20 velvet dress that could be cut in half or handkerchief skirts that be could transformed with a gros-grain ribbon waistband, I became crafty about my maternity groove.

The relief that came with adapting these curious vintage pieces and finding flattering shapes that actually felt pretty was my first revelation in yummy motherhood. For every problem that pops up, or out, there is a creative solution. Despite the tempting idea that maternity style can be bought in a box with an A-line frock and neat little black leggings to help you cakewalk through it, the truth is that bodies, lives, and personal vanities are far more diverse than that. If a girl *hates* leggings in civilian life, why should she suddenly assume some Marcel Marceau identity at eighteen weeks? I never imagined that I could look better and revel in dressing up as an urban belly dancer/Storyville Madam/Grecian naiad when I was pregnant, but it happened. My maternity gave some of the best style ideas and jiggle-proof solutions I've ever had, and two more amusing assets besides.

I will tell anyone in the first year of mothering to hang on to her pregnancy rights (the cravings, the emotions, the attitude, and, yes, even those ten pounds) and to fixate less on going back to what she was before. Once you're a mother, it's all about more. You can't be less now; you have come through your fertility rites, and, frankly, size 6 holds little substance. It isn't easy to be expansive in a culture that is constantly urging women to contract, shrink, and diet to the point of disappearance, but that is probably the greatest challenge of Yummy

Motherhood: to feel scrumptious every step of the way. Proudly so. Pregnancy is the milestone we carry up front. This is the most glorious moment to be all of your many selves. Never will you occupy so many variations of one body in such a short space of time. And, hopefully, never will you feel so free, in high heels, in overalls, or in nothing at all.

2. THE BODY BLOSSOMED
Seven Yummy Self-image Secrets

People tell you that carrying a baby is sexy, liberating even, and it is hard to believe them. The physical inconvenience and the inflated scale are not images we associate freely with pleasure. But pregnancy *is* hot, as well as heavy.

For me, the first inkling of the rampant sensuality to come arrived while watching the Oscars on TV in 2004. Uma Thurman held the red carpet for ransom in a black evening dress that was almost all bustline. Her ivory bosom was of the quivering, milky caliber that could reduce the entire Italian national soccer team to prayer.

Cleavage as silencer. It was not a thought I had entertained since Lady Diana Spencer all but fell out of her black taffeta corset dress getting out of a Rolls-Royce on her first evening debut with Charles. Big, deliberately exposed boobs are such a taboo in so many contexts, especially for the career girl; yet on a pregnant woman, magnificent breasts take on a mythical resonance that transcends social mores or private inhibitions. They are not the distorted, cartoonlike, massive silicone orbs on a rail-thin body: the Hollywood norm. They are not prurient, comical, or simply decorative. Maternal breasts are vital function wed to divine form. Organic to the whole body in full bloom, they exist in proportion to a gorgeous swell that rises like a prelude at the clavicle and explodes into a full rapturous overture at the belly. I wanted them. The fleshy ankles could be dealt with.

It wasn't until I occupied a completely barrel-shaped body that I got to enjoy total freedom from scathing self-criticism for the first time in my adult life. Usually the mirror is a minefield where faults are cataloged in running order. When pregnant, I saw my looking glass as an unfolding memoir of gestation. I was way too busy gently caressing my sculptural orbs and shiny, remarkable bulge to let the eye drift down to the outrageous deposits of fat on my derriere and thighs. When I did catch a fleeting eyeful lumbering out of the bath or struggling to wriggle into a slipper, I'd greet the fecund blubber as future food. Baby food, that is. "Ahhh, milk for little Marcellino" is a lovely thought to have when confronted with a sea of dimpled skin. That's how I saw it and how I still see it. Pregnancy ought to dilute every woman's unrealistic body image or tendency to mentally self-mutilate, forever. For the first time, perhaps one feels the power of occupying the body from the inside out and not in that anxious state of being on the outside looking in.

The sheer primal force of creating life out of flesh is too profound to squander on anxiety about bulk or even on the constantly shifting caprices of fashion itself. When you are pregnant, it doesn't really matter what is "in" that season. You can adapt, ignore, or totally reinvent style, and it's the best time to do so. To truly enjoy every month and every moment of your term in style takes certain basic pieces. More important yet is a philosophy of pleasure and acceptance that will carry you through your best and worst moments. It is highly probable that others will foil your joy with fleeting remarks, silly pet names, or irrational fears. When my mother first saw me showing, she called me a fat teenager. Nice. One well-meaning coworker exclaimed in front of an entire office, "Oh but you're *huuuuggge!*" And husbands can't help but be occasionally awful. *Lump.* That was my name for the last ten weeks of my term. "Lump!" he exclaimed with vigor, slapping me on the rump and observing that I did not simply have a visible panty line but, in fact, four bottoms dissected by a pair of bikini briefs stretched to the limit.

Secretly, I think people (men especially) are confronted by the potent power of pregnancy, and they deflect their awe with deprecation. But one can only pity those who fail to marvel at this brief journey of transformation. It's an adventure so much deeper than sheer size, and the beauty of it dwells in the physical intimacy between you, your skin, and your child.

Nine Yummy Self-image Secrets

1. *Dress for your dreams.* Fantasy and romance are rarely terms we associate with maternity style, but this is the moment to dress like a Charlotte Brontë heroine, a Greek goddess, or a saucy Shake-spearean wench. Even if only on Saturday nights. Let's face it, you have the rest of your life to wear the classic patent leather pumps, little black dress, and pearls.

2. *Balance basics with small luxuries.* Like shopping for "normal" fashion, it pays to balance designer items against less expensive basics. Get your denim Capris at good old Gap and splurge on a ruche-fronted poplin shirt and a keyhole peasant blouse from a designer you adore. Try to know the difference between a disposable necessity and a piece that can live on for another year or three. Well-made stretch fabric pieces in silk, lace, and cotton that button or unzip in front are your friends.

3. *Tend to the details.* Grooming is a mood booster and a body smoother. Control your hair, and you can control the world. View

pampering as a pleasure with great cumulative benefits for your skin, hair, and nails. Once the baby arrives, your makeup bag might gather cobwebs, so now is the time to preen mindlessly.

4. *Change your icons.* Create a collage of positive pregnant images and put them in dime-store frames around the house. It sounds almost childish, but every time you see these Gustav Klimt earth goddesses and rosy baroque nymphs, you'll get that extra reinforcement of how precious and brief pregnancy is.

5. *Build a strong foundation.* The day you find a bra and panties that don't laugh at you is the day you can truly revel in a pregnant body. Avoid colors that look elderly or surgical. Add your own lace if you have to and wear underwire on special occasions when the monobreasted look becomes stale. Pumpkin Wentzel, the designer behind the label Pumpkin Maternity, told me about the importance of good underwear during your gestation. "If you are wearing pretty and supportive undergarments, it makes dressing more of a joy. I became a fan of the thong during my first pregnancy, but I can also understand women loving those baggy 'granny' knickers at full term." A mother of two, Pumpkin says the best thing about pregnant style is actually overcoming niggling body issues in favor of the *big* picture. "Having your body change in ways you can't control allows a woman to let go of a lot of self-obsession. This selflessness is the first step to becoming a parent." Amen!

6. *Keep a salty sense of humor.* Fertile, fabulous, full figured, and free spirited—there is nothing more attractive than a woman owning up to her changes with grace and a belly laugh. The funniest item I found on the mommy market was a T-shirt that read "Got Breast Milk?" Getting the chance to wear that would make all of the hard work worth it!

7. *Accessorize your adventure.* Don't be the pregnant plain Jane! Accent your new boobs with a velvet-trimmed shawl for evening or a double strand of faux emeralds. Wear anything now that might become a liability later on: chokers, chandelier earrings, trailing ringlets—all of which will be impossible once baby starts clutching.

8. *Think and plan* big. The rare moments of humiliation that happen in a pregnancy usually occur when clothes suddenly stop fitting. This can literally take place in the space of days. Running out for juice, you can't do your coat up. Suddenly you can't zip up your boots over burgeoning calves. A favorite knee-length skirt becomes a mini. To avoid feeling like you are experiencing puberty all over again, plan to have larger pieces at hand. This is especially true of bras, pants, outerwear, and, in the very last weeks, shoes. Have some larger stretch ballet flats or even chic Chinese slippers at the ready!

9. *Cherish your body every day.* So much of how you look clothed reflects how you feel naked. Start with the talk you give yourself when confronted with a mirror. Are those habitual barbs aimed at your butt or belly really relevant anymore? In their place, say affirmations (even if you begin by only half believing them!), chant a mantra, or simply hug yourself. Making up kooky rituals in the shower, writing a body journal, or belly dancing to Bjork are all baby steps on the path to physical self-acceptance. In the process of learning to look at yourself with love, you will be amazed at the warmth and beauty of your gestating body as it blooms, and this should quickly replace any anxieties you may be harboring about body image. In pregnancy, *everything* is perfection. With this single truth in mind, think of all the compliments you can pay yourself for the few seconds that you share with your reflection each day. When you send love to your body, the baby is listening, and he really doesn't care if your jeans fit properly or not.

3. WHAT TO EAT AND WHY

Creating the Pregnant Power Pantry

I can hear the collective groan or even the sound of fingertips skipping over this very page to get to the sex chapters. *Stop!* I promise this is not going to be the bit where I righteously tell you to eat your greens. Pregnant women are always being told to chomp broccoli stalks nonstop. They are told to down five servings of vegetables (not including parsley), six servings of grain, four servings of protein, five servings of fruit, and eight glasses of water a day. Not to mention also squeezing in oily fish, fatty calcium-rich cheese and yogurt, and a double serving of protein. Technically, these maxims are important, but they make for very dull reading and a seemingly laborious existence. First, it sounds like a full-time job to persevere through so many food groups; second, your nausea might have you stuck on doughnuts—end of story—and third, it's very hard to make excellent nutrition suddenly integral to your life if you have never been a particularly diligent eater. For the habitual grazer, the massive food pyramid might seem suffocating, and for the junk food queen, salads aren't comfort food, they're compost.

But nutrition is not just "a nice idea," it is the building blocks of the human life beating inside you as well as the cornerstone of your own wellness both before and after the birth. Every molecule that you ingest is sculpting your baby. Eating well is a big deal, but you can make it a pleasure—even a relaxing treat. The energy you conserve through a diligent food plan during pregnancy will dictate how well you feel for years to come. Many wellness experts compare nutrition to a bank account where health is the balance and pregnancy is the best time to start saving. Once you give yourself the gift of nutrition, your child benefits three times: in utero, through your breast milk, and then growing up dining at the family table.

FORGET FOOD NEUROSIS: FEAST LIKE A PREGNANT WOMAN

The first step to good eating is to shift your mind-set from calories to nutrients. A healthy diet is not a diet at all: it's a series of empowered choices based on energy that, over time, become habitual. To master nutrition now and for the rest of your mothering life, it's best to eliminate the connotations of good and evil, fat and skinny, innocent and guilty, and simply know which foods give your body the best benefits, the most vitamins, and the most vitality. So-called fatty foods such as bananas, avocados, and hummus are critical energy builders for both pregnant and nursing mothers. Carbohydrates, so fashionably demonized by modern diets such as South Beach, the Zone, and Atkins, are critical to pregnant health, and they help quell the nausea of the first trimester. Pasta and rice (especially the whole-grain, wild, and brown varieties) are great with heaps of mixed veggies and lean meats, and even the occasional bowl of calcium-rich ice cream can contribute. I said *bowl* though, not *pint*.

WHOLE FOOD FOR MUMMIES

The easiest way to eat better is to banish the foods that have the least nutrients and find creative, flavor-packed ways to replace them. To make my life simple, I avoid fried foods or anything made with bleached flour or refined sugar. And I try to eat four different fruits and four green things (from apples, to cilantro, to celery, to haricots verts)—and at least three of these raw—a day. This sounds *much* simpler than it seems. I have tried this principle while traveling in the Wheat Belt of the Midwest, and while stuck in airports and at certain malls, and, yes, I have gone hungry. Corporate food chains run on white bread, sugar, and fat. If you want to combat the urge for a bucket of nuggets, a chili dog, or a Krispy Kreme, you need to be armed with your own movable feast.

When pregnant and while nursing, I carried nuts, dried apricots, dried instant miso soup and noodles, fresh apples, bananas, energy bars, and herbal tea bags. My handbag looked like a mini health food store, but I loved the positively Girl Scout stealth feeling of always having vital fuel at hand.

When eating out, I chose any entrée that has two or more veggies, one protein, and a grain. Pregnancy is a time when you crave sexy rather than sensible foods, but even pizza can be healthy if the toppings are fresh and veggie heavy. Don't feel shy at Asian restaurants to ask for extra greens, extra garlic (for immunity), or extra ginger (for digestion). Many Chinese restaurants now offer brown rice, which is more than three times richer in vitamin B than white rice, and the only grain that naturally contains vitamin E. Soups make an excellent choice at Italian restaurants because they often include meat, fresh herbs, beans, veggies, and some cheese, all in one bowl.

Admittedly, it took me years to convert to whole foods and to get in the habit of checking labels for preservatives, fat, and sugar content, but after awhile you can literally "vibe" if a food is going to love you back or not. The more colors in a salad, the better it will be for you. The more raw foods (from fruits to nuts to sprouts) on a plate, the more complex nutrients and fresh enzymes you will be ingesting. Foods resonate with the energy they possess. Heavy, greasy, sticky foods make me feel stale. Perky, frisky, fresh foods make me feel alive, and anything with a shelf life that goes beyond one year makes me wonder if it was embalmed for the Egyptian afterlife! Preparation also plays an important role in getting the most from food: Try a few weeks of eating grilled, steamed, and baked foods, and you'll find that the greasy taste of a deep-fried batter or piece of chicken just tastes bad, and not in a good way.

SUPER-SIMPLE ACCESS TO SUPER FOODS

Folic acid is the same thing as folate, a water-soluble form of vitamin B_9 that is crucial for the production and maintenance of new cells. Antioxidants are like the body's foot soldiers, defending our cells against free radicals—the damaging reactive molecules that trigger the main diseases of aging. While it is tempting to simply scarf down a prenatal multivitamin and a folic-acid supplement and hope for the best, it's much more sensually satisfying and physically beneficial to eat a wide diversity of dark-skinned fruits, berries, green vegetables, and mineral-rich foods such as sea vegetables and raw nuts. All of these foods are packed with folic acid and antioxidants but have many more complex rewards besides. To me it makes perfect sense to eat living foods while growing a living organism, and the easiest way to do so is by making super-food smoothies and making some aspect of your regular diet raw, be it with cold veggie soups, big salads, or smoothies.

The recent attention given to so-called super foods is linked directly to their antioxidant content. Acai berries, goji berries, and raw cacao beans (whole or ground) are rich in goodies and easy to assimilate into breakfast drinks whipped up with a blender at home.

Anny Fodor is a holistic health counselor and nutritional healer who advocates eating plenty of fresh, locally grown or organic produce as close to its natural state as possible. Her studies with leading nutritional and healing experts David Wolfe and Deepak Chopra led her to the strong belief that the consumption of a diversity of foods is key to growth and wellness.

Of course this leads to the question of how a Brazil nut tastes with a brussels sprout. Fodor's solution is smoothie recipes that combine foods that might seem odd paired on a plate into a surprisingly tasty and exotic health shake. Using coconut water (a natural hydrator) or nut milks (a rich source of vitamins) as her base, she makes green juices using fruit. "The sweetness of fruit cancels out the sometimes blandness or bitterness of the greens. If you don't have fresh greens on hand, chlorella or spirulina are very good options. All fruit is fine, but the more color the higher the antioxidants; I love all berries, dark grapes, figs, kiwi, mango, peach, and plums. Freezing the fruits before blending gives a very smooth texture! Freezing is also a very economical way to purchase and store organic berries, which are often prohibitively costly."

Throw all ingredients into a high-powered blender and smile—you won't even think about the kookiness when you feel this alive!

My Sweet Mornings Smoothie

1 ripe mango
2 tablespoons of spirulina
¼ cup of raw cacao nibs
1 cup of coconut water

Anny's Afternoon Delight Smoothie

5 sprigs of parsley

2 cups of kale

2 cups of berries (blueberries, raspberries, strawberries, etc.), fresh when in season, OK frozen when not

Small handful goji berries

Juice of 1 whole lemon

¼ cup of fresh ginger (great for nausea)

1 cup of fresh apple or orange juice

I found even more yummy recipes on the website of my favorite local juice bar (www.urbanspring.net) and in the book *Raw Food, Real World*, by Matthew Kenney and Sarma Melangailis. While I do not recommend any strictly raw or extreme vegan diet during pregnancy, many wonderful and complementary food and recipe ideas can be found in raw, vegan, and vegetarian cookbooks. Why dump a steaming pile of chard on your plate when you can make it sexy with raisins, sliced carrots, roasted yams, a sprinkle of sesame seeds, and some mustard dressing?

NAUGHTY, NAUGHTY CRAVINGS

Repeat after me: *Cake is not a food group.* I well recall the raging appetite of pregnancy, a time in your life where food almost feels like an hourly preoccupation, and the daily dose of French apple tarte Tartine feels justified on whatever grounds you can concoct: emotional, physical, biological, recreational. But the truth about cravings is that while some are based on sound nutritional needs, many more are based purely on lust.

Being pregnant is really the only time a woman can be socially accepted as full figured—OK, very large—and with that green light, it feels great to plunge into eating without censure. But (big butt) the more pounds you gain from calorie- and sugar-laden foods during your term, the harder it will be to make your way back to civilian threads. To be brutally honest, I ate like a sow during my pregnancy and took two whole years to deflate my thighs. I wallowed in a sea of boiling hot custard for nine months and ate bacon club sandwiches at midnight. My best friend, who developed gestational diabetes in her first trimester, was sworn off sugars, and the difference in our postpartum shapes was extreme. She wore jeans; I wore a guilty little smile.

Retrospectively, I have no guilt about the passionate gluttony; I simply feel that nutritionally my diet could have been stronger and that my borderline sugar addiction could have put my health and the baby's at risk. Gestational diabetes is a temporary condition where a pregnant woman's body produces too little insulin to process sugars to energy. While it is not proven that excess sugar causes this condition, it helps to be conservative about sweets. Older mums need to be particularly vigilant, as generally the metabolism over thirty-five is slower, and the reserve of nutrients built up through a year of wise eating works to allay much of the inevitable exhaustion of mothering.

I refuse to moralize about cravings—they are one of the most delicious aspects of carrying a baby—but there are many highly healthy ways to satisfy them that contribute to the job of building a child and salvaging your own well-being. Choose fruit and nut breads instead of muffins, low-fat muesli cookies instead of fudge, and add whole dried fruit to your own baking. Also, make parfaits from yogurt, raw honey, and fruit rather than eating packaged puddings or ice cream. Or, take a small bite of what you fancy, then have a trusted friend bar the fridge door.

BUST THE BOOZE

Many women party hard only to find themselves pregnant some weeks later. In fact, the wild and boozy conception sex story is a common

one. Whatever the context, you need to curb your drinking from the moment you test positive; every clean day will make a difference.

Though many abide by an occasional tipple, alcohol simply does nothing but harm to your unborn baby. It is a completely nutritionally empty, sugar-heavy source of calories and a depleter of vitamin B that will only deepen your sense of fatigue and possibly depression. The risks outweigh the benefits, and any alcohol you consume will pass directly into the baby's bloodstream through your placenta—a perfectly horrible thought. Guinness has iron and is fairly low in alcohol compared to wine, so if you get the urge, I say reach for a small glass of dark stout or ale and have it, English pub style, with a steaming lamb sandwich or ploughman's lunch of cheddar cheese, brown bread, and chutney or pickled onions. Hard liquor is out. You'll have plenty of time to drink cocktails in broad daylight once the baby is at preschool. Just kidding. In fact, the habit of drinking less has ongoing benefits for young and older mothers.

Once you're a vital go-go-go mama, the last thing you'll ever want is a hangover. In fact, the sleep deprivation feels a bit like being hung over for two years straight, so why compound it? Develop a taste for juice-based spritzers and classy nonalcoholic mocktails now, and they can become second nature later. A motherhood spent leaning on the nightly fix of wine to get through or reward a hard day (and there will be thousands!) is a gradually depleting routine. In many ways, the first three years with a child are like a sustained marathon, so whichever "treats" hold back your performance, it's best to monitor them during the conservative and enriching period of pregnancy. Consider this your moment of concentrated poise before leaping from the blocks.

COFFEE, TEA, OR ME?

Caffeine in pregnancy needs to be ingested with extreme moderation, if at all, as it has been linked to miscarriage, low birth weight, and less serious health issues such as maternal insomnia. Another problem with coffee is that it often rides sidesaddle with a sticky bagel, sugary cake, or bar of chocolate, none of which has the rich benefits you need to be hoarding for your baby. Caffeine also inhibits the body's absorption of iron and taxes the central nervous system, and it isn't good for baby even in small quantities. Get over your latte addiction with chai tea with steamed milk or have cocoa instead. Cocoa has 70 fewer milligrams (mg) of caffeine than coffee, and the milkier you make it, the better for your calcium intake. If you still want tea, opt for white (pearl jasmine) or green tea, both of which are rich in antioxidants.

THE SOUR TRUTH ABOUT SUGAR

Sugar is all pervasive in the American diet. The average adult eats 150 pounds of sugar a year, mainly in the form of candy, chocolate, alcohol, dairy products, baked goods, sauces, processed food, and soda. Especially soda. When you have a soft drink, sugar spikes insulin in the blood, creating a false surge of energy (the sugar high), and then rapidly plummets, making energy crash in the body. Too much sugar debilitates the absorption of vitamins and minerals and disrupts the healthy function of digestion, meaning that even more nutrients are drained from our diets. It's also very fattening. While fat and carbohydrates are demonized as the culprits of an obese society, it is sugar, so childlike and seemingly innocent, that is plaguing our health, promoting medical problems such as type 2 diabetes, breast cancer, arthritis, migraines, and cardiovascular disease. And the cruel blow is that many women crave sweet tastes very badly while pregnant. I know I did. But in order to maintain optimum nutrition and avoid gestational diabetes and unneeded weight gain, sugar has to be rationed strictly.

The rewards are immediate. Replacing one sugar-based treat with one of the following alternatives will have you eating better straightaway: whole fresh fruit; a yogurt smoothie; organic dried fruit; a bowl of nuts; a slice of healthy whole wheat bread with honey, banana, and ricotta cheese; or a generous piece of 80 percent dark chocolate. Sweet

23

foods are addictive, socially ritualized, and emotionally comforting. They make us feel babied, perhaps because breast milk is so sweet, but the real babying right now has to be for your own immunity and long-term health.

FEAST, NEVER FAMINE

Many believe that the foods we crave (and eat) in pregnancy stay with us afterward and make us fatter, though it certainly doesn't have to be this way. Once you have the building blocks for an easy, fresh, vital diet, you can eat pretty much the same way for the rest of time and not gain too much excess weight. The recommended extra 300 calories needed during pregnancy increase to 500 calories while exclusively breast-feeding, but the optimal vitamin, mineral, protein, and healthy carbohydrate needs remain the same. Being calorie savvy is irrelevant if the content and quality of your food is compromised. So instead of worrying about fat content, develop a habit of using complementary replacements: fresh for frozen, whole instead of processed, brown instead of white, high-calcium whole dairy rather than low-fat and low-calcium. Drink less sugar and caffeine, and you will instantly get better hydrated through herbal teas, pure fruit and veggie juices, and water. Eat more fruit, and you will crave less refined sugar. Grill, steam, and bake more foods, and you'll be addicted to the clean, distinct tastes of meats and vegetables and turn your back on the lardy, palate-crushing weight of deep-fried crusts and batters. Balance proteins with carbs, and you'll feel full and less likely to snack. And in the whole process of making friends with food, the kitchen can become the site of sensual adventure and family nurturing that is healthy and joyous rather than ladened with anxiety, secrecy, and guilt.

Nothing feels better than flinging open the fridge door and grabbing anything you desire, knowing it will do you good. A little planning and a lot of self-love will make this a reality. And, yes, the strawberry

Häagen-Dazs is OK too; it's a good, simple treat for when the sugar fairy comes to bite you on the ass, and you just can't resist. Just be sure to gobble it up with fresh bananas, fresh strawberries, and almonds: You're on a folic acid trip, Mama, and it's for life!

NATURAL BEAUTY IS ALWAYS JUICY

Water is the cornerstone of maternal health, from the thirsty months of pregnancy right through your nursing, and afterward, when the body replenishes itself from all the hard work. Water remains an important constant for breast milk production, healthy hair and skin, balancing the nervous system, swift elimination, and overall energy. Even when you don't eat perfectly, you can remember to drink and keep the body fresh and flushed. To get radically hydrated, I gradually increased my intake of water by a glass a day by placing full jugs and tall bottles all over the house. We bought a water purifier to save on the cost of bottled spring water, but you might find that a large office-style water cooler delivered to your home is also an excellent idea. Keep it in the bedroom later in your pregnancy, when treks to the kitchen lose their appeal.

GETTING IT ALL ON ONE PLATE

I find I eat best when I combine foods in a bowl rather than laying them out on a plate. A Thai beef salad with broccoli florets, chunks of orange, slivers of toasted almonds, some cilantro, and a twist of lemon with a sesame oil dressing amps up the iron because vitamin C complements its absorption. But the fun part is, you are not staring at a plate where all of the flavors are segregated and the ingredients are arranged clinically. Look for books on bowl food, original salads, casseroles, and soups. I like *Complete Vegetarian Cookbook,* by Charmaine Solomon, and *Ani's Raw Food Kitchen: Easy Delectable Living Food*

Recipes, by Ani Phyo (for the smoothies). Any cooking method or recipe that keeps all the nutrients in the pot, steeping in the juices they were cooked in, or that combines unlikely and contrasting ingredients (feta cheese, walnuts, and green apples!) are usually the ones that are good for you.

SHOPPING LIST FOR THE PASSIONATE PREGNANT PANTRY

My golden rule for nutrition is "Plan what you need, carry what you want, and banish the rest from house and handbag." So think about candy all you like, but eat the healthy cashews in the bowl! I made a rule to eat only seasonal fruits and vegetables, from local growers farmers' markets, if possible. The less distance produce has to travel, the more likely it is to be fresh. I couldn't afford all organic, so I concentrated on the foods with edible skins: beans, grapes, pears, apples, and plums, which I bought sparingly, as organic produce tends to age more quickly. I bought the fruit for my midnight binges in bulk. I recall eating a watermelon a day or nine oranges a night in the second trimester. Only you can define what feels "normal" about your tastes and appetites now.

For day-to-day well-being, I set up a very basic home "pharmacy" with both fresh ginger and ginger tea bags for the nausea. I put several tea bags in each handbag so I would never be caught short, and I also included a gentle herbal antinausea tablet (some women find ginger chewing gum and lozenges help). A prenatal multivitamin with folic acid (0.4 mg to 0.6 mg) a day is recommended to protect the baby from neural defects and spina bifida. Supplements provide great security for pregnant women, but they are only a complement! Don't slack on healthy eating. Food is always the best source of nutrition and energy.

I built my pantry with enough condiments and dry goods to be able to make food with only a handful of ingredients. If I have green curry paste and a can of coconut milk, I can make a curry literally from two chicken drumsticks, some cilantro, and a sweet potato. Ready-made healthy tomato sauce and pesto are also great meal builders, as marinades for meats, on pasta, or even on whole wheat pita with melted cheese and sliced fresh veggies as a mini pizza. Surprisingly, shiitake mushrooms sautéed with ginger and miso stock satisfy sugar cravings and increase nutrient intake. So do baked yams or thick-crusted sandwiches of cherry tomatoes, cheddar cheese, and avocado. When I'm in the supermarket I ask myself: Can I eat this ingredient more than three ways? Is this ingredient low in sugar, salt, and artificial ingredients? Can I rub this on a leg of lamb or bake it between lasagna sheets? If the answer is yes, I buy it no matter how much it costs. When you're pregnant, you're distracted. When you're a mother, you're exhausted, and multipurpose wholesome ingredients become key.

Foods to Avoid

- Steak tartare, rare meats, bloody lamb: *Toxoplasma gondii* is a parasite found in soil, cats (for example, in cat litter), and raw or undercooked meat. Clean kitchen utensils thoroughly when preparing raw meat, and eat all meats cooked to an internal temperature of 170 degrees Fahrenheit.

- Leftovers: Salmonella is not a town on the Amazon. To avoid this harmful bacteria, let food live in the fridge for one day max, then toss it. Learn to buy and prepare quantities that avoid waste.

- Raw eggs in any form: Foods prepared with raw eggs include Caesar salad, eggnog, and hollandaise sauce. It's best to avoid them.

- Raw shellfish: This can pose the threat of transmitting the hepatitis A virus. Prepare seafood swiftly (the same day) and always store very cool.

- Mercury-heavy fish such as marlin, mackerel, swordfish, grouper, shark, saltwater bass, croaker, halibut, tuna, sea trout, bluefish, and lobster pose a risk to pregnant women if eaten in quantity. To see the full list of mercury contents in fish please refer to www .americanpregnancy.org under the heading "Mercury Levels in Fish."

- Food from damaged tins: If a can looks swollen, it's likely to be contaminated with bacteria. Be diligent about use-by dates and broken seals of any kind.

- Frozen food that has been thawed and refrozen: Bacteria can proliferate in foods that have altered temperatures, hot to cold to hot again. Plus, it just isn't nutritious at this point.

ANNA'S IRON-RICH SCRUMPTIOUS DE PUY LENTILS

Digestion is a very volatile process while you're pregnant. Some women can digest plenty of meat to get the iron and protein they need, and others cannot. Lentils are an excellent, inexpensive vegetarian alternative. They taste amazing hot like a soup or served cold on toast or with salad the next day. This is a dish that keeps in the fridge for up to three days and always makes me feel robust, energetic, and deeply nourished. And once baby is a little older, it's a great complement to a juicy glass of Oregon Pinot Noir.

Take seven cups of De Puy French lentils and soak them overnight covered in cold water in a lidded pot or bowl. The next day, finely chop eight cloves of garlic and dice three small carrots, sauté in olive oil until lightly browned, about three minutes. Then add seven large bay leaves. Toss for a few seconds in the hot oil and then add the lentils and one 32-ounce carton of organic chicken stock (veggie stock is fine too). Simmer till the stock reduces, then add two large cans of organic whole stewed tomatoes and salt and cracked black pepper to taste. Stew for about twenty minutes, then add a splash of good red wine, and simmer on very low heat for another fifteen to twenty minutes until the lentils are tender and the tomatoes have formed a thick red sauce. Serve with sprinkled chopped fresh parsley and crunchy buttered French bread hot from the oven.

4. STYLE LUSCIOUSNESS

Maternal Chic Divided by Three

When I fell pregnant, I fell in love with the idea that I would have a pagan fertility goddess belly. My vision of coming to terms was that of a very glamorous Teletubby with lipstick and a ponytail. No sooner than I flung my pregnancy tester into the bin I was imagining what it would be like to be a human pillow, and probably like a million other women on the planet had done before me, I raced into the living room and stuffed a scatter cushion up my jumper in an attempt to visualize the change. At just five weeks gone, it's very hard to imagine the expansion of every inch of your body. *Every inch.* The models in maternity magazines serve as no guide. Giraffe tall with sticklike arms and legs, they merely look as if they have eaten a basketball. Early adventures in shopping were equally confusing. Tiptoeing into maternity stores, I was shocked to see prosthetic bellies hanging in the change room that looked just like…scatter cushions. "Pregnancy is

great," my agent reassured me. "It's like one big science experiment." Did that mean I'd be wearing a lab coat?

If this is your first baby, it is very hard to assess the subtlety of the challenge ahead. There are many nuances to dressing a body that is changing every day, week, and month. One style will *never* do for all. Some women have the height and the proportion to wear very clingy thingies bought mercifully cheaply at "real" clothing stores. The tall girls who are expecting look good in pants, and the rest of us are left flicking through books on Renaissance art. In the first three months of your term, you do not usually have the ripe, fulsome gut to match the bulging thighs, brimming bosom, and dimpled derriere, and one can easily feel as if they have been plunged into a second puberty. This is what I call the "fat teenager" phase of pregnancy, and the best time to comfort yourself with favorite pieces that still fit you. From early on in a pregnancy, one really must avoid any piece of clothing that reminds you of childhood or *The Golden Girls*. One must also ignore well-meaning input from others. Strange items and advice will come flying from all directions. My French neighbor suggested wearing jeans with the zipper half undone! Perhaps that works in the Pigalle at twilight, but I tried it at Pastis and simply looked drunk. My mother plied me with many pairs of crushed-velvet drawstring pants and large artist's smocks that made me feel like an earnest silken pear. Starched men's shirts arrived in discreet paper bags from friends, which I gave directly to my husband. Shopgirls suggested overalls, track pants, and dresses that looked like Lycra pillowcases. I felt like a big-boned girl from a Gauguin painting being urged into an Edwardian nightgown by many caring, invisible hands. Often, I felt lumpen and sad.

Of course, I was not alone. Most freshly pregnant women of average height and "weight gain tendencies" reach a stylistic stumbling block straightaway in their first trimester. Mine was that I was not tall enough for true maternity chic (the Upper East Side Manhattan standard of tailored gray flannel pants, a turtleneck, and a big, lush cashmere poncho) and yet not full-blown enough for proper tent wear (the Mexican dresses, the Moroccan robes). It is in the second trimester, when you finally have your "badge" in place, that the world of clothes revolves around your middle like the earth around the sun.

Weirdly, I decided to base many of my fashion ideas for the next six months on a supermodel half my size. It's life's great irony that even the thinnest woman on earth becomes your sister once she sprouts a bump, and so it was with Kate Moss. No matter that I lacked bone structure or couture connections; I simply loved her maternity look, which was rich with whimsy, rock, and romance. The trick with maternity style, of course, is to wear things you'd die for anyway.

Kate made pregnancy look *fun* by wearing delicate printed chiffons, gypsy layers, Missoni halter tops, frayed-hem denim skirts, Grecian-style pleated evening dresses, simple but divine art deco–looking shifts by Lanvin, and pastel duffel coats. More like a dream-sequence fashion parade from *Funny Face* than a drab march of duty. I concede that supermodels and actresses do not live real lives. They spend hours in counsel with stylists and vintage-clothing dealers inside the vast crypts of their walk-in wardrobes. They have Silvia Venturini Fendi design their diaper bags. But they give ordinary women more daring ideas about how to dress. Emboldened, I teamed plain long-sleeved T-shirts with my collection of chunky metallic eighties disco belts tucked under my bosom and just resting (like a Christmas ornament) above my bulge. Feeling positively reckless, I wore halter tops and vintage beaded cardigans over slip dresses and low-heeled silver snakeskin pumps in broad daylight.

One of the joys of pregnant dressing is that you do not have to pursue aggressive camouflage or skim trouble spots as vigilantly as before. Yet the rules, like the rest of you, expand so widely that perhaps for the first time in your life, you can really afford to experiment. For once in our lives, we can burn the rule book: The big no-no's of chic, such as horizontal stripes, big polka dots, and crazy large-scale floral prints, look cool on a pregnant belly. And anything that draws emphasis to the cleavage—a massive decorated choker, a low-cut crocheted poncho, radically diagonal stripes—is a good buy, for both now and naughty moments in your future yummy existence.

THREE STAGES OF STYLE

First Trimester

Puffy, sore breasts, perpetual bloat, a thickening waist, and stubbornly swelling thighs. The first months are so tumultuous with subtle (but potent) change that few will be preoccupied with what (or what not) to wear. If you have decided to conceal your pregnancy until three months, then suddenly you will be looking at clothes with an eye to discretion. If you are on a budget, you will be wanting to stretch your everyday clothes to the limit, and if you are not sure just how big you might become, it seems very hard to plan at this point.

PS: Two Hot Shopping Tips

1. Trawl your favorite maternity fashion websites for the sale items. I found great evening wear at A Pea in the Pod, and pieces such as fall/winter coats and sundresses are also greatly reduced at the end of each season.

2. Look for labels that base their maternity lines on "normal" clothes. I think it a stroke of genius that Topshop UK (www.topshop.co.uk) offers many of its everyday collections in maternity sizes, and it's probably a trend that will go global very soon.

Second Trimester

Depending on who you are, you will either greet the arrival of a real belly with delight or mild horror. Many women who are very thin feel interrupted by a pregnancy and lament the loss of their everyday uniform (usually jeans). Women who are already heavy might feel overwhelmed by the extra bulk of a belly. Short girls might start to feel like those perky circular guys on the M&M's commercials. Thrusting all of those complex issues to one side, please appreciate that energy-wise, health-wise, libido-wise, and weight-wise, this is the golden age of your pregnancy and a great time to be very active, social, and organized.

Third Trimester

The third trimester is the last great hoorah and often the time of the most accelerated growth. Clothes will literally be useful for a week at a time and then discarded. This is the best time to borrow maternity wear, because these pieces will be too big to recycle (no matter how much fudge you've eaten) and too expensive to buy for such a brief shelf life. One great idea is to form a rotating Yummy Mummy clothing club, where the same bag of maternity clothes grows with each hand it passes into and is kept in perpetual rotation. Everyone who borrows from *the bag* adds fresh items, and removes, repairs, or replaces items that are too threadbare.

PS: A Note on the Final Weeks

The bigger I became, the more I enjoyed dressing, until the last weeks when—quite honestly—nothing on earth felt right except nighties, socks, or nudity. Late pregnancy can lead to desperation dressing. This was the moment when I crumbled and accepted "pseudo" trousers into my life: horrible discount store leisure slacks that were a mutant pajama—part legging and part yoga pant. This blatant slob wear allowed me to wear dresses as tops and kept my thighs from knitting together permanently.

5. THE BRIDE WORE STRETCH LACE

Fearless, Fabulous, and Fecund

I t takes guts to be a pregnant bride. First, you're up against a truck-load of tradition. Physically, the bride who's expecting is the literal embodiment of putting the cart before the horse. No matter how rampantly bohemian you might feel with a virginal veil and a fecund belly, a shroud of taboo will follow you like a cloud of Fracas down the aisle.

Glossy bridal books will all but ignore you. Vera Wang, in her beautiful coffee-table book *Vera Wang on Weddings,* devotes one paragraph to pregnant bridal fashion but, tantalizingly, no images. Who ever heard of a society wedding where the bride weighed more than the cake? In a similar collusion of tradition, materialism, and conservatism, bridal magazines allude fastidiously to the etiquette of the expectant bride (nonchurch weddings, whimsical invitations, combined baby and bridal showers), but again, the gowns we see are wasp waisted. Blooming, blushing betrothed maidens with big, veiny bosoms and very flat slippers are the stuff of fifteenth-century Dutch paintings, quite the opposite of the hypercontrolled modern bride. Micromanaged down to the muscle tone, modern wedding style seems to be about everything but fertility. Flip through *Martha Stewart Weddings* magazine, and you will see a chic regiment of brides in control: A stiff duchess satin gown, a pointed three-inch Jimmy Choo heel, a taut, lacquered updo, and a prim bouquet of white tulips tied as tightly as a tourniquet leave little room for a bulge.

Even if the social stigma of a shotgun wedding has lessened, taboos of a more subtle nature have taken its place. Weddings have come to compress Holy Communion, graduation, the debutante ball, and a mock royal coronation into one. Increasingly, it has become *the* day of manic perfectionism, where a woman looks thinner, richer, and more groomed for the photographers then she ever will again in her lifetime.

The raw emotion, flushed flesh, blooming body, occasional nausea, and sheer unpredictability of being pregnant blow the lid off this princess fantasy. I mean, who wants to fuss over gift baskets, color coordinated confetti, and sugared almonds tethered to bamboo chairs with tulle when a small foot is poking between your ribs? The logistical challenge of organizing an event and then starring in it is much worse when your back is aching and clouds of fatigue drug your days. Emotionally, you might be feeling more vulnerable or sensitive than usual. Or more violently hostile. Pregnancy is a great disinhibitor, so there's a strong chance you'll tell several relatives to "bloody shut up!" midsentence. Physically you're also on a way more visceral plane. Pregnant women can smell to the core of the earth, a faint breeze of lilac can make them weep a bucket of diamond tears, and food is either an emergency or a source of intense revulsion. So just imagine how offensive a chicken vol-au-vent might seem.

For all of these reasons, getting married while expecting will give you a very different experience. By necessity, the event needs to be sim-

pler, cheaper, smoother, and shorter than what you may have planned. And, if the marriage has to preclude the birth, you might be planning a ceremony and reception in record time.

One of the hidden advantages of a shotgun wedding is the speed with which your plans all fall together. Consider it streamlining by default. With a baby on the way, you are not going to obsess about the size of a fondant orchid or the thickness of the paper stock for your invitations. A small disadvantage might be compromising the length of your honeymoon or the remoteness of the destination. You might also have to compress baby and bridal shower into one, or run two registries sidesaddle. And you will definitely have to give some intelligent thought to the dress. Unlike so many brides who are shrinking by the second and having their dresses continuously, nervously taken in, you will be sprouting and stretching and needing room both in front and behind.

Many famous women marry pregnant. Your mother might have; mine certainly did! Yet even though a recent British survey of bridal shop owners revealed that 1 in every 5 brides is pregnant, the options available for off-the-rack dresses remain lean. When it comes to maternity bridal, it pays to follow the lead of a French empress instead of a Victorian queen. Napoleon Bonaparte's bride, Josephine, trotted down the aisle in 1810 in a sheer, gauzy very-high-waisted gown with prim capped, puffed sleeves and long gloves. It is still a perfect look for a woman well into her second trimester, but for the very pregnant bride, even more grace of line and skill in proportion are needed. A dress in a stretch fabric or a bias-cut silk will look good if your shoes, hair, and accessories are streamlined. In terms of the cut, you must avoid like poison ivy high necklines, backless models, and ruffles.

Jessica Iverson, an innovative maternity bridal designer from Santa Barbara with a successful online bridal salon (www.maternity-bride.com), started her label because she could find nothing to wear to her own wedding at seven months and counting. The result is a collection of very simple, rather summery gowns that flatters many degrees of bulge. "It's an understatement to say there's a lot going on being pregnant, so the simpler the dress, the more classy the look, and all the more fitting for flat shoes beneath the gown," Iverson says. "This is not the moment for something really trendy; you want to feel as comfortable and fresh and as uncluttered as possible."

Just because you are getting hitched in the family way does not mean you must wear sage green and abolish traditions you hold dear. A glowing bride of any skin tone looks better in white or ivory than biscuit or apricot, and the something blue could be something very witty such as a little stork embroidered onto your veil or a single pink satin bow sewn to the hem of your gown if you are expecting a girl. Symbols of the coming baby can also make a special contribution threaded through the reception decorations, on the invites, and even on the cake. How sweet to put bride, groom, and baby on top of the icing and to make a guest book just for messages to the baby.

Striking the balance so that it is still your BIG day and not just your *big* fat bump is important. You might ask everyone involved in the ceremony and reception speeches not to ask you—or worse still, divulge—if it's a boy or a girl or to keep offering you a chair at the edge of the dance floor. No bride wants to feel like an object of pity, no matter how swollen her ankles become. Equally, it should be the groom's job to shield his lady from too much aggressive in-law focus or to let her retreat regularly from the party into fresh air and silence when it all gets to be too much. Pregnancy is like a cocoon of inner contemplation, and so much of wedding ritual and obligation is the opposite of sanctuary.

In terms of entertaining the guests, don't be ashamed to organize a much shorter reception or to even bypass a dinner in favor of afternoon cocktails or something even simpler, like a grand tea party. Don't be afraid to be extra selfish as well, demanding two wedding nights instead of one and spending more on your honeymoon than anything else. If this is your first baby, then your honeymoon will be the last chance to be truly alone with your husband for some years. Swim naked, sleep all day and talk all night, order fruity mocktails with little umbrellas, and pose poolside.

Loaded with all this sensible advice, a girl still needs to search her soul to know if this really is the best moment to wed. If being pregnant will make your very private dreams fall sideways or render something special into a blur, think twice. For some women the notion of a wedding and a pregnancy is too psychologically intense and physically demanding. Water weight *and* the weight of the commitment are heavy. Not to mention the pressure on the groom to perform as both new husband and impending father. To mitigate against the claustrophobia of so many milestones being crammed into one moment, you might opt to elope (for the sheer privacy) or to shelve the whole shebang. After getting our license at city hall without any pomp or ceremony, I was engaged and booked for a March wedding when I found out I was due in June. I weighed the stress of the wedding against the stress of a first baby and decided that postponing the wedding was the better option.

I admit that my inner Cinderella was crestfallen. So much of the magic of matrimony is that mutual step into the unknown, into the fresh pastures that beckon, untainted by the habits of well-worn domestic routine. I wondered at the necessity for a wedding at all once the baby came, if it would seem like an inverted ritual or simply a gaudy, needless expense. However, cutting the cord before tying the knot only deepened our commitment to connubial splendor and arduous fidelity. Fear of the future doesn't figure once you've been in labor on a gurney, staring up at your husband dressed in pink surgical scrubs. Parenthood is marriage without the cake and the tinsel; it's the hard-core union with far fewer photo ops. By the time we get to that ice-cold champagne toast we will have earned it. As it stands, my son will be three years old at my wedding, just big enough to pop out from under my silk skirt and frighten the priest.

A Head-to-toe Guide for the Full-blown Bride

- Bridal makeup is tremendously personal. Some women want to look like a freshly scrubbed milkmaid, and others follow the lipstick lead of Dita von Teese. You want to glow but you don't want to look . . . slippery, which is a challenge, since pregnant skin often brings pigmentation, blotches, enlarged pores, and perspiration. For these reasons, spend serious time finding a base that you trust and a powder that is light, reflective, and translucent.

- The intensity of your makeup depends greatly upon the light; will it be dappled stained-glass chapel light or glaring Mexican sun? Natural makeup looks best on skin that already has plenty of color or delicate freckles. Richer lipstick and smokier eyes suit the bride who is being photographed against a dramatic backdrop such as snow, a gray city landscape, or in black-and-white film. One of the great cheats of the 1960s bride (be she Earth Mother or Stepford Wife) was individually placed and custom-clipped false eyelashes. With subtle but foxy Bambi lashes, you'll be ready for your close-up.

- Hair in pregnancy can be gloriously full, so why not break with the chignon convention and wear it loose and wavy? If your dress has bare shoulders and a gracefully low neckline (V, cowl, or sweetheart) try a slightly 1940s wave and a side part. Somewhat deconstructed hair can be made more formal with a fresh gardenia behind one ear or with glittering barrettes. If you do choose to wear your hair up, try to avoid a tight or lacquered look. You don't want to look like a well-groomed pincushion or a Russian doll now, do you? And do ditch the tiara. Who wants to be the pregnant princess?

- The length of your veil should be dictated by the bulk of your belly. I say the bigger the bulge, the longer the tulle, because a fingertip veil or shorter will just look comical (and I mean Off-Broadway funny) with a rotund tummy up front. A longer veil and especially one that frames the face with a lace, pearl, embroidered, or crystal edging keeps the eye flowing over your whole glory and not just stuck on the most dramatic feature you've modeled to date.

- Upper arms in late pregnancy can get a trifle meaty. A shrug, a chiffon vintage ballet jacket, a mantilla (worn as a wrap), or a custom-made bolero in a lively guipure or bobbin lace are flattering foils, and look best with a strapless dress that has a simple or straight neckline.

- Sheer, fluid fabrics move with the body, while matte satin and duchess silk satin encase it. To avoid looking as stiff as marzipan icing, choose a gown that slides and glides over your form instead of tailoring the tummy. Bias cut could work, especially in the first trimester, but Empire and Princess lines and even a ruched goddess dress are the sure winners for heavier brides-in-waiting.

- Fear not the diamonds! A pregnant bride has a lot going on and needs simple details to look elegant. For this reason, she should skip carrying a handbag, wearing gloves, or staggering about in beribboned boots or fussy shoes. Place your accessory vote on jewels: a seed pearl choker, a mabe pearl necklace (you fertile moon goddess!), some diamond drop earrings, or even an Edwardian-style chandelier necklace that dances upon your burgeoning bosom. Forget piety; go for the glamour.

- Pay attention to proportion when choosing your bouquet. A big belly looks best with a wild bouquet of romantic trailing flowers that flow down vertically (think Pre-Raphaelite Ophelia) rather than a tightly bound posy or a small lace-trimmed bunch. In fact, avoid anything that looks tightly bound, especially around the wrists or ankles.

- Because you have girth, you also need to create the illusion of length to your line. Try a trailing wispy sleeve, a flowing floaty veil, ribbons dreamily suspended from your bouquet, or a hairstyle that features a few flyaway strands.

- Given the circumstances, it seems timely and seemly to work a little sensual abandon and romantic whimsy into your look: plenty of lace at the décolletage for a church wedding, a fresh flower bracelet on one wrist for a field wedding, gold Indian sandals and a smattering of toe rings for a beach wedding. A cold, classic Puritan look à la Jackie O. is not really your friend right now. Do chic minimalism later. On this day you are a pagan queen, no matter who your God is.

- Call me ruthless, but bridesmaids need to fall in line with the expectant bride, and that means no skintight sheath dresses, wasp-waisted corsets, or tight sash belts, please. It is the bride's prerogative to choose dress styles that fit with her theme, and her attending maidens must submit. Play up feminine delicacy rather than vampish excess. Classical themes—ivy-embroidered hems, chiffon handkerchief sleeves, art deco dresses, balletic layers, and soft but not sickly pastel colors—are going to look better than an army of chicks in red satin leading a pregnant bride. Anything that reminds you of *The Rocky Horror Picture Show* has to go. Socially, symbolically, and visually, the belly is really statement enough.

- Lingerie for the big, *big* day is a tough call. Big boobs need support, and it is hard to squeeze a proper panty liner into a flimsy lace thong. And the more pregnant you are, the more protection you will need. There might be leaking milk and more discharge and sweat than usual. Icky but true. For this reason, choose a comfortable and supportive foundation for the wedding and reception (in a fiber that breathes) and slip into the horn-bag she-devil knickers for the wedding night.

PS:

- Pack several different kinds of baby-doll slips, peignoirs, sheer pj's, and kinky undies. That way you can keep reemerging from the honeymoon suite loo in ever-glorious variety.

- High heels are bad for pregnant spines and hips, and worn regularly they can seriously displace your posture. But tripping down the aisle in a pair of three-inch Louboutins is not so naughty if you have some kitten heels or flat satin slippers for the reception. But—don't forget!—your center of gravity has shifted, so you better look and see if you can still walk (rather than cakewalk) in heels. A stately gait is probably more important when walking down the aisle than an illusion of height. You're round, you're booby and bouncy; just accept it.

- Some rituals can bite dust when you are carrying a baby. Don't let anyone lift your skirt and prize a garter off your thigh, unless you are getting hitched at a Renaissance fair.

- If you need to find a "going away outfit" for retreating from the reception, make sure it is as fabulous as an evening dress and absolutely *not* your regular maternity wear. Spend a little extra on this outfit, as it will definitely be in the photographs.

- Speaking of photographs. Ask for several portraits that are just head shots of you and your husband. You will adore the "my big fat pregnant wedding" snaps, but you will cherish the classic pictures of just your faces just as much as the more freaky conservative in-laws will.

- Expect your rings to be much looser after the baby comes and even to need altering at the jewelers. Everything swells in pregnancy, and especially digits. Despair not, my damsels, the fluid fairy will liberate you postpartum.

6. CONFESSIONS OF THE HORNY PEAR

Boudoir Secrets and Plus-size Pleasures

Flaming desire and pregnancy. For some women, it's a union as palatable as onions and chocolate. The saucy heroines of romance novels are rarely pregnant. Maternity magazines never—I mean never, ever—run inviting cover lines such as "Your Best Orgasm Yet!" I have seen only one film in which a pregnant woman had wild, moany intercourse at the foot of a walnut tree, and of course it was French! All I can say is, what a glaring omission. With respect to the women who have nine months of nausea or body issues so heavy that they feel numb to the possibilities of pleasure, there is also the possibility that pregnancy can be the most erotic adventure of your life.

Perhaps it's a prelude to the fallow weeks and months after giving birth, perhaps it's the last big bang before lending your body over to the care of a needy little being, or perhaps it is simply nature's reward for the long and heavy burden of carrying a child, but the erotic charge of pregnancy is a most peculiar pleasure. To begin with, there are the dreams. I had afternoon tea with a very quiet young woman in her thirty-third week of pregnancy. With an amused smile, she informed me that she had dreamed the night before that she was making love to the furniture in her house, systematically grinding into the couch, table, and chair like a cat. She didn't go into detail, and she didn't have to. I remembered it too well. The exhausting nights with Johnny Depp, Daniel Craig, and Denzel Washington pounding through the cloudy bedroom of my unconscious, leaving me spent morning after morning.

"The sex," I would say wearily to my husband, "is exhausting me."

"What sex?" he would reply, deeply puzzled.

How could I explain the sex in my head alone? The desire and satiation that pulsed with a thudding weight through my blood, the pressure of the baby's head sending silvery shivers between my legs, and the constant heat at the tips of my engorged breasts.

"The sex!" I would say with urgent emphasis and brazen contentment, although I probably meant "the sexuality." For pregnancy, in my experience, was the most sensually heightened year of my life. Perhaps it was the wedding of food and fertility. The joy of a ravenous appetite quenched by bowls of custard and guiltless feasts of cake and hot tea. Perhaps it was the challenge of actually making love with this tremendous orb floating between us. Perhaps it was the power of the belly itself, as blatant and symbolically potent as an erection, and far bigger than anything else in the bed.

Unlike many other women, I felt my size gave me strength. It was as if I had become the vast, round stone fruit of Roald Dahl's surreal storybook *James and the Giant Peach*. Careening down the street, I felt a majestic sway, as if my belly were a crinoline skirt tilting its arc flirtatiously at the world. Despite the normal inconveniences of sciatica, incontinence, and swollen feet, I felt the surge of having 40 percent more blood coursing through my system. Everything felt pumped up and softened, as if touched up and plumped out by Renoir's brush. Thanks to a heavy dose of estrogen, the hollows of my cheeks, the lines in my face, the texture of my skin—all looked a decade younger. And as my body swelled in its ripening grandeur, an outrageous chorus of chemical changes made every nerve ending tingle. Parts of my anatomy that were once mildly sensitive became almost radioactive.

In a word, *nipples.* I could have written this entire chapter about the revelation of breast sensitivity during my second and third trimesters. By the first week of my second trimester, I would shake in my Ugg boots if anyone brushed past my breasts. In a hot second, I was dry mouthed, sticky knickered—imploding with lust. If I held my hand less than two inches away from my chest, I would experience a rush of heat that would enter through my tightened teats (as rigid as raisins) and course through my blood like hot milk. It was like lactation inverted.

The hormone responsible for your best and most fierce feelings during pregnancy and way beyond into as many years as you wish to breast-feed is oxytocin. Dubbed the love drug, it is a multitasking hormone that can stimulate uterine contractions (from orgasm to early labor), increase arousal, and generate that honeyed warmth of "postcoital bliss." Oxytocin is a pregnant woman's pleasure but is not exclusive to her. It can be released in the body by seeing one's lover (or baby) or touching their skin. In the case of breast-feeding, oxytocin amps up the blood flow during a feed, creating a naturally warm place for the baby to rest his head, and is even said to intensify the nutrients of breast milk, while simultaneously calming the mum with a beatific high. The prelude to all of this in pregnancy is a special relationship between nipple stimulation and uterine contraction. Pinch your boobs while pregnant, and you could feel anything from a faint tremor in the core of your belly to a wild, piercing heat that surges like a hot wire from the nipple to the uterus and, like a line of flame, directly along to the clitoris. It's all connected, of course, and it helps back up my theory that enjoyable labor and courage in birth are born of pleasure rather than pain.

Pleasure for a pregnant woman is usually an activity that has *not* been suggested by an expert. Anything even vaguely clinical or "good for me" has rarely appealed, and most pregnant women are being told what is good for them almost hourly. I was told to "go massage [my] perineum" by the midwives at my birth center and was given a very rough diagram that looked like Venus, the moon, and Saturn but was supposed to represent the vagina, the perineum, and the anus. I recall opening up the pages on the bus and feeling mortified at the exposure. When I got home, with my apricot oil and my knickers round my ankles, I got to stretching that tender but very flexible skin between the two orifices. I had been told to stretch away until I felt a burning sensation. "How unpleasant," I said to no one in particular and promptly gave up. Everyday masturbation would do the same trick and feel a whole lot more comfortable, so I tried that instead.

Egged on by the theory proposed by writers such as Sheila Kitzinger and Ina May Gaskin that pleasure calms both mother and child and makes labor faster and easier, I goose-stepped my husband to the bedroom almost every night for a month before I gave birth. As my due date came and went, my efforts became more intense and more perfunctory than kinky. Yet the side effect of constantly touching and arousing myself "down there" was one of deep connection with my baby and the coming birth. Some women make love and many masturbate during early labor to both bring on the contractions or to merely get in touch with the idea of opening up to full dilation. For several nights before giving birth, I excitedly frigged away in prelabor, hoping (half terrified) for accelerated momentum. I am sure the vision of this is profoundly unappealing to many—a woman up in the middle of the night, squatting in the middle of a Persian carpet in a vast white nightgown, looking like a beached killer whale grinding her belly into the sand. But birth has tremendous erotic power, a fact that has been stripped away by an increasingly clinical approach to a deeply primal act. Perhaps I would hesitate to liken my labor to an orgasm (more like coitus interruptus), but many women have experienced intense arousal in their contractions and the dramatic release of their child from their body.

And yet, it simply isn't fashionable to describe such an odyssey at a dinner party. Sex in our culture has been divorced from its consequence, and the deeper a woman journeys into her pregnancy, the farther she travels away from its true source. The cultural taboo on pregnant sexuality is illustrated well on the Internet, where a woman can either find pregnant pornography sites or dry medical facts pertaining to safety and hygiene but very, very little editorial exploration, philosophy, or art about the subject. When I googled the words *pregnant sex,* I yielded such helpful advice as "Do not let your partner blow air into your vagina" and "Enjoy more shallow penetration closer to your due date." Sensible words that left me high and dry. In my mind was the holy vision of a rosy-fleshed woman with child, russet ringlets streaming to her hips as painted by Gustav Klimt, but I could find so little of that spirit: so dreamy, introspective, and luscious.

Spiritual Midwifery, the bible of natural birth by Ina May Gaskin, now in its fourth edition, is illustrated with grainy black-and-white photos of couples making out during labor. The first time I saw these tender bearded men cradling topless Madonnas, I tittered self-consciously. Taught that birth was pain, pushing, and poo on the floor, it was hard to visualize a John and Yoko–style love-in on my own B-day. And yet over the course of the pregnancy, I began to understand the link between sensuality and courage. My husband's touch got me through my whole journey from the day I tested positive to the terrifying moment of the C-section incision. Words of encouragement ring on deaf ears when you go into that soundless void of early labor. Yet a featherlight caress can echo through your body like a sound current through water or a bell through stone. Kissing, embracing, and nipple tweaking are definitely home-birth etiquette. It was hard to imagine the profoundly private freedom of having my husband oil my perineum (yow!!) or work my nipples over in a public ward with a big clock above our heads and three detached staffers in scrubs standing

by. And yet right up until my emergency transfer from the birth center to the labor ward, Ina May's sweetly radical, sexually open, and emotionally intimate model of birth stayed with me. That way the father of my child played a vital physical role right until the end.

Once they had strapped a monitor around my belly and punctured my back with an epidural, the eroticism was gone, and so was my sensitive and deeply private ongoing conversation with my uterus and vagina. By the time I was asked to push the baby out the next morning, I was utterly spent from a night hooked up to a fetal monitor in a darkened ward and completely without sensation from the waist down. It's very hard to push a baby out with a numb bum. It's hard to even care. Shortly afterward, my son was declared "stuck in the birth canal" and was delivered via emergency C-section. It was a long, long way from the gentle vision I had nursed through my pregnancy and completely opposed to the ideals I held about being utterly in touch with every subtle physical sensation.

Birth outcomes are hard to control, especially if you are thirty-nine years old with a baby that is three weeks past his due date. But despite the highly invasive way Marcello was delivered, my sexed-out pregnancy bore me in good stead. My labor, which lasted a good eighteen hours, was not unbearably painful—in fact, it was very peaceful and empowering. I had craved the contractions as the fruit of so many hours of waiting and visualizing. When they came, I felt at one with the baby, swimming through the same stream of blood and instinct and struggle. Perhaps I wouldn't have had quite as positive a perspective if I hadn't spent considerable time devoted to sensually nurturing my pregnant self. So much stood in the way of feeling truly sexy—the weight, the water retention, the discharge, and the backache—and yet I always found ways to link this baby back to his source, back to the heat and the mystery of conception. I still had a clitoris, even if I couldn't quite reach it.

In the same way that happiness is not simply the opposite of misery, pleasure is not just the opposite of pain. It is a choice as much as an action, a mind-set as much as a moment. While it is very easy to be cynical about pregnant sexuality, everything changes when you see it as a state rather than an act. Pregnancy is the purest sign of union; it is truly woman in full flower, and it was, in ancient times, the prerequisite for the first sex symbol. Have we come so far from those pagans and their crude little Venus statuettes? Can anyone really desire a body full-blown with flesh, blood, milk? The answer begins and ends with you.

7. DREAM NURSERY
Building Utopia on a Baby Budget

Everything is softened for little people: Mozart is simplified to a few robotic chords, color is paler, and faces, places, and things are fatter and fuzzier. Disneyfied. Purified. Watered, and dare I say, dumbed down. So it goes for the nursery, the room where a baby first experiences his world in microcosm and communes with his mother round the clock. Often this is the room that makes a sharp U-turn from personal style and the contents of which remain at the mercy of mass-produced furnishings and muted, almost neutered palettes. For new babies, the nursery is meant to be a soothing sleep factory with soft edges. Yet what of Mummy? Can she survive in a space decorated solely with fuzzy duckling wallpaper borders and gingham dust ruffles? Isn't it better to go quietly bonkers in a room that you can stand?

THE PRENURSERY:
BABY'S FIRST MONTHS

The place where a baby sleeps can be very fluid in the first six months. Legend has it that as infants, the Fendi sisters dozed in drawers in their parents' Rome leather store. My own mother bedded my brother down in a wooden drawer full of blankets back in the sixties. In his first five months, my son slept all over the joint; I watched him breathe next to my face in a plastic bassinet on wheels that I rented straight home from the hospital, then in a Moses basket placed on top of the bed right next to my pillow in a zip-up carry bassinet with reinforced sides. The kid liked to rock. Literally. So the idea of setting him adrift in a vast immobile crib seemed silly. And impractical.

The whole concept of a nursery is predicated on separation, a concept somewhat unnaturally cold when a newborn needs your scent and skin so badly. I gave no real thought to a nursery for nine months, as it seemed so much easier to feed my son and sense his many needs right next to our bed, on top of our bed, or right in it. He loved being changed, or fed, or played with in the middle of everything. He loved sleeping near the TV. He loved watching me cook from his vantage point in the center of the kitchen or lying under the backyard tree that I had festooned with old Christmas decorations that flittered in the breeze. At night I wanted him very close. The idea of placing a newborn "down the hall" (albeit hooked up to a monitor) for me just generated more work compounded by the stress of uncertainty. The transition to a real nursery seems more comfortable when a baby has outgrown a bassinet and night feeds, and this could be anywhere between six months to two years, depending on your parenting philosophy and your baby's personal needs. For families who choose to cosleep, the nursery might be more important as a playroom than a bedroom.

THE BARE-BONES NURSERY

When we finally moved Marcello into his own space and crib at ten months, it was en suite to our bedroom, and we pulled the door off the hinges. Psychologically (if not aesthetically), it felt right. Looking at that twelve-by-six-foot room, I saw endless potential and promptly bought four gigantic rainbow-colored woven-plastic buckets, a beat-up vintage bookshelf (to paint white), and at last . . . a big white crib. It took a long time to commit to a changing table, and an armoire was out of the question. The idea of those three big, fat chunks of varnished furniture in such a small space reminded me way too much of a photograph by Diane Arbus. Yet many mothers are convinced that they are not performing their duty without purchasing "the suite." Clustered together into a congested trinity, traditional nursery furniture can look like dollhouse decor on steroids. The sleigh-bed crib that holds sway over the market is somewhere between a massive lyre and a varnished coffin. Flicking through catalogs and websites that sell traditional nursery furniture makes me ask myself, whose tradition? Bram Stoker's? Liberace's? Cher's?

For some inexplicable reason, nurseries remain the one room in the house that modernism and good taste forgot. Oddly, the perfectly round or square crib have become an urban status symbol because of their rarity. Two companies, Stokke and Oeuf, dominate the market, and mainstream versions of their deluxe offerings fall short by default of needless whimsy. JCPenney copied Stokke's round crib but added finials for a canopy—the curse of the traditional nursery strikes again. The price of a modernist crib is enough to make you choke on a Cheerio: $700 and up. Yet having the crib (and, yes, the crib bedding) you really love, much like having a very strong stroller, is not an extravagance. The baby's bed is the focal point of the nursery, the starting point for all decor dreams and, if handled well, will survive successive children. Divide the price by five years (and more than one child), and then rationalize it to your budget.

BE A TIRE KICKER

Some mothers fret over the materials used for a crib. Wood or metal? Cast-iron cribs were introduced in the mid-nineteenth century in Britain and in the colonies, as they were believed to be more hygienic (and less humid) than wood. The fancy, formal balustrades of a metal crib are really cosmetic, though. To me they look like miniature Victorian holding pens, and the image of a soft skull hitting the sides doesn't appeal. At the opposite end of the spectrum, wood veneer can warp, chip, and simply snap over time, especially if the crib is bought secondhand. I bought two cribs on craigslist. The first collapsed within weeks, the second is still standing. A preloved crib needs to be a strong one and the top of the range. Don't rely solely on its appearance; rap the side of a railing with your knuckles to test for real solidity.

Find a bed that has a fluid side rail, adequate storage, and the ability to convert to a toddler bed. I avoid pull-out drawers beneath, because toddlers love to sit in them and get fingers stuck in them. Install a very generous, thick bumper (babies can pogo at one year) and one or two Lovies blankets, soft toys, or cloth books to comfort your little frog when alone.

The following important information is from the National Safety Council. For more detailed information about bumpers and so on, go to www.nsc.org/library/facts/cribtips.htm.

- Dispose of antique cribs with decorative cutouts, corner posts, or lead paint.

- The space between the slats should be no more than 2⅜ inches apart to prevent infants from getting their head stuck between them. Cribs manufactured after 1974 must meet this and other strict safety standards.

- The corner posts should be the same height as the end panels or less than 1/16 inch higher than the end panels.

- No cutout areas on the headboard or footboard so a baby's head cannot get trapped.

- The top rails of crib sides, in their raised position, should be at least 26 inches above the top of the mattress support at its lowest position.

- As soon as the child can pull himself to a standing position, set and keep the mattress at its lowest position. Stop using the crib once the height of the top rails is less than three-fourths the child's height.

DON'T FORGET THE BREASTAURANT

Other than the crib, the other critical investment for your own comfort and much yummy bonding is a comfortable and supportive nursing chair. Any small sofa-style or slipper chair that can fit into a tight space will do; it doesn't have to be a gargantuan, ugly glider or a ye-olde cushioned rocker. Arranged around your chair should be an ottoman or footstool for elevating exhausted legs and a small table always stocked with nuts, chopped fruit, your daily dose of postnatal supplements, some organic dark chocolate, a thermos of "mother's milk" or fennel herb tea, and a two-liter bottle of water. And (for long feeds) some brain-fluff magazines or short poetry volumes. Some might think it excessive to have such a complex feeding station set up in the nursery, but I am here to say that in the middle of the night, dreamy and depleted, you will need all of the inspiration you can get. And, as your brains sweetly siphon out through your nipples, the easy access to vitamins, liquids, or food becomes welcome routine.

TO MATCHY MATCH OR NOT TO MATCHY MATCH

A baby room that does not jar the eye is ideal. But who really can sustain an all-white or pale-pastel nursery with a toddler in residence? A far better idea is to use white or pastel furniture (the most common stuff available at thrift stores and malls) and bounce brighter colors off it. Lime green and lemon yellow was not my planned color scheme, but when I found some vintage fabric at a yard sale, I had some curtains and a crib sheet made to cut the incongruity. Yellow in a nursery is energizing for all those early mornings and looks cleaner over time than powder blue or cherry red. Instead of focusing on matching exact fabrics, I let color echo through the room, tying the curtains with lime green grosgrain ribbon and making a "screen" in the open doorway from ribbons and cotton pom-poms in shades of lemon, saffron, olive, and lime.

A fast way to decorate the walls was to slice up a favorite children's calendar (ours was Miffy), place each image on a brightly colored cardboard mount, and complete with a cheap, white, or wooden dime-store frame. The simplicity of the lines detracted from the inevitable clutter of toys and clothes, and the calendar cost less than $20. I think the most important gift for a growing child is a room that balances repose with inspiration. If you get too lost in a theme—dinosaurs, Elmo, sailing boats, Thomas the Tank Engine—what room does this leave for the child's own budding obsessions, experiments, and inspired chaos?

COLOR

The best baby room I ever saw had Schiaparelli pink walls decorated with a concentrated burst of about sixty small, richly colored images of flowers, insects, animals, and exotic wonders of the world. The pictures were cropped to focus on the most brilliant aspect of each image: the heart of a lily, a pair of bejeweled Indian dancing feet, a butterfly wing, a rose in bloom. I imagined the tiny girl who woke up in this room every day, alert to the vivid beauty of the world without a pastel Beanie Baby in sight. Some might have been shocked by such intensity in a child's room, and think the smaller the baby, the more tranquil the palette choices should be. This said, vivid pastels such as bright saffron, lilac, canary yellow, and chartreuse lend more energy to a small room than pink or blue.

I have seen very few wallpapered nurseries; most parents opt for a conservative border trim along the picture rail. Yet wallpaper could be the cheapest and funkiest way to create a space that is creative and joyful. Vintage 1960s wallpapers with very large, almost psychedelic flowers suit small rooms and look quite witty on one wall of the room; say, just behind the crib, rather than all over. Color can also infuse a room through the use of sheer, layered organza or taffeta curtains (babies love to see them flutter in the breeze), a square of sari silk suspended over the crib, or a veil of brightly dyed lace hung as a wall panel. Bedding needs to be calming, but soft toys look very delicious in bright, unexpected shades: Hot-pink elephants and blue teddy bears have more fun.

CREATING A FUNCTIONAL SPACE

I call my domestic route in our tiny nursery the cow path. Every day I tread a predictable route from crib to changing table to bookshelf to floor to crib. As in a galley kitchen, most mothers pivot in an ever-shrinking circle in the nursery, and their ease is based on access.

The nursery needs to be designed for the way you move within it. Diapers, baby care products, quick changes, socks, and wipes all have to be in one place. I use baskets to store folded clothes and bins to sort and store toys. One bin for soft things, another for wood, and another for plastic. In each bin I place Ziploc bags to gather up small bits and pieces that could get lost . . . or swallowed (blocks, buttons, Legos). Favorite books, toys, and clothes can be clustered in one spot and rotated weekly. Shoes, hats, sunscreen, spare pacifiers, and travel books need their own area (usually a shelf nearest to the door, where I keep a spare diaper bag, fully packed for times when I am too stressed to pull together the daily routine). Clothes often add to the confusion of a small nursery. Allocate one section in your own wardrobe to coats, jackets, and baby dresses (they pack down to nothing or hang in small clusters) and place a few days' clothes at a time in baskets. I share a dresser easily with my son and lay out clothes the night before for both of us, to save time.

MURALS, MOBILES, AND FOCAL POINTS

There will be no avoiding clutter in a baby room. To create a visual core to a room crawling with stuffed monkeys, you need to make one bold statement. A beautiful Mexican tree of life painted on the wall above the crib, an oversized Calder-style mobile hanging from the center of the room, a gigantic Bruno Munari screen print of an apple, or a length of Marimekko fabric hanging like a tent above the crib all create an illusion of space and clarity missing from most fluffy, ruffly, traditional nurseries. For respite, ideas, and online dreaming check out www.marimekko.com, www.moderntots.com, and www.designpublic .com.

CLICHÉ SMASHING

Gingham and *broderie anglaise*. The American mother cannot get away from these two visual viruses of nursery decor. They line baskets, creep along dust ruffles, and climb the walls as trims, curtains, bedding canopies, and even picture frames. If one is not living in the Hamptons, where whole houses look like wicker and white picnic baskets, then a more worldly alternative must be found. For lack of viable alternatives, I went along with white wicker baskets that came in sets of two at Pottery Barn and Target, but promptly gutted their *Gidget*-style gingham linings in favor of solid colors such as lemon, lime, and fuchsia, and used vintage floral dress fabric and even hand-blocked Indian printed cottons for the bumpers and bedding. One standard pillowcase becomes two child-size cushion covers when halved. Two cloth table napkins can almost line a small basket, and one standard sheet is enough to create a small duvet cover and dust ruffle. To get around the god-awful gingham diaper holder, I chose plain canvas and trimmed it with thick rickrack. And when faced with a bedding set that had to be gingham due to a total lack of choice, I settled on navy and white—the most chic, visually positive, and French-looking option at hand.

8. UTTERLY SCRUMPTIOUS NAMES

Hundreds of Reasons Not to Call a Child Jane or Steve

We named my son Marcello many months before he was born. His daddy and I were virtually living on the dusty old IKEA couch where we had conceived our son, like two inert hibernating bears. We were watching *8½*, Federico Fellini's epic about cinema and infidelity, the sort of film a couple can watch only if they have something as solid as a pregnant belly to bind them together. Marcello Mastroianni was dancing with a light soul at the end of the film, and he seemed just the right sort of madman-child to name our son after. His face was sophisticated, but his chin and eyes were winsome, timelessly elfin. And so it was.

Mahrr-chell-oh. I had always fancied a name with lots of vowels and a whiff of the ancient. Marcellus was a Roman general, hopefully not excessively cruel. No one on either side of the family bore this name, and it's always good to be first. Plus, if you are going to give a baby a name that is Italian or African or Hebrew, make it magically, excessively so. Zacharias has so much more music than Zach. So why hold back?

Names, I have always believed, hold a spell for those who carry them; they are both a promise and a blessing. The process of naming a baby begins as a lovely, creative exercise and often devolves into a weary concession to diplomacy (as so much of parenting tends to do). On a social level, we worry about our kid being the one with the weirdo name in roll call. Beck, Björk, Moon Unit, Zowie. And on a family level, we are still under sufferance to pay homage to our kin (but isn't that what middle names are for?). Despite all this external pressure, naming remains a territory where the mother really ought to hold her ground. After all, this is the name you will utter a million times over decades. This is the name that frames a face and a life, so why not go out on a limb or tempt the gods with a little whimsy, exoticism, poetry, and madness? The kid can always go out and change his name to Jack or Clint later on.

In the meantime, I suggest that all mothers begin to populate the world with names of beauty and strange brilliance. Good places to get inspired for names are in a book of Greek myths, a volume of Shakespeare (I adore Miranda from *The Tempest*), the pages of an atlas or a botany book, or, more simply, in a baby name book in a foreign language—the French have the most soulful, womanly, poetic names for girls; the Italians have, I feel, the most powerful, majestic names for boys; and non-Western languages have names of rich spiritual portent and ancestral meaning to many, especially if the baby has a mixed heritage.

Some meticulous mamas might need a system to arrive at a short list of names. I can think of several. The first might be to narrow down the name to a specific letter in the alphabet, since parents often unwittingly choose names of the same initial and the same number of syllables as their own. No wonder my husband loves his son's name;

Marcello/Matteo ring together like an echo. In choosing a name from a specific culture, say, African, why not draw up a list from specific parts of the continent? In the brilliant book *The Best Baby Names in the World* (by J. M. Congemi), there are names from eight different African countries to choose from, complete with easy phonetic pronunciations and meanings. Zahra, a delicate name that evokes the desert, actually means "blossom."

Many parents who adopt a baby from another land choose a name from that birthplace. Chinese names do tend to be very brief, so it's tempting to bind two names together for richer meaning: Li means "elegant," Ling means "bell," and Li-Ling has a ring to it. Some foreign names have a distinctly Western sound but a different spelling. Fei (pronounced *Fay*) means "empress" in Chinese, a good start for any little girl.

Exotic names have never been fashionable. From 1900 to 1960, the most popular name in America for a girl was Mary. Digging around through the lists of the thousand most popular names for each decade from the U.S. Bureau of Statistics, I found that the older the name, the wilder its nature. Ella, Bella, Bessie, Minnie, Maxine, Opal, and Violet were all popular girls' names in the 1900s, and all rather brassy and adventurous in their own way. In 2005 the number one name was Emily, and standing at number five was Olivia. I was tempted to think this was because of Olivia the piglet in the popular children's book and not Olivia Newton-John.

Why is it that we are all so prudent with our vowels and our cultural references? What do we fear in a wild or unusual name? Other than a flirtation with French names in the 1920s, American mothers have rarely strayed from their English ancestral roots, even though ethnic names, without doubt, have the most music, especially Indian names. My favorites are Chandra, which is Sanskrit for "moon," and Lalita, which simply means "pretty." Hebrew is the lushest source for girls' names beginning with Z (Zahava!) and boys' names heavy with poetry and mythology. Spanish also has some zingers, including Zaneta, Zarita, Zaviera, Zerlina, and Zelia, which means "sunshine."

Famous British Yummies have a tendency to give their daughters names that sound like cake shops: Daisy Boo, Fifi, Trixie Belle, and Poppy Honey spring to mind. This is delicious if your darlings go to a posh private school where everyone is called Apple, and if you are sure your child wants a baby name for life. Botanical or operatic names are a nice compromise; I think I'd rather be an Allegra or an Aria than an Apricot or a Plum. My weakness for names that suggest flowers exposes the Victorian romantic in my soul. I would have loved to have been a Peony or a Camelia, and perhaps if my mother had called me Willow, I would have grown that little bit taller and been just a little less clumsy. Names have power; they are dreams yet to be lived out by the dreamer. Picasso had about twenty names from first name to surname. All you need is one, so make it a doozy.

Uncommonly Pretty Girls' Names

Adelaide, Adelle, Agatha, Aisha, Allegra, Amelie, Anooshka, Antigone, Arabella, Ariel, Aurora, Aviva

Bailey, Basia, Beatrice, Bebe, Bessie, Biba, Billie, Bliss, Blossom, Brave, Breanna, Brigitte

Calypso, Capri, Celestine, Christa, Clea, Clementine, Coral, Corinthia, Corrina, Cosima

Daisy, Danica, Demeter, Diandra, Dido, Domino, Donatella, Dorothea, Dublin, Dusk

Edie, Elaini, Electra, Elisabetta, Ella, Eloise, Emerald, Emiline, Epiphany, Estrella, Eva

Fern, Fiorella, Flame, Fleur, Francesca, Frederique, Freya, Frida, Fuchsia

Gala, Genie, Georgianna, Germaine, Gia, Gigi, Gimili, Ginger, Giovanna, Giselle, Gogo, Gracie, Gwynevere

Harriet, Hattie, Hayley, Helene, Heloise, Hespera, Hyacynth

Iman, Imogene, India, Indra, Inez, Irini, Isadora, Isis, Isla, Isobel, Ivonne

Jade, Japonica, Jasmine, Java, Jemima, Jerusha, Jonquil, Joy, Julietta

Kahsha, Kalani, Kamala, Kameko, Kaneisha, Karolina, Kaya, Kazuki, Kelila, Kenya, Kiki, Kristiana, Kyoto

Lark, Laure, Leaf, Leatitia, Leda, Liberty, Lila, Lilith, Lisette, Lorca, Lorelei, Lotus, Luella, Lulu, Luna

Madeleine, Madrigal, Magenta, Mallory, Marguerite, Marie-Laure, Marisol, Matilda, Maude, Maxime, Maya, Mia, Mignon, Milena, Mimi, Minnie, Mirabelle, Mischa, Mona Lisa, Murielle

Naiad, Natasha, Nepal, Nerida, Neroli, Nico, Nile, Nina, Noelle

Odetta, Odile, Olabisi, Olivia, Olympia, Ondine, Oona, Opal, Orchid, Orla, Ornella, Ozara

Paloma, Peggy, Persephone, Petra, Petulia, Plum, Poppy, Portia, Posy, Prudence

Queenie, Querida, Quest

Rae, Rain, Raisa, Ramona, Raphaela, Raven, Regine, Rilke, Rita, River, Romi, Rosalita, Rosealba, Roxy

Scheherazade, Serafina, Serena, Seville, Shakti, Shaquilla, Sheba, Shiva, Sibilla, Sienna, Simonetta, Sofia, Solange, Soledad, Soraya, Sorrell, Stella, Stevie, Storm, Sylvana

Tamilla, Tatum, Thea, Thelma, Therese, Thierry, Tilda, Toni, Torillyn, Trilby, Truly, Tuesday, Tula, Tulip, Twylla

Ucella, Una, Unity, Ursula, Uwimana

Valentina, Veda, Velvet, Venetia, Venus, Verushka, Victoire, Viola, Violetta, Viva, Vivien

Wanda, Wilga, Willow, Windsong, Winsome

Xanthe, Xara, Xanthe, Xaviara, Xenobia, Xyla

Ynez, Yoko, Yolanda, Yseult, Yvette

Zahra, Zalika, Zarita, Zelda, Zephyr, Zizi, Zooey

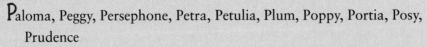

Unusual and Striking Boys' Names

Adonis, Alberto, Alden, Allesandro, Alvaro, Amos, Anders, Andreas, Ansel, Antoine, Apollo, Aquila, Aramis, Ari, Armand, Arno, Aubrey, Auden, August, Austin, Avery, Axel

Baird, Balthazar, Barnaby, Basil, Bayard, Bello, Benoit, Benton, Blaise, Blake, Brooklyn, Burgess, Byron

Carlito, Carmine, Cedric, Cesar, Chayton (means falcon in Lakota), Che, Claudio, Clemente, Conrad

Daniel, Danius, Dante, Danton, D'arcy, Darius, Dashielle, Davide, Diego, Dieter, Dillon, Dimitri, Donato, Donovan, Dov

Eduardo, Elias, Emery, Emilio, Enrico, Ernest

Farrell, Federico, Felix, Fielding, Finnegan, Firth, Fletcher, Floyd,
Foal, Forest

Gabriel, Galahad, Garcia, Gerard, Geronimo, Giancarlo, Gideon,
Giles, Giotto, Gustave

Harper, Heathcliffe, Henri, Hilliard, Holden, Humphrey, Hunter

Indigo, Innis, Inrik, Ira, Ivan

Jasper, Javier, Jean-Claude, Jett, Johanne, Jonas, Jules

Kane, Kaspar, King, Kiran (Sanskrit for "beam of light"), Kristophe

Langston, Lawrence, Leonardo, Leopold, Leroy, Levon, Lido, Lionel,
Luca

Makoto (Japanese for "genuine"), Marcel, Marlon, Marvelle,
Matteo, Maurice, Merlin, Midas, Miller, Milo, Misha, Mitchell,
Mitchum, Morell, Moss

Neptune, Nicolo, Night, Nikita, Noah, Noel

Ogden, Olivier, Olmo, Otis, Ottavio

Pancho, Paolo, Patch, Paz, Perry, Pierce, Pietro

Quincy, Quinn

Rafael, Ramon, Raoul, Rashid, Ravi, Reynolds, Rhys, Rio, Rollo,
Roman, Romney, Rugby

Sailor, Samara, Satchel, Seal, Seamus, Sebastian, Sergio, Seven,
Severin, Silas, Silvio, Sinbad, Sirius, Sky, Sol, Stefano, Storm,
Sunday, Sylvan

Tarot, Teirnan, Theo, Tiberius, Treat, Tristan

Uri

Vaile, Verity, Virgil

Wagner, Warner, Wilder, Winslow, Woodie, Wylie

Xavier, Xiao

Yani, Yohann, Yojef

Zeus, Ziggy, Zorro

9. PREGNANT PAUSE

The Essential Last-minute Lists

In the quaking wake of birth, it's nice to know where your black eyeliner pencil, your extra-large satin pajama bottoms, and your dove gray Ugg boots are. Along with monster, surfboard-size pads, I wisely packed some rather Edwardian lace peignoirs, starched Indian cotton nighties, and even a length of blue grosgrain ribbon to twine around my tangled mane for "receiving" at the hospital. I was exhausted but looked fuzzy round the edges for the photographs, and on really bad days, I knew there was a fresh nightgown to absorb those crazy lactation night sweats with grace. Most women give birth in hospitals, and some in freestanding birth centers, but for those who have their babies at home, some clear-eyed planning for the birth and the immediate moments and days that follow also demand meticulous lists. Birth is a lot like going camping; you need lots of dry clothes, chunky, comforting socks, and something sweet and very particular to eat in the darkest hour of the adventure.

HOME BIRTH

Women organizing a home birth will confer with the attendant midwives, support team, and/or doula for their needs. Some order home birthing kits from respected sources such as Mama Goddess Birth Shop (www.mamagoddessbirthshop.com) and Everything Birth (www.midwifesupplies.com). Many of my friends who home birthed used a simple inflatable toddler pool, not so much to water birth (they lack the depth of those great birth-center spa pools) but for pain relief. For those who are not planning a home birth, it's still not a bad idea to have materials and basic information at hand in case the baby decides to come fast and furious right where you are.

It's hard to predict where you will actually birth the baby, but a very firm mattress or a mattress with a firm board placed beneath it will help support you during labor. Make up the bed with plastic sheeting (some use a shower curtain, with fresh bedding on top). It sounds wild, but you also might need some plastic sheeting for the room where you are planning to labor and birth. Cover what you value, including rugs and sofas. And clear a generous amount of space so that you can move around. For the actual moment of birth, a sterile sheet should be provided by the attending midwife.

Basic Needs for the Birth

- inflatable bathing pool
- boiled water in a sterilized jug
- kettle, and backup kettle (if large quantities of water are needed)
- six clean towels
- box of overnight pads
- sterile gauze pads
- breast pads
- antiseptic fluid
- unscented soap
- antiseptic soap (for hands and thighs)
- two large plastic bowls

Basic Needs for the Birthing Mother

- three thin, open-fronted nightgowns
- two pairs of bed socks
- small sponge to moisten lips and face during labor
- lip balm for dry lips
- hot-water bottle or ice pack for lower back pain
- snacks, sandwiches, barley sugar candies, diluted fruit juice
- music that you love and gentle lighting

Ask for:

- Only the people present that you want there, someone manning the phone and door to ensure your privacy, someone to make calls when guests are welcome, and a sign on the door if needed. Unlike a hospital, there are no visiting hours at home, so it's up to you and your support team to lay down the law and ensure your rest—and the baby's sleep.

- Food instead of flowers; you may be in no mood to cook after all your good work, and a freezer stocked for a week with nutritious soups and stews is gold right now.

- Someone to do rounds of fresh laundry and basic housework straight after the birth.

- Extra towels and bedding, in case yours are all gloriously used.

BIRTH CENTER BIRTH

Pack:

- All of the things listed for the hospital (see below), as well as more personal touches such as a birth ball, a swimsuit for your partner if a water birth is planned, towels, a plastic camera or video camera, your own small bouquet of flowers or meditative objects or images to focus on during the birth.

Ask for:

- Someone to cover the clock while you labor. It really aids a natural birth to get inside your own sense of time and to not feel pressured to "dilate one centimeter by the hour," as is standard hospital protocol. If you are progressing well and want to turn your energies within, have all flashing appliances and timekeeping devices obscured.

- Music you love (many birth centers allow CD players for the birth). My friend Sam gave birth listening to Arvo Pärt's "Für Alina," which is a little like giving birth to Philip Glass. Deep, cyclic rhythms can deepen your sense of calm and concentration. I myself could have done with the Doors' "Riders on the Storm."

- An electric oil burner, plus one object from home that makes you feel completely relaxed—even if it is a poster-size image of Hello Kitty.

- Plenty of fresh hydrating snacks (barley sugar candies, fresh fruit, frozen juice cubes).

- Something fizzy to drink straight after the birth: pink lemonade for you, champagne for your doula/midwife/family and friends.

HOSPITAL BIRTH

Pack:

A Labor Bag Containing

- flower water facial spray (lavender is calming)
- small sponge
- lip balm
- bed socks
- old T-shirt, singlet top—forget the bottoms; you're giving birth!
- appropriate massage oil. I found a sexy and calming blend of calendula- and chamomile-based labor massage oil at Earth Mama Angel Baby (www.earthmamaangelbaby.com).
- hairbrush and elastics
- snacks
- birth plan

Hospital Bag Containing

- five nighties and two pairs of pajamas (it sounds like a lot, I know)
- breast pads
- three nursing bras
- one really comfortable dressing gown
- gentle natural soap (liquid is best)
- makeup and toiletries (tinted moisturizer and a bit of blush might be as far you get)
- small hand mirror (handy if you can't move too fast)
- mountains of sanitary pads
- tissues
- slippers
- trashy magazines, uplifting poetry, and one holy book
- an eyeshade
- a going-home outfit that doesn't make you look like Jack Nicholson in *One Flew Over the Cuckoo's Nest*
- pocket money
- health insurance card
- phone card, address book, cell phone, and charger

Ask for:

- Flowers in just the colors you love. Like a crazed diva, I said no orange flowers, and for once in my life it felt justified.

- Fresh food. (Avoid chocolate, as it can give you migraines after an epidural or simply the deep dehydration of labor and birth.)

- A copy of the newspaper printed on the day of your child's birth. This is a great talisman and a reminder that the world is in fact still turning outside the labor ward!

PLANNED CESAREAN BIRTH

Pack:

- A rose, lilac, lavender, or chamomile water to be sprayed in a mist near your face or on your pulse points by your partner or attendant before the surgery. The scent of flowers is enormously calming in a sterile environment.

- A camera. You won't be seeing the baby emerge (few women gaze into the wound at the point of incision and birth), but your partner can shoot the birth just as he or she would at a vaginal delivery. It took me a while to get over the blood-and-guts side of things, and I'm so grateful for these shots now, as I was too emotional at the time to recall the first sight of my baby.

- A medically approved laxative! The constipation and abdominal bloating after a C-section is the terrible secret of this surgery, and I am here to tell you that first movement is no symphony. Consult your doctor on an approved laxative and foods that will help you get regular.

- Pillows from home and your pregnancy pillow help you manage your wound *and* your baby.

- High-waisted granny knickers to keep you feeling secure rather than exposed about your healing, bandaged belly.

- A teddy bear of your own that is well worn and not a gift for the baby . . .

- Nightgowns instead of pajamas; you'll be feeling very belly sensitive.

- Slippers with good grip for balance; you cannot afford to fall over!

- An inspiring image or card of a mother and baby from the animal kingdom. I could have really used this when I got my short dose of baby blues, and this can happen after any kind of birth.

Ask for:

- Healthy, hearty food: raw juices, fibrous salads, fresh fruit, green juices, liquid chlorophyll (to flush out all the drugs), and a decent liquid-vitamin supplement. Major surgery plus the stress of birth need substantial nutritional support post-op, and hospital food does little if anything but dehydrate a new mother.

AND FOR THE BUBS

- disposable diapers
- baby wipes (love that meconium!)
- two comfy going-home outfits
- a muslin wrap or fleecy cotton wrap in colder weather
- a tiny beanie for his/her wee little nog

10. BIRTH

Your Brilliant First Act

My Birth Prayer to All Mothers

Give the birthing mother a soul sanctuary, a huge set of loving
hands to shelter her from doubt, misunderstanding, ignorance,
fear.

And give her deep, peaceful sleep to make her body strong.

Guide her to a community of experienced, like-minded women to
bolster an unshakable faith in the innate wisdom of her own
body.

Grace her with the right to retreat into a deeply private and primal
state of mind, to face the challenge of birth with an open heart
and an energized spirit.

And just for one day or maybe two,

give her nerves, and balls, of steel.

SUMMONING FAITH IN A SEA OF DOUBT

Birth is the most dramatic first act of your life. It is the first real sacrifice and the first initiation in a chain of giving acts that will echo through all your mothering days. Birth is obsessive. When pregnant, it's easy to fixate about birth and barely give a thought to the concrete reality that comes after, of having and caring for a baby. Birth is introspective. As the belly gets bigger and bigger, thoughts and dreams turn inward. Birth is heroic, rousing strengths and passion you may have never known.

And for many, birth is fearful. The days and weeks before birth are full of excitement for some and apprehension for many. I recall being ravenous for images, information, and personal accounts of birth, and, in equal measure, terrified. For over nine months, I had bonded with my belly, partly not wanting to let go of the creature sleeping so snugly within and partly not believing I could. Perhaps my son sensed this and stubbornly stayed in place, not making a move till three tough weeks past my due date.

The simultaneous desire and ambivalence a first-time mother feels toward birth seems natural to me. Birth asks a woman to go from the known into the completely unknown in a relatively short space of time, and every day of pregnancy leads up to a climax you cannot time, predict, control, or anticipate. It is impossible to taste, feel, or sense birth till you've done it yourself. Just as reading romance fiction is nothing like falling in love, studying birth books won't get you there either. For this and many other reasons, I'd rather speak about birth in a way that is spiritually and emotionally supportive rather than clinically descriptive. Especially as I am not a doctor.

The language of birth, in this society, is the language of medicine. Once the baby is born, he will have a face, a name, an identity within your family. He will be yours. But until that moment, he remains the fetus to be delivered, and you, his mother, the patient. I sensed this deep disconnect and loss of autonomy in almost every prenatal visit I made to the hospital birth center where I planned to have my birth. On the way to these appointments, I would sing to my baby, talk to him, and stroke his long legs coiled against my ribs. At each exam, I could barely contain my joy. "You won't be laughing when you're in labor," said one examining nurse sternly, and I felt my curiosity and confidence begin to ebb.

Pregnant women spend a lot of their energy deflecting the fears of others. And it is truly exhausting to reassure other people about your safety and well-being, when you are trying to salvage some of that courage and certainty for yourself. It takes huge emotional strength to filter out the prevalent message that giving birth is dangerous and unpleasant. Modern birth is portrayed as fearful; movies and TV depict the pain of labor as unbearable. Celebrities promote the idea that a completely anesthetized surgical birth by C-section sidesteps that pain. And the current standard of hospital care treats all births as high-risk procedures. A tour of the average labor ward, prior to your birth, will reveal an impressive and intimidating array of equipment available to assist, monitor, and intervene with a birth.

As your due date gets closer and closer, it may become harder and harder to silence the feeling that birth, your birth, is slipping out of your hands. And it is true that normal, natural birth, without drugs, scalpels, bells, or whistles involves proper effort and diligent planning by the birth mother—as well as fortitude in the face of official objection, familial pressure, and a prevailing sense of deep distrust. The paradox is this: Birth is natural, but natural birth is not widely supported, respected, or well understood.

To stifle the naysayers and build up your emotional reserves, please write down these words and put them all over your home:

The female body is an extraordinary mechanism designed
for the efficient birth of not just one but many babies.
I am physically designed to give birth alone or with the
loving assistance of others. The more I listen to my body,
the stronger I become.

For the vulnerable pregnant mother, the world is a mirror that needs constant polishing for a clearer reflection. Late in my pregnancy, I wanted to be only with people who believed in the female's ability to push out a healthy baby. I spent time with experienced mums who were up front about the pain of labor and birth but who reassured me that I could handle it. I watched plenty of videos of women in labor, comfortable at home, going through their moves, leaning on partners and furniture and moaning that deep, secret life grunt, which has a guttural depth somewhere between orgasm and a cat's yowl. I *loved* looking at old black-and-white photos of the British birth activist Sheila Kitzinger dancing on a table the night before one of her many births, looking exultant and free. And I spent time swimming in a small lap pool, imagining my body submerged in the water as the baby's body floated with complete trust inside me.

Keeping up your confidence and spirits. Practicing relaxation. Having faith in a physical process you've never experienced before. Not letting the quite natural fear of birth completely eat you alive. All of this takes great grace as the days of waiting for the baby drag on. All eyes are on you, and the pressure starts to intensify. The extreme lack of privacy that characterizes modern birth starts before we labor; with extra sonograms booked if the baby is late, many well-meaning strangers asking when the baby is due, and anxious, inquiring phone calls and e-mails flooding in, it can be hard to get into a state of relaxed concentration. Yet shutting out all the white noise to prepare for the moment of labor is crucial for birth. For the pleasure of it, and for the hard work.

The night I finally went into labor was incredibly exciting. I remember kneeling on the floor, gloriously relieved to know the baby was coming, awestruck with the crazy force inside my uterus sending waves of sensation through my spine like a thumping wave crashing to shore. Resting in bed between heavy rushes of contractions and soaking in a small bathtub to ease the pain as they became more intense, I managed well. My personal experience of labor was that the more privacy I had to get on with it, the less pain I felt. The presence of a good

experienced doula did not impinge on this sense of privacy. And I re-call with gratitude the space she gave me as I labored long. Twenty hours into my labor the idyll ended. I was in the hospital labor ward, surrounded by many strangers coming and going and arguing about how to work a new fetal monitor. I lost my inner dialogue of steady pain management and succumbed to unbearable levels of discomfort. The baby, also, may have lodged in a difficult place; it was all going by in a blur. When I accepted an epidural, I lost physical contact with my baby and became completely concentrated on the equipment being used: the tube in my back, the fetal monitor blinking in front of me, and the clock on the wall. The hospital staff and my doula, Anna, had tried hard to help me deliver my baby vaginally. But so many things stood in the way, the most basic of which was that I could no longer feel my sphincter. I was given two chances to push. I failed, and Mar-cello was delivered by C-section. As a result, my best memory of birth, my strongest and most romantic memory, is the long labor I enjoyed trying to open up. If I can offer anything to an expectant mother, it is the fact that you *can* love your labor and let it guide you in its wild and primal way to a strong and healthy birth.

Labor is an amazing ally in birth. It paces you, telling you when to rest and when to breathe hard, and it toughens you for the incredible tension between external and internal sensation: that alternation be-tween deep internal stretching and almost breath-crushing contrac-tions. I can understand why many women find labor claustrophobic. It is very *raw* and *total*. Like an orgasm that doesn't stop or period pain that enters every fiber of your body. It is also a great disinhibitor that makes you surrender everything: appearances, good manners, ego, fear, and sometimes the control of your bladder and bowels. It's heavy shit, and it's wild. I can understand why many women would want to numb their labors—or to soften, shorten, or even artificially speed them up. It's emotionally painful to lose control and to totally open up and lose your façade to pure primal function. Nothing in our lives pre-pares us for this. Fashion contains the body. Good manners suppress it. We are forever lowering our voices and crossing our legs to be ladylike, so who told us that to give birth, we have to open our mouths and our vaginas at the same time and *let it all out*—blood, sweat, yelps, screams, tears, and all?

The hospital is a hard place to be a wild woman. That is why more and more women are enlisting the help of a doula or birth assistant during their deliveries and asking their husbands or birth partners to advocate for their wishes. This is not some flight of self-indulgent fancy. When a woman feels safe, she births well. And when she feels free to move, make noise, and spontaneously respond to the needs of her baby, she births more easily. The work of birth, physiologically and emotionally, is hard. But the many obstacles, external anxieties, rules, and invasive procedures of modern medicalized birth can make it so much harder.

Until natural birth becomes the model for all births in America, as it is in Western European countries such as Holland (where one-third of the population safely home birth their babies, and midwife care is the norm), women will have less support to birth vaginally, without heavy pain relief, in the physical position (and location) of their choice.

Until natural births become more mainstream and supported by our culture, many of them will continue ending up as emergency surgical births. I don't write this to add to your fears but to urge you to make informed decisions and creative choices about the care you choose for your birth, the coping methods you'll apply for your labor, and the ideals you hold for the treatment of your body and the baby's during and directly after delivery. In many ways, birth is the first milestone choice of many choices you will make as a mother, and it *can* be an empowered one, no matter what the outcome.

TAKING THE HURT OUT OF C-SECTIONS

Cesarean section as an emergency can come as a shock. Changing your birth plan at the last minute is a profound development. But because of the very real fact that one in four mothers will deliver by Cesarean section, it is prudent to be aware of the procedure and ready for it as one birth outcome. Ideally, most healthy women can avoid a surgical birth by choosing to labor longer at home, resisting unnecessary induction, and enlisting the assistance of a midwife or obstetrician who supports vaginal birth even in the face of a perceived challenge (such as twins, posterior presentation, larger babies, and overdue babies). *Mothering* magazine has an archive of very well-written articles on this subject (www.motheringmagazine.com), but my simplest advice for addressing the possibility of a Cesarean is talking about it *a lot* with your health-care provider and, if you don't want a C-section, stressing your desire for a vaginal birth in every context and especially in the labor ward itself.

While a Cesarean birth is more dangerous and not ideal, it is important to remember that it is still a birth, and in the context of an emergency, a miraculous one at that. My sharpest memory of the moment my baby emerged from my body was a clock on the wall that said 11:15. My husband said our son smelled like raw clay when he was born and gave a strong, lusty cry. I was too angry to notice. The time we had together as a family was a matter of minutes, before my husband and son left me alone for suturing and many long hours of recovery.

Happily, my experience is no longer the model. Family-centered Cesarean birth is a new trend in many hospitals and is an approach that honors the process as a birth as well as a surgery. A family-centered Cesarean allows the husband or requested family member or even a midwife to be present, the baby is brought immediately to the mother, and, in some circumstances, the baby stays with the mother during recovery. The surgery is conducted as a birth with respect and calm rather than detached chatter from the surgical team. If you are having a scheduled C-section, it is reasonable to have a birth plan that encompasses some of these ideas. To ask for simple things such as silence or encouraging information about the procedure as it is happening is extremely empowering for the birthing mother. When (after the birth) my hospital room was filled with laughter and jokes about staff holidays, I removed my oxygen mask and firmly asked my surgical team to tell

me about the stitches instead, and this act was reassuring and focusing. Perhaps it gave that team pause to remember there was a new mother under the arc lamp as well as a patient!

My good friend Ruth had ongoing back problems and consequently knew through most of her pregnancy that she had to have a C-section. A devoted attachment mother, she made peace with this outcome by imagining the hospital as an extension of her own body (!) and by loving rather than fearing the hospital staff. This courageous leap of faith made the day of her surgery a true birth where she felt honored, protected, and, most important, present at the delivery of her son Harry. The little canvas screen that divides a mother's view from her surgery can do much to make her feel as if she is invisible, and ultimately irrelevant, at her own birth. Whatever the medical staff and your chosen birth partner can do to make you feel connected is vital to how you feel at the moment of birth and how you view it for years to come.

Just because Cesareans have become standard (and prevalent) practice in American hospitals does not mean that our responses to them must become standardized. Every birth, like every baby, is entirely different and entirely unique and personal to the mother birthing. Make it as intimate and beautiful as you can. Something as simple as a spray of fresh lavender water on your face before the surgery might be all you need to feel human and womanly in a sterile realm.

SOME SMALL THOUGHTS ABOUT THE BIG ISSUES OF BIRTH

Pain and Fear

Everyone has a different pain threshold, but undoubtedly pain has a deeper impact when anticipated and feared over time. The energy spent worrying about the pain of childbirth would be better invested in learning deep-relaxation techniques, reading birth stories, devising your own pain relief methods, and visualizing the goal of labor rather than morbidly focusing on the process itself. The more support you get for your fears of labor, the better the experience will be.

The terrible dreams pregnant women have at the end of their terms are like clearinghouses for the unconscious, unburdening our souls of all the "what-ifs." The truth about birth is that it is accompanied by risk. But not more so than acts of everyday living. Every time I hold a sharp knife, go near a cliff's edge, or approach oncoming traffic at a crosswalk, I summon instinct, reflex, caution, and faith to keep me alive. The same survival instinct applies to birth. Trust yourself and give all your energy to the baby rather than to your own natural fears.

Pain Relief

There is no medal for giving birth without pain relief. Every woman must judge the needs of her own body in birth against the health and safety needs of her baby. For this reason, it seems sensible to at least try natural labor and ease into the rhythm of it before asking for drugs to take the edge off or numb it completely before you are well into dilation. The disadvantage of a spinal block, or an epidural, is that it can slow labor and the rate of dilation, increasing the risk of further intervention. This said, I have many friends who vaginally birthed successfully using epidurals and other forms of pain relief. My main objection to the use of drugs during labor is that all pregnant women are asked to refrain from substance abuse for the full nine months and are then invited to flood their system (and the babies') with narcotics during labor and delivery. Think closely about anything that will jeopardize the breathing, feeding, motor function, or food for your newborn.

Location, Support, and Focus

Choose a place to give birth where you feel safe, and try to find an ally in that place who can consistently attend to you during your birth. In the presence of many uninvited or unknown people, you'll want to focus on the one person who is guiding your birth. In some circum-

stances, that person might wind up being you, but I strongly suggest considering appointing a primary support person who can comfort you and advocate for your needs during labor. A doula is a birth attendant who can help you labor at home, accompany you to the hospital, and provide much-needed postnatal advice and assistance. Her presence may not guarantee the birth you want, but she can certainly help you stay focused on the work at hand. The same help could also come from a friend, family member, partner, or trained midwife. Check with your hospital about its protocol regarding the presence and participation of an outside midwife at a birth. Ask hard questions about the rate of Cesarean section births and the rate of episiotomy. These are crucial facts to gain before a birth.

Finding a Doula

If you feel you need more support, empathy, and information before, during, and after your birth; if you feel you need an extra person at hand to advocate for your wishes or birth plan; if you simply need a woman to be with you during your birth who is *not* a friend or relative, you might do well to invest in the services of a doula. A doula is not a trained midwife and she is not authorized to deliver a child, but she can be a great complement to a midwife for a home birth or birth center birth, or a calming presence at a hospital birth. My doula, Anna Urbanski, a mother of three, provided me with reading material, shared vital insights in late pregnancy, and was the source of laughter and strength through a long labor and subsequent medical birth. She stayed all night during my induction and was there for me after the birth. Visiting my ward and even accompanying us home, she helped me make sense of my birth and gave solid and uplifting support in the weeks that followed. New motherhood is costly, but this sort of support is a very worthy expense. If you are considering using a doula, want to know more, or want to locate one in your area, try the website of the respected organization Doulas of North America: www.dona.org.

Laboring at Home

If you feel well, are in good health, and are not bleeding, it could be a good idea to labor peacefully for as long as it is safe in the comfort of your home. The model for labor care at most hospitals is based on the Friedman curve, a conventional medical standard that dictates a woman dilate 1.3 centimeters an hour to successfully deliver her child. Those who fail to dilate fast enough can be induced or given a deadline to birth naturally. But birthing by the clock can inhibit labor, decrease the confidence of the birthing mother, and invite unneeded intervention. Talk to your doctor or midwife about how long you can wait and how far you'd like to progress before coming to the hospital.

Hang-ups

Imagine taking a shower in front of four men in lab coats and pissing on their shoes. Imagine opening your legs really, really wide and letting a massive red rose made of blood and skin blossom out of your butt, all in a perfectly white, sunlit room. Imagine moaning in orgasm loud enough to wake up your whole street. Then imagine all of this and more for giving birth. The most important thing to leave at the door is the urge to be "nice" or birth "properly." For goodness sake, woman, just piss on those shoes and get on with it!

Control and Surrender

Some mothers might want to plan their labor—including choosing the type of pain relief—well in advance of the birth, giving themselves a sense of security and control. But no matter what you plan, a sense of deep surrender is needed to get through birth with acceptance and joy. The more you study and learn about the birth process, the more you might want to forget the technicalities in labor, "get out of your own way," and let your body and primal instincts drive. Giving up rational

control during a birth is not an act of passivity; sometimes it can actually give you even greater strength. For more on this please refer to *Birthing from Within,* by Pam England and Rob Horowitz.

Pleasure

Not many of us prepare for joy in birth. We might secretly hope for it, but rarely do we openly believe that birth can be pleasurable. Guess what? It can be a gas as well as a pain in the ass. Laughter in birth—and, in fact, any gesture that opens the mouth wide—helps the cervix dilate. The only way to make your vagina smile is to let your mouth do it first. Howling, groaning, and singing wildly all work too.

One of the main tenets of sexual birth is that the horny spirit that made the baby is the same spirit that will bring him out. If the very thought of making out during labor makes you laugh, try it anyway. Or at the very least, concede to the erotic possibilities of a huge dilation. Some women actually climax at birth. And even if there are only seven of them on the face of this earth, I want to meet them and shake their hands.

Healing

There is a lot of stress on mothers to not dwell on a birth in the first days postpartum but to briskly "get on with" the job of new mothering. No matter what your birth is like, every woman needs time to heal and reflect afterward. To find her feet and to forgive, or simply absorb, whatever path her baby chose to come to her. The women who experience injury in birth need extra, tender care, and for the many women who have unexpected, violent, or difficult births, there might be rage and pain that need to be channeled so they do not deteriorate into depression. Well before your birth, establish trusting relationships (at least two) with people you can share your birth experience with. People who know how to heal through simple acts of caring and can just hear you out are gold for your soul.

Resources for Planning a Better Birth

BOOKS

Active Birth: The New Approach to Giving Birth Naturally, Janet Belaskas

Birthing from Within: An Extra-Ordinary Guide to Childbirth Preparation, Pam England and Rob Horowitz

Mothering Magazine's Having a Baby, Naturally: The Mothering Magazine Guide to Pregnancy and Childbirth, Peggy O'Mara

The Complete Book of Pregnancy and Childbirth, 4th edition, Sheila Kitzinger

Ina May's Guide to Childbirth, Ina May Gaskin

The Natural Pregnancy Book: Herbs, Nutrition and Other Holistic Choices, Avira Jill Roum

Birth Right, Susan Ross

WEBSITES WITH EXCELLENT BIRTH STORIES

For birth stories that are very diverse, check out www.motherstuff.com.

For birth stories that involve healing after a Cesarean and vaginal birth after a Cesarean, have a look at www.birthrites.com.

For images of pregnancy and the postpregnant body in all its many forms, try www.theshapeofamother.com. It's a pretty radical departure from what the magazines convey as a postpartum ideal and offers home truths and great blogs.

Part 2

STYLE SURVIVAL FROM
YEAR ZERO

11. BABYMOON OR BUST

Getting Through Those Mad First Six Weeks

B ringing home a newborn is so much more than the physical act of putting the key in the front door and gingerly lifting a bundle over the threshold. The first weeks of mothering can be, in their own way, more confronting than birth itself. In a strange way, it's a lot like being held hostage. You no longer choose when you eat, sleep, or even urinate in a timely fashion. You carry on a perpetual vigil caring for the tiny unknown creature, and on top of it all, there are people knocking on the door, calling on the phone, and poking their nose into your pain, your pleasure, and your shock. External advice becomes a hum of ongoing white noise. I think that of all of the adjustments of mothering, the first week and weeks that follow are the keenest challenge, the steepest learning curve, the most potentially humiliating, often most fulfilling, and certainly the most surreal of your womanly life. No matter how delectable the infant or how deep the relief of having made it, no matter the brief moments of silent communion, there is this sense of accelerated demand and a deep state of unknowing that makes it all just terribly . . . raw. And the longer you have spent in the hospital, the more interventions involved in your birth, or the weaker your state, depending upon the ease of your pregnancy, the less confidence you might feel finding your feet.

I had so wanted to be robust and resilient. And in this spirit of ignorant passion, I began my at-home mothering days with a very short-lived zeal. Free from the maternity ward after ten days of very slow recovery, I went a bit bananas. Off the painkillers and out of pajamas, on day one I flung on a front pack and power strutted to the nearest park, promptly bursting two stitches. C-section, schmee section, I really wanted to show my husband that I was competent and cheerful. Oh yes! All the while feeling as if a bandit had left a steak knife somewhere inside my stomach. The big, fat white lie of new motherhood is how confident one is supposed to feel doing things we have never done before. Even though handling a newborn comes very much step by step, nothing felt basic or inherent to me. My husband would tersely wrap Marcello's tiny body as tightly as a falafel roll, his purple screaming head floating above the swaddling cotton. I was bad at wrapping, hopeless at soothing, rough at getting the gnashing jaw clamped onto the cracked nipple, and had a hobbled gait. It was very tempting to feel I was a bad mother. Doomed.

Wounded, exhausted, defeated, and half-crazy from the three-hour cycles of sleeping, nursing, nappy changing, settling, and quietly crying myself back to sleep, I seriously wondered how the earth came to be populated at all. At really desperate moments in that first week, I wanted to pound on my neighbor's door and ask the pretty blond Yummy, "How did you do it? How on earth did you get through this?" Fatherhood hit my husband just as hard. He felt guilty that he couldn't nurse, was tense from the constant crying, and utterly baffled by my rage. The Madonna and child never looked like this.

Having read mainly natural-mothering books that raved about the fuzzy days of an intimate babymoon, I was completely unprepared for the physical demands of postoperative mothering. The energy and joy that I had wished in these moments, plus the necessary courage, seemed to be seeping out through my wound. My badge of disenchantment. All most books tell you about recovery from a C-section is no lifting or driving for six weeks. And that's it. The most instruction that books give about the first two weeks with your baby is to never shake a newborn, to support its fragile head and floppy neck, sleep when the baby sleeps, and fill up the freezer. But I can tell you that you need a truckload of faith, very, very patient family and friends, and a rock-solid belief that things will get better. There's just no point to counting the days until they do; time is not on your side. The noticeable turning point for settled calm in a baby is said to be twelve weeks. That's three corrosively long months. I will never lie and say these are easy days, but they are critical to the journey and preparation for every pleasure that is to come. And if you can cover the basics of keeping the baby at a comfortable temperature; feeding him at least eight times in twenty-four hours; bedding him down safely on his back without toys, cords, ties, pillows, or excess bedding (see the American Academy of Pediatrics recommendations at www .aap.org and other tips at www.kidshealth.org); and being loving and gentle, you are not getting it wrong. You are simply getting it done.

Feeling like a failure as a new mother comes as a very deep blow after ten months of anticipation, yet the truth is, there is no such thing as success in those early days. It can be terribly hard to believe that everything will be OK, and in that sleep-drained, doubtful mind-set, both mother and child can be locked into an endless cycle of tension. It seems awfully disheartening at the time, but a twelve-year-old girl could settle your kid from a crying jag simply because she's not you.

One totally artificial but very real pressure is the desire to look in control in the eyes of others. My first family lunch out of the house, at two weeks postpartum, was a tearful, embarrassing fiasco. I wore a dress that I couldn't nurse in, the room was bright with sunlight, and everyone was so excited to see the baby, but all he did was wail. The compassionate, perhaps pitying, looks and barbs of advice that came flying across the restaurant table made me feel I was not a natural.

There must be a reason that many cultures sequester the mother at home for the first six weeks or longer. The world can wait. In the first month of mothering, I felt best simply alone with my son, staring at him asleep, feeding him in the dead of night, and lifting his bowed legs like the wings of a Thanksgiving turkey; or lying in bed, the three of us shipwrecked in love and tender trepidation. Anxiety was constant: I remember standing in the shower listening to the water hissing and squealing through the pipes and believing it was the sound of a roaring cry. The house seemed to ache with whispering and gently closing doors. Of course, to mothers of two, three, and more, this description of horror can bring only a wry smile. There is only one first time.

Blood-and-Guts Basics for Brand-new Mothering

- Conserve energy. You might be on a big high from getting home and think it a fine idea to hose down the yard. Resist! You need long-term energy and sustenance now.

- Limit all visits to the most useful hands-on friends or relatives you know, or establish a fixed visiting hour just like in the hospital. Never feel the need to entertain or serve guests in the first month.

- Don't apologize! For the state of the house, for the way you are dressed, for the baby crying, or for the baby being asleep. This is not an exam or a TV show; it's your house. Expect and command respect simply for getting on with things as best you can.

- Ignore any advice that goes against your grain, and don't just let anyone seize your baby. This should be a slow time of deliberate and gentle movement and soft gradual adjustment (for the baby, as well as for you).

- Sleep like a newborn. Eliminate a sense of normal time and forget about "sharing" the evening with a movie or meal with your husband. If you are feeding on demand around the clock, you need perpetual rest. There'll be plenty of time for dinner and date nights later on. The evening hours between six and midnight are best for banking on snatches of well-earned rest. Sorry, Dad.

- Praise your partner for whatever help he or she can give you. It's all hands on deck right now, and a spirit of teamwork is needed from the very first moments of parenting. That way, neither exhausted, wrecked parent can get locked into a cycle of blame. And believe me, the resentment starts now.

- If your partner is on limited leave from work, make sure that you have emotional and practical backup for when he or she returns to the job, and try to understand the huge reality gap that might grow between you from the moment the front door closes to the moment he breezes back in. Try not to hate him because he's not there in the trenches with you, lost in the poo and the wipes. Fathers feel a tremendous loss at missing the first months at home with their new babies, so try not to assume they have the easier job—even if, on many levels, they actually do. Parenting is a series of heavy compromises and trades, and the number of nights you'll wish your husband could lactate will amaze you.

- Find small ways to baby yourself: soft-lined slippers, pretty comfortable clothes, a brand-new fashion mag on the nursing table, healthy snack bowls all over the house, and one really decent soaking hot bath (or shower with candlelight) a day . . . or two.

- Try to leave the house without your baby for a few minutes each day. Even if that means flinging open the front door and stretching out your aching body, opening your heart to the vastness of the sky, and seeing people going about their lives. Realize that the concentration of these weeks will dissipate in time.

- Count the blessings of small mercies: a healthy child, a kind word, the sound of rain on the windows as everyone sleeps, a well-made little bed or a tidy changing table. Whatever pocket of order you can create inside the storm is your moment of sanctuary.

- Give yourself points for getting through each day and even indulge in a little new mum blogging if in need of commiseration.

- Have well-written support material at hand for all your burning questions. Don't be ashamed if *Breastfeeding for Dummies* is your constant bedside reading.

- Get external support for your routine: Make sure that everyone who visits you replenishes nursery, kitchen, and bathroom supplies and pitches in with the cleaning, laundry, and cooking.

- Leave the house with baby in tow when you're ready, and only then. The first ventures out with diaper bag packed, stroller navigated, and pajama top hidden under clever trench coat feel like lunar expeditions. Take short walks with the front pack or sling first. You have nothing to prove to anyone!

- New mothering is a time of soul searching and perpetual second-guessing both for yourself and for your baby: Google all you want (from breast-feeding positions to wound management and nutrition), but don't overload yourself. Draft a list of questions for the hospital midwives, your GP, or your mum, and then seek second opinions. Often the overwhelming nature of the job can make you need way too many second opinions for essentially basic issues.

- Treat any new skill gained as a personal milestone, including changing a diaper on the backseat of a car!

- Slap on a little lipstick, some cool barrettes, or a smudge of eyeliner. Even pajamas look better with a coquettish touch of style. This is an issue of soul survival, not manic maintenance.

- Enjoy massaging your baby, singing to him, dancing him to music, reading to him, and simply holding him while he sleeps. The more contact you create each day, the deeper the bonding. Love dispels doubt, so build that faith with private, tender, cherishing acts.

- Ease up on your routine to meet your own pace. A dirty diaper is not the end of the world; make that cup of tea first if you really feel the desire.

DEALING WITH BLUES—
AND FEELINGS OF A DARKER HUE

Expect dark days. Baby blues—a slump where tears and heavy emotions seem to flow—can come about three days after birth and last for up to two weeks. But I am hesitant to put a number on the days that feel foggy or flat or just unsettled in the first weeks and months of mothering, as so many individual influences come into play: Exhaustion, medication, sleep deprivation, trauma, and hormonal balance all have a role. One particular pill for blood pressure I was asked to take after giving birth made me black with despair and violently angry. Luckily, I managed to recognize its impact and request another prescription almost immediately. Keeping an even keel in the first weeks is helped by tending to your own health diligently. Try to stay well hydrated; have friends bring whole food to the hospital, and ensure optimum nutrition with a supplement that includes omega-3 essential fatty acids; try to have daily exposure to sunlight; set up strong emotional support from a variety of friends and family; and sleep whenever and wherever you can.

All of this will help lift the baby blues, but it will not be enough if you are suffering from postpartum depression, which is said to affect 15 percent of American mothers. Stars such as Courtney Cox Arquette and Brooke Shields have suffered from it, and social awareness about it is rising. If you suspect something is very wrong in the first weeks or even months after birth, don't chance your health—reach out immediately. Listed below are symptoms of PPD and some sources of support for your recovery.

- emptiness and lack of connection with the baby
- feeling restless or irritable
- feeling sad, hopeless, and overwhelmed
- crying a lot

- having no energy or motivation
- eating too little or too much
- sleeping too little or too much
- trouble focusing, remembering, or making decisions
- feeling worthless and guilty
- loss of interest or pleasure in activities
- withdrawal from friends and family
- having headaches, chest pains, heart palpitations

Postpartum depression can be subtle or very violent and clear. It can come on anytime in the first year of your mothering and is a temporary condition that can be treated. There is no shame or failure in seeking treatment. The most dangerous thing a woman suffering from PPD can do is to isolate herself or suffer in silence. The Postpartum Support International organization has an excellent, very well laid out website (www.postpartum.net), an emergency help line(1-800-944-4773), and links to support groups across America.

- If you have a history of depression, I recommend reading a little about PPD, not to scare yourself but to be prepared for any unexpected lows. A very sound and comforting book on the subject is *The Mother-to-Mother Postpartum Depression Support Book* by Sandra Poulin.

One of the greatest sorrows of suffering from PPD is the huge gap between how a woman expects to feel as a new mum and what she is actually suffering through. Emotionally, the unspoken expectation that every new mother is joyful weighs especially heavily on those who do not feel well after birth. One very moving line I read on the www.postpartum.net support page is actually the mantra commonly used in recovery from postpartum depression, and it's a great one: *You aren't alone. This is not your fault. You will be well again.*

12. BREAST-FEEDING

Going with the Flow

THE JOY OF BRAZEN BREAST-FEEDING: GIVING SUCK AS THE MOOD STRIKES

I have always seen breast-feeding as masterpiece material. Leonardo da Vinci, Raphael, and Picasso shroud the breast-feeding mother in a spiritual haze, first as a Madonna, then as a woman. Because the woman nourishes from her body, she is always a sort of goddess. Contemporary culture has no equivalent image that approaches that peaceful, dignified, replete divinity. Breasts are presented as either sexual or functional, and the bras that house them before and after maternity illustrate this duality well. Maternity bras rarely feature the frills and decorations of lingerie; they are there to do a job. Nursing bras are terrifying, often porridge colored and thick with elastic and harnesslike straps. Armed with pillowy breast pads that shield the pliant bosom from the world and de-eroticize the weight of the flesh and the flow of the milk, we struggle to free aching nipples from layers of respectability.

Sometimes we don't want to be herded into a mother's room or a crowded café corner; sometimes we want to be with our babies and with everyone else. And sometimes the hunger of a baby is an emergency in itself, and there's no time to tastefully shroud your bosom. On a bus one afternoon, enjoying the warm sunlight on my bare shoulder and nursing my son to sleep, I fielded the glare of a harried office worker. I smiled and said, "It's a little bit of bosom or a whole lot of noise. You choose!" Too often, it's not just the child that is expected to be seen and not heard. Never mind that breasts are *everywhere* except where they are needed most: in a baby's mouth. Why is it considered normal to sell a car or an ice-cream cone or a can of Budweiser by exposing breasts, and obscene to unsheathe a nipple to nurse?

Breast-feeding is pure, but its raw sensuality bites at the puritanical heart. Before we have babies, we sport cleavage as a weapon of seduction, and afterward, when the breast is at its pinnacle of heavy, potent glory, there is some confusion of decency over its display. Breast-feeding in public is completely legal in all fifty states, with the exception of babies over the age of twelve months in Tennessee! Yet the image of a woman actually doing so freely is less common here than in Europe, Asia, or Israel. Standing at the checkout at Whole Foods Market some years back, I stumbled across the front cover of a magazine, which featured a beautiful photograph of a big, pale breast with a cheeky baby firmly attached *and* smiling while suckling. One could not have wished for a more in-your-face celebration of the bare, milky boob. Seeing mouth to nipple made me instantly want to reach for a big bar of white chocolate, to gorge on molten, sweet milk, and dream.

Of all the aspects of being a new mother, I loved the subversive power of nursing best. Breast-feeding brings that little bit of nature, primal force, and tender generosity into the rational mechanics of everyday life. It is a form of care so explicit and eternal that it can't help but humanize any situation, which comes in quite handy in a breathless, brutal city like Manhattan. Nursing at will wherever and whenever she and the baby please is just about the most ancient and the most modern stand a mother can make. And it's important for one reason alone: Mothering is felt by everyone, but it is rarely seen. Society makes very little space for mothers, so we have to claim that space ourselves. What better way than engaging in a little gentle lactivism?

Nursing engages all the senses and at its best can transport both mother and child into a very private moment of fused ecstasy: physical, emotional, and sensual union. I suppose that sounds quite a lot like an orgasm. The body certainly releases the same hormones while nursing as during orgasm, and that heavy dose of oxytocin (which doctors call the love drug) deepens the bond with every feed. Breast-feeding in comfortable, adequate privacy, unpressured by the constraints of time, creates a bubble of bliss and a circle of heat and intimacy around the two interlocked bodies involved. I think it is nursing's kindred spirit with the erotic that goads some parties. Sin always belonged to the body, specifically Eve's. Rosy apples and engorged nipples share the same flush and pose the same invitation. So even though a woman giving suck was depicted as holy throughout history, there have always been those eager to step in and stop too much of a good thing. Breast-feeding is about spontaneous touch, nudity, physical union, and rapture available anywhere and anyplace day or night. It's an amazing freedom that every mother should be able to try, enjoy, and fiercely protect.

BREAST-FEEDING 101

Why Breast-feeding Will Rock Your World

Breast-feeding is beautiful on so many levels. Environmentally, it generates no waste. Physically, it helps your uterus shrink back to normal size. Emotionally, it bonds you to your baby by pumping your body full of the feel-good hormones prolactin and oxytocin at every feed,

and it gives you plenty of skin-to-skin contact, ensuring that you are holding bubs tight several times a day. Practically speaking, nursing is an entirely mobile way to feed a baby without the fuss of bottles, measuring cups, and so on (ideal for long-distance travel and getting out and about—even attending concerts!). And in terms of good health, the benefits for your baby and for you are manifold: For baby, breast milk has the perfect proportion of fat, carbohydrate, and protein. It also has powerful antibacterial properties, disease-fighting antibodies, multivitamins, nutrients, pacifying and calming properties, and, remarkably, it adjusts in temperature to suit the baby's needs. Breast milk is highly digestible, taking the stress out of trying to nourish and hydrate a sick baby, and does not generate as much mucus as formula. Breast-feeding has been linked to reducing the cases of many common childhood illnesses, including asthma, pneumonia, influenza, ear infections, bronchitis, and German measles. Think about it: Before vaccines, breast milk was designed to protect a baby's health and build his or her immune system, passing on the mother's antibodies and nutrition with every feed. Long-term breast-feeding also helps Mum. Some studies have revealed that nursing reduces a mother's risk of contracting ovarian and breast cancers, as well as osteoporosis. For a more comprehensive list of the health benefits of nursing, have a look at the remarkable article "101 Reasons to Breastfeed Your Child" on the website of the nonprofit organization Promotion of Mother's Milk (ProMoM) at www.promom.org.

Another more subtle but very important benefit of nursing is that it is a lifestyle that keeps you "nice" rather than naughty for just that little bit longer, obliging you to eat well, not drink or smoke, and rest in order to keep up your supply. By becoming a mini ecosystem, you might be taking better care of yourself than usual, and you'll be burning up to 500 calories a day, so losing the baby weight is less of an issue. Given all this good news, I think that the initial discomfort, struggle, or "weirdness" of breast-feeding is a small sacrifice to make for such massive gains.

Getting Started

After I gave birth, I waited four days for my milk to come in, agonizing as I pumped the liquid gold of my colostrum into a tiny bottle from a massive, old, electric, hospital breast pump. I wept terrible, jealous tears watching nurse midwives give my hungry son formula to silence him in the middle of the night, and panicked that I would not be able to nurse. When, on morning four, my breasts finally exploded into bowling balls, soaking the bedsheets, I had a surprisingly tough time getting Marcello's frantic little mouth and darting tongue to latch on. When his mouth missed the mark or I failed to disengage him without his biting and dragging, my nipples cracked and blistered. I was the one standing at the back of the room during the hospital's daily screening of the "How to Breastfeed" video, weeping and feeling like the cow who couldn't milk.

In the hospital where I was recovering, there was a very persistent, very patient lactation consultant. She was the one who got me to place my baby's head at the two o'clock position and to literally plunge his open mouth onto the nipple so deeply that he would not be able to bite. She also taught me to tickle his chin to stop him from dozing on the breast, to stroke his cheek to get him to suck harder, and to stick a finger in to disengage his mouth without tearing or dragging my shocked skin. In the brief time you get at the hospital, seek all the help you can with establishing a good attachment technique. Don't worry if some of the advice or disparate information you receive overlaps or contradicts itself; I found that when I got home and was nursing on my own, the strict technicalities of feeding and attachment gave way to improvised personal methods that worked just as well. If my back was well supported in a good chair or with many pillows in bed, if my son was relaxed and didn't have to reach or stretch too far for the nipple, if we had privacy to fumble and flail to get started, we were usually fine.

Aside from attachment, another big nursing concern is the quantity of milk and the frequency of the feeds. In my first year, I found that every baby has his or her own feeding style. My son guzzled hard and fast on each breast for the first few minutes, and lolled or dozed after that, requiring coaxing for good, vigorous sucking over a sustained amount of time. He was the five-minute feeder and fed more frequently but always swiftly. Two other girlfriends had very greedy, hungry babies that seemed to suck for a good thirty minutes on each breast. At times it made me anxious. But, a year later, all our children leveled out at similar weights. Unless your baby is underweight or failing to thrive, I say trust the amount of milk you are producing and don't get caught up in measuring each feed. Often in-laws and one's own mother will obsess about the use of bottles or even request more pumping, so they can "see" what your baby is getting each day. Unless you are physically away from your baby for stretches of time or need extra sleep, feeding directly from your breast is best and the far more relaxing and spontaneous option. A contented, full baby usually wants to sleep and is smiling, burping, or spitting up the excess.

Some Common Obstacles

PAIN

Breast-feeding is blissful. Eventually. At the start, there can be terrible pain from engorgement, the discomfort of night sweats, and cracked and blistered nipples from the baby biting or pulling off too roughly. To counter biting, you need to plunge the nipple deep enough into the baby's throat to make sure it is not dragging or slipping out. Taking the time to learn how to attach is the most critical answer to avoiding pain.

This said, nipples still get a raw deal from nursing, and nasty bouts of recurring mastitis can end your breast-feeding career. Mastitis is an uncomfortable inflammation of the breast that occurs when milk ducts become engorged and blocked. Symptoms include red, swollen patches on the breast or nipples, fever, or flu symptoms. Depending on the severity and discomfort of your condition, try to massage the milk out even if you are not nursing for a spell, and also try to heal your nipples by applying your own breast milk to them and letting them air-dry between feeds, as breast milk is rich in antibacterial agents. If using ointments, try lanolin-based ones only, as these are safest for baby. Cleaning or scrubbing your breasts between feeds is not recommended; instead, use a soft towel moistened with warm water and massage them regularly to keep engorgement and blockages at bay (go to page 121 for more mastitis ideas).

CULTURAL ISSUES

I illustrated this chapter with an African-American nursing mum on purpose, as this is one part of the mothering community prone to avoid, abandon, or prematurely cease nursing. The renaissance in breast-feeding brought back by organizations such as La Leche League International is not universal. Yet. The online magazine *Mommy Too!* (www.mommytoo.com), written specifically for black mothers, features a regular column about breast-feeding by the magazine's editor, Jennifer James. A working mother who nursed both her daughters for two years each, James wants to reassure women of all cultures and backgrounds that breast-feeding is healthy, manageable, and fun. "Through my blog and site," she told me, "I want black mothers to understand that, yes, black moms do indeed breast-feed and that it's not weird or 'hippie.' I want mothers to understand the healing and bonding benefits of breast-feeding."

When James shared with me some of the cultural and practical obstacles facing black mothers, I found many convergent issues true for all moms new to nursing. "Most black women [with babies] work," says James, "and finding the balance between pumping and working can be difficult and trying, especially as many black mothers are raising children alone."

Breast-feeding, then, becomes one extra burden for single black moms to carry. "It becomes easier," James says, "for many black women to simply formula-feed their infants, especially when there can be many different people who watch their children, from day-care workers to their extended family. And, in some black communities, there is a stigma, especially among some black men, that a child who breast-feeds is taking away their women." In other words, some fathers simply don't want to "share the breast." Surely every mother from every culture faces many of these issues and obstacles to some degree. My husband is Italian, and, after a while, he wanted my boobs back too!

Resistance to nursing can begin with a free package of formula given to you on the day you leave the hospital, a discouraging word from your own mother, a lack of support from your partner, or simply the demands of returning to work. And trying to pump. Websites that support your point of view and friends who share your values really help with the effort of nursing. An important asset of the La Leche League website, www.lalecheleague.org is that it is also fully available in Spanish, Italian, Russian, and Chinese.

WORK

If you are returning to work early in your nursing career, it is critical that you are given the privacy, support, time, and inherent right to pump in comfort at work. To improve conditions for pumping and not have to do so in the misery of a bathroom cubicle or the exposed area of your own desk, it helps to make requests before your maternity leave and team up with other working mothers who share your office or workplace. Please do not underestimate the effort involved with pumping or the possible interference of office politics. Remember that what you are doing for your child is not an indulgence or a waste of anybody's time. And taking time off to nurse a sick child is less efficient than nurturing him through pumped milk. *Nursing Mother, Working Mother,* by Gale Pryor, is an excellent resource for pumping moms.

How Long Is Too Long, and How Much Is Enough?

No research has revealed that the constitution of breast milk changes over the duration of months or years, though many women, and even some doctors, will tell you that breast milk has the most nutrients in the first six months, and its benefits lessen after one year. Yet the World Health Organization (WHO) recommends that babies nurse for a minimum of two years, so these theories clearly haven't been proven. The conventional recommendation to wean at one year is based on the fact that solids are introduced at this age, that many women return to work, and that weaning fosters independence in a baby. But many attachment parenting and breast-feeding advocates will argue that secure, spontaneous nursing, rather than forced weaning, is the real source of security and confidence in a child. I am no militant, but I feel it is high time that the arbitrary dates for weaning be questioned and that longer breast-feeding (where convenient and possible) be encouraged. Letting a child nurse a few months longer does not harm him. In fact, it gives him extra affection, nutrients, calming hormones, and antibodies. On top of that, it is a ritual and a relationship that are highly personal to the needs of the mother and the child. I say, if it feels good, what is all the fuss about? I promised myself eighteen months of nursing and ran over by six months. In that time, my son had only three colds and one ear infection. He was calm and easily soothed, traveled on four twenty-six-hour long-haul flights to and from Australia without tantrums, slept well, and ate well. We felt very close, happy, and connected.

There were times when it was an effort to keep going and times when my supply ebbed and dipped, but we persisted, in part for the gazillion scientific reasons but mainly for the love of it. Of all the so-called duties of motherhood, nursing can to be the most pleasurable and the most relaxing. For however long you choose to nurse your child, and even if you are, in fact, using a bottle, it is an irreplaceable time to cherish the incredible closeness of holding your child and communing eye to eye, skin to skin, and heart to heart. This is the stuff of dreams and cupids.

Got Milk? Seven Ways to Increase Your Supply

Many women give up nursing earlier than they need to because of a sudden dip in their supply or because of the strain of keeping up with the demand of a particularly hungry baby. But, in truth, you needn't be a gushing fountain to nurse successfully beyond the first critical months. Any breast milk you give is an asset to the baby and provides a powerful oasis of calm for you. But anyone who aims to nurse long needs a game plan. Luckily, this is easier than it seems; healthy changes in diet and diligent hydration, better sleep, and even a weepy movie can restore the delicate balance that supports good supply.

STAY HYDRATED

New nursing mothers need to drink twelve glasses of water or fluid a day, or roughly one tall drink for every time the baby feeds. That's a little more than three quarts! Seems like a lot, but you'll be parched without it. Measure your level of hydration by looking at your urine; the darker it is, the more dehydrated you are. Make water readily available at every feeding, and drink before, during, and after. Do not skip hydrating when you're tired, and avoid caffeinated tea and even decaf coffee, to ensure that your body keeps all the precious fluid it needs. Also eat extra servings of salad, raw fruit, and fresh fruit smoothies.

BE A TEA BAG LADY

I suggest carrying fennel tea bags in your handbag. I drank four cups of Traditional Medicinals "Mother's Milk" Tea for almost eighteen months. Whether it was a placebo effect or not, I'll never know, but it worked for me. I also found Weleda Nursing Tea and vervain tea excellent, and delicious alternatives to the caffeinated drinks I craved. Be careful with mint tea; it's tasty, but contraindicated for nursing, which means it's not recommended. I have been told mint dries up sup-

ply, and in some cultures it is imbibed at times of weaning. My rule of thumb is to avoid any herb (including chamomile) not designated for nursing women.

GO GREEN, VERY GREEN

I drank a large glass of green juice made of veggies and parsley three times a week and watched my milk supply double. Greens work! But you need them in potent quantity. A lettuce-leaf salad alone is not going to boost your supply, but a whole bulb of fennel, eaten raw, will really help. Make a salad of avocado, cilantro, cucumber, fennel, green apple, alfalfa, lime juice, and a splash of olive oil. If you don't like the taste of alfalfa, try taking it in tablet form, as it is a very powerful milk booster. Augment your greens daily with fresh soups, lightly steamed kale and spinach, green juices, and wheatgrass. Not only will you have more milk, it will be better, packed with nutrients and minerals for Junior.

PS:

This is the time to be very diligent about the quality and cleanliness of your own food: Avoid foods with traces of pesticides, as these poisons become highly concentrated in breast milk. Milk thistle tea can help diminish the presence of pesticide residue.

PUMP TO THE MUSIC

Pumping and then bottle-feeding her breast milk can make a new mother anxious about her supply and fixated on that little line on the side of the bottle that reads 20 ml. Some say that pumping can decrease your supply because you are decreasing flesh-to-flesh contact, which is said to help keep the milk moving. But pumping also sets you free when you need to work, go out, or get some extra sleep. If you are pumping at the office, make a "mood board" of nursing images, pictures of your baby, and colors that relax you. Visual signals can help connect you back to the source and make you forget even the most sterile corporate environment. Avoid pumping just before you have to rush out the door to work or an engagement, and instead use the overflow from a particularly strong feed. Try to pump during quiet, relaxed times in the day, and pump to beautiful, "flowing" music (Ravi Shankar!) or try pumping in the bath, gently massaging the breasts and stimulating the nipples with hot water. I found this best when supply was low between five and eight p.m. in the evening.

PUMP AND DUMP

If you have had a little wine with dinner, don't forget to pump before turning in for bed. That way you can flush out the tainted milk and ready the breast for more lattes later in the night.

FEED THROUGH MASTITIS

To help heal occasional engorgement, place baby in different positions for each feed to make sure that all ducts are being used, avoid wearing tight-fitting or underwire bras, regularly massage your breasts in the direction of the nipple, give more frequent feeds (or pump to reduce the excess), and, to naturally soothe an inflamed breast, try wearing half a raw cabbage leaf against it overnight or fill your bra with steamed comfrey leaves as a homemade natural compress. Hot wet towels can bring some pain relief, as can cool. Sounds medieval, but it's best to try natural solutions before reaching for antibiotics. If home remedies don't work, see your health care provider as soon as possible to avoid pain and complications.

TAKE MILK BREAKS WHEN YOU REALLY NEED THEM

This is a controversial point, as some babies can develop nipple confusion or reject the breast from too much bottle feeding, but when things are dire for your own health, a balance between breast and bottle can be struck. I think it's better to supplement feeds with formula and persist with breast-feeding than to give it all up in a moment of doubt or weariness. While it's true that sucking keeps the milk flowing, sometimes a woman needs to rest or repair her immune system or simply stop worrying about milk to continue nursing. At nine months, I went to the hospital for surgery and didn't nurse for two days, but simply pumped the polluted milk out of my body. I still had my milk; it just took a little coaxing, faith, and courage to return to normal.

Resources

BOOKS

The Nursing Mother's Companion, Kathleen Huggins
Wise Woman Herbal for the Childbearing Year, Susun Weed
The Womanly Art of Breastfeeding, La Leche League International
Fresh Milk: The Secret Life of Breasts, Fiona Giles

SUPPORTIVE LINKS

Kellymom (www.kellymom.com) provides a nationwide lactation consultant directory, an excellent Q&A section, and breast-feeding troubleshooting as well as information on more obscure topics such as tandem breast-feeding, herbs and breast-feeding, and nutrition.

La Leche League International (www.lli.org) has a detailed multilingual website with very thorough cultural and medical information resource. The site also lists local support groups.

13. GUT REACTION
Primal Mothering for Prudes

Before you have a baby, the act of mothering is opaque, a mystery deepened in equal measure by fear and fantasy. Many books will equip you with the clinical facts and the technical skills of swaddling, burping, and holding a baby. Other more rare and precious volumes will allude to the spiritual and emotional journey of birth and early mothering. But no matter what you read, nothing can truly prepare you for the specific needs, abrupt challenges, violent changes, and peculiar passion involved in having your own child.

We all start as one mother and become another. My "imagined" and ideal mama-dentity was a replete Earth Mother as depicted in the seminal 1970s natural-birth guide *Spiritual Midwifery* by Ina May Gaskin—I was to be a tuned-in hippie goddess giving natural birth with freedom of movement and no compromise, and would proceed to cruise through the first year making bread in a cheesecloth dress and breast-feeding on demand to the tune of Van Morrison's "Astral Weeks." The romance of this image gave me enormous strength during my twenty-hour labor and came crashing down after an emergency C-section. I had been so focused on my drug-free water birth that I had no ballast for its absolute opposite: a full hospital experience of extreme intervention. I found myself stoned off my tree under searing lights as the doctors stitched my uterus, and my broken dreams, back up. I felt like Persephone stolen from the ripe wheat fields of spring and plunged into a clinical underworld where a screen divided me from my emerging baby. It was a bad place for an aspiring Earth Mother to be.

Looking back, I see the conflict between my own projections (funky Amish farm-style) and how I eventually birthed (medical emergency style) serving as a metaphor for the extreme polarization of mothering methods today. At one extreme is a highly modernized, mechanized, and medicalized culture of pregnancy, birth, and child rearing. This school of thought is so prevalent, it's not until you break it down that you see how much like science fiction modern mothering has become. We take it for granted that technology can support and in some cases supplant the work of the mother. A profound blessing for many, but a mixed one. Eggs can be harvested and frozen, sperm can be banked or donated. Fertility can be boosted by drugs, conception assisted by in vitro fertilization technology, and one can choose to carry the successful embryo in her own womb or select a surrogate. The pregnancy is monitored by three-dimensional sonography (Tom Cruise bought his own machine!), and gender and any early abnormalities can be detected by sophisticated blood work and the extraction and study of amniotic fluid. Birth can be induced to be "timely," or labor can be bypassed altogether, and a woman may have elective Cesarean section on the date of her choice.

The role of outside technology and expertise is so mainstream now that women can plan and order everything, from the egg, to the birth suite, to the preschool, before even laying a finger on her husband. On a practical level, this is great for women who feel the need for control,

predictable outcomes, and a watertight schedule. But, on a cultural and even physical level, women have lost some of their sense of agency in the creation, delivery, and raising of their own children. Don't expect to talk for a long period of time with an obstetrician, a fertility specialist, or even a sleep-training night nurse about instinct. Modern, mainstream mothering is driven by facts, not feelings. I remember going to my prenatal appointments and trying to talk about what I sensed in my own body while the hospital staff politely ignored me and stared instead at test results, ultrasounds, blood work, and dates. Especially the dates. Maternal intuition isn't credible because it is no longer trusted. And no longer fashionable.

Fashion is an important force to consider when it comes to birthing and mothering styles. From the 1920s to the early 1970s, breast-feeding was not fashionable, so very few women did it. After giving birth, a mother was given pills to dry up her milk and immediately taught to bottle-feed her baby formula. That lack of choice seems horrible and sad to a contemporary woman, but many times the same sense of defeat and medical dominance now applies to birth. Today it is hard to name one celebrity who has not had a C-section. And celebrity creates consumer demand. Can it be a coincidence then that in some regional areas of Brazil, the statistic for rates of Cesarean births are as high as 90 percent, and the rate in the United States is approaching 30 percent? I predict a movement of a return to normal, natural birth in the same way that breast-feeding was reclaimed by women in the seventies, but before the tide changes, mothers still have so much to contend with and much to reclaim.

As long as birth and mothering are seen as a series of technical obstacles, the craft and the feeling of it will be lessened. I recall the regimentation of learning to care for my baby in the hospital. The bathing area plunged each newborn under an infrared heating lamp with overhead lights so blinding that the babies wailed. Lying in my metal bed, staring at my newborn in his plastic and metal bassinet, I dreamed of someone coming to teach us how to wear a baby sling or to sing to and massage our infants—instead of the stress of three hourly feeds, fanatical hygiene, and methodically tight swaddling.

Once home, I was overwhelmed by the options of equipment designed to help me cope: vibrating bassinets, musical night-lights, video monitors, strollers festooned in dizzying amusements, and high-tech papasans designed to soothe with three different speeds of vibration; then, a few months later, the play gyms, doorway bouncers, walkers, and capsulelike activity centers where my baby was expected to content himself for longer and longer stretches of time. It was easy to feel as if my arms were obsolete. Some of my friends had their offspring watching *Baby Einstein* videos at a few months old. I heard of a TV network called BabyFirstTV, designed expressly for babies under two, with content developed by "leading experts: pediatricians, psychologists, and educators." Why, I began to ask myself, were the experts never just plain old moms, the only qualification I needed to see? So many of my experiences, through pregnancy and in the first weeks of mothering, made me want to buck the system; I didn't want a fancy stroller wedging a void between my baby and my body, and I didn't want to rely on a pile of books imposing their many systems. No, I wanted to learn to rely on myself and follow the cues of my child to forge the way forward. Clearly I was not alone in this rebellion.

In answer to a modernity gone berserk, many mothers are turning toward other, older, much simpler, and more intimate ways. Some call themselves eco-moms, others primal mommies, and many connect with the idea of attachment parenting. Evolved from the studies and writings of psychologists John Bowlby and Mary Ainsworth in the early 1950s, attachment theory is anchored in the concept that mother–child bonding is the vital and central force of healthy infant development. In simple terms, attachment mothering is monkey love: You sleep with your baby, wear him on your body, feed him on demand for as long as the child desires, and integrate him into almost every aspect of your life. By extension of the principle of natural living, foods, clothes, entertainment, and domestic tools are made from the healthiest and most natural materials available. The TV is switched off and replaced with plenty of reading, music, and interactive play. Many attachment mothers choose to homeschool their children, so the connection, the ideology, and the commitment truly become a life's work. Staying at home for a long, long time is a given.

Some attachment moms call themselves natural moms, drawing the line in the sand and perhaps even posing a challenge to those with more traditional or mainstream views. It's sad and silly to find the need to draw such distinctions, as all mothers are "natural." Yet one comes to understand why natural mothering, and natural family living, has become such a tenacious backlash movement. In many ways, the natural mother is trying to escape Big Brother. From the sacred peace and privacy of her pregnancy to the privilege and responsibility of educating her young, she's trying to get back her primal instincts and personal truths. And primal is not a feeling one gets when lost in the aisles of Babies"R"Us.

Attachment mothering is hard-core in the way that it stresses availability, both emotional and physical, for such a long time. Precluding any notion of work outside the home, it can seem a bit class specific, speaking to affluent women who don't need a double income for several years or who can afford to buy organic food, wooden educational toys, and alternative tuition. It costs a lot to be an Earth Mother, no matter how frugally you budget or how remotely you choose to live. And because many of the natural mothering websites, magazines, and books lay down guidelines for living that smack of fundamentalism (lots of lists, plenty of don'ts), it can be tempting to reject or feel rejected by this way of life. I recall picking up Jan Hunt's book *The Natural Child: Parenting from the Heart* and stumbling badly at the first tenet of her highly positive if prescriptive list "Ten Ways to Grow a Happy Child." Her first commandment was "Have a happy birth experience." Raw with the shock of an interventive birth, I felt like I had no chance at the primal connection. If you've had a C-section, carrying your new baby, co-sleeping, and perhaps even successfully breast-feeding are all potentially very tough. Or simply impossible. It's tempting to think that primal mothers are the lucky ones

that got their birth "right," or didn't get depressed, or breast-fed easily, or fell wildly in love with their infants at first contact. It's vital to understand that every mother has a fresh chance to connect with her baby or child from the moment she decides to, bad birth or not. I know some moms who came to attachment way after a full year or decided to apply the principles later on, simply by becoming more intimate, physically and emotionally available, deeply attuned, and creative in their mothering.

The very words *natural mother* throw up a lot of cultural baggage, negative stereotyping, and pain. Is the opposite of a natural mother an artificial one, or simply a bad one? I entertained all of these doubts—when I slept apart from my son, pushed him in a cavernous stroller, supplemented breast milk with formula, and felt that black, hollow sadness that came with exhaustion, confusion, and way too many postnatal medications. Sometimes I felt like the plastic Earth Mother, the hippie with a Bugaboo, and only trial and error could carve a middle path between full-on "monkey mothering" and necessary compromise. The first time I tried to carry my son, I busted my surgical stitches (hence the stroller). Once, when we coslept, he rolled out of my bed and fell flat on his face. Yet the few natural choices I did make for my son worked wonders for him: breast-feeding for two years, using predominantly organic foods, very little TV, no sleep training, no war toys, no refined sugar, and plenty of time running around nude. When I finally was able to carry Marcello, it created a chain of responses that made us closer on the whole. Smelling his skin and listening to his breathing and burbling deepened my sensual and emotional connection with him and helped me see the world from his own delicately budding sense of awareness. I learned his language so much faster.

Sleep training was my first testing ground to forging an alternative way. My local pediatrician, an advocate of the Ferber method of making a baby cry it out and self-soothe alone in a darkened room, suggested, "Stand at the side of the crib with a face like a robot and don't make eye contact while your baby cries." When I frowned, he added: "Whatevva you do, don't touch him, don't pick him up! Don't soothe him! It's tough love, but it works, and he'll be sleeping through the night in under a week." He meant well, but his advice was completely counterintuitive to the trust I was forging through touch and swift response with my son. The price I paid for willingly feeding my son through the night for more than two years was exhaustion, but the benefit was deep and total connection, as well as the occasional discovery of a fever or cough.

On the night that I cowered beneath my son's crib gently rocking its wooden rim with two fingers, I listened to him sob for another hour and felt a violent pain in the pit of my stomach, literally a scream from the womb. And from that moment on, I vowed to act on instinctive response. And this became my compass for all decisions concerning Marcello. Gut reaction. Blood wisdom. Strong feeling. Choosing bliss over pain. This revelation didn't just arrive in a cloud of motherly love. Instinct, like intuition, takes time to excavate, buried as it is under the rubble of social mores, fashion, conformity, fear, and personal doubt. Happily, the instinct to hold a baby close leads to more rewards than just feeling good. It is rich with health benefits for mother and child. The hormone prolactin surges through the mother's body during skin contact, caressing, and breast-feeding, deepening what pediatrician Dr. William Sears calls "motherly feelings." Nursing also promotes deeper sleep for both mom and baby. Frequent skin contact and loving play have been linked to advanced neurological development. Babies literally live on love, and bloom and thrive from your touch.

Mothering "by hand" is hard work, though, and the temptations of shortcuts and convenience are always there. Babies are primal, but society is not. And stuck in the middle of this absurd gap is the modern mother, who is being pressed to accelerate her child's development and independence with every manner of instinct-blunting tool.

I think the most important message of the natural mothering movement is that there is nothing arbitrary or "routine" about mothering. Every moment is precious, personal, and irreplaceably formative. For a very brief moment in time, a new baby needs *all* of his mother, and the natural thing to do is to give that all, the best way you can afford

to. Try to see the sacrifice of your body, income, and time as a sacred moment in your life. And then comfort yourself with the knowledge that for everyone, mothering is completely exhausting.

As a loose experiment, I closely observed two good friends with diametrically opposite mothering styles raise their babies. Mum number one was primal to the max: She home birthed in an inflatable tub; massaged her baby with oils; did baby yoga; wore her child in a perpetual papoose; didn't use a pacifier; seemed to have her breasts popping out at all times for both comfort and feeding; refused TV; co-slept; and made her own organic baby food. Whoa. Mum number two had less time and more faith in modern speed: She weaned early; bought every gadget and brain toy under the sun; pushed a super-stroller replete with toys, snacks, and music; used part-time day care; sleep-trained; and took pleasure in rushing at every milestone like an Olympic marathon runner. She was proud when her son sat through an entire episode of *The Simpsons* sitting on a miniature couch like a miniature man. Both women loved their kids with a deep passion and both were burned out, singed at the edges at seven months, utterly spent by the essential task. So you see, mothering is intensive by nature, even if you do not choose to mother intensively.

Blazing your own trail through all the dogma, right and left, and following your heart and senses as much as your logic, will not protect you from the fatigue of the job. But it will help you stand by your choices and know that they were truly your own.

PRIMAL MOTHERING FOR PRUDES 101

For mothers who are time poor, money poor, or geographically isolated, there needs to be an alternative to the alternative—a middle way that helps you get closer to your baby without being soldered to him 24-7. There is no magazine for the semi-attached mum or the part-time pagan. I read attachment magazines knowing that I don't completely fit the mold: I need to work out of home, I use at-home child care, I occasionally pop in a DVD, and I sometimes settle a fight with a plastic toy. Sometimes we bend. Sometimes we snap. And sometimes we simply succumb to the absurd needs of the moment. Peggy O'Mara, the editor of *Mothering* and natural-family-living guru, wrote the mantra "Trust your body. Trust your baby. Trust yourself." And I gratefully follow her cue. Here are some helpful ideas for the journey.

Birth

Natural birth is not the only gateway to natural mothering. Many women who face a surgically invasive or intervention-heavy birth can request the centering comfort of a doula or partner, and respectful, informative behavior from the hospital staff. Asking for immediate and prolonged skin-on-skin contact with the baby at birth (swaddling is not always critical)—and even, in some cases, immediate breast-feeding—is a possibility for some women. Drug-free, peaceful, and private birth is the ideal, yet for every alternative, there are ways to humanize, personalize, and empower your birth. Seeing it first and foremost as your own sacred rite of passage is primary to feeling strong and connected.

Breast-feeding

If you cannot breast-feed, it is possible to still co-sleep and hold your baby in a deep skin-on-skin embrace, with intimate face-to-face closeness and plenty of eye contact at every feed. Touch is a form of food in itself for the souls of mother and child. Assess all allergies and nutritional needs before choosing a formula and consider goat's milk as a whole-milk alternative for toddlers, as it is gentler on the stomach.

Co-sleeping

For nervous nellies who don't want a newborn in the bed, a co-sleeping cot that attaches to the side of the bed is ideal for night feeds, hearing

and seeing your baby, and general closeness. Sleeping in the same room is still much safer than installing a separate nursery too soon.

Baby Transport

Find a front pack that supports your lower back. When graduating to a backpack, find one that distributes baby's weight evenly. Metal-frame carriers are best for long trips only; all-fabric fits the body best. I found my Ergo sling comfortable right up to twenty-five pounds and beyond. Be prudent about the amount of time spent wearing a baby, though, as you need a strong and protected spine for all the years to come. A few hours a day is beautifully bonding, and convenient too.

Touch

Bathe together, dance together, give massages, and share family hugs every day. Touch is the primal language you share before words and will remain your secret code with your child forever.

Responsible Consumerism

Read the labels on everything! Reduce the level of packaging, plastics, and chemicals entering your home. Choose products made with natural/organic ingredients, essential oils, and sustainable materials.

Healthy Eating

If you cannot afford organic food, join a food co-op or bulk shop with friends, try to buy seasonal local produce, and try growing your own herbs, sprouts, and small veggies in a windowsill planter. Apply your own high nutritional standards to what baby eats.

Medications and Immunity

The best approach to accepting anything medical for your baby is to be completely informed in your consent. Try to research what is in every medicine, vaccine, and treatment, and do not be embarrassed to seek broad opinion and data to inform your choices. Despite the expertise of doctors and specialists, each mother has a deep sense of her child's particular health profile, sensitivities, and progress. Many mums know their kid has a problem before anyone else can detect it, especially when the symptoms are profoundly subtle. Follow those feelings. Regarding the controversial subject of vaccination for immunity: Some mothers vaccinate and leave it at that, believing their child has blanket protection. But health is a holistic reality. Be proactive about immunity from the vantage point of offering the complementary supports of breast milk such as fluid; vitamins; excellent, clean food; fresh air; sun; and love. These are vital complements to whatever other avenues of health building you choose. Also view food as the original medicine. It astounds me that no one has made the connection between sugar and illness in children. The single most loving and natural blessing you can give a child is to keep them as sugar-free as possible for as many years as possible, and to instill them with a passion for fresh, whole fruit.

Closeness and Time

Women who work, women who have health problems, women who live alone or share custody, all face challenges for giving enough time to their children. But attachment is not just a matter of clocking hours, it is also the art of being completely present, loving, and consistent for the time you have to give. Create rituals that allow you to slow down and completely tune in to your child's mood, needs, and feelings. I find getting down on the floor together can usually melt any distance or tension I feel after being apart from my child within a few minutes.

Education

The natural informed mum doesn't send her kids to a school based on geography alone. Instead, she researches her child's school curriculum to see if there is enough magic in there and if her values are echoed. A happy home life often leads to a love of learning. And children learn what they live, so work hard to make your home an inspiring, creative, spiritually uplifting place, and try to find a day care, preschool, or kindergarten that feels the same way.

Be as Mad as You Wanna Be

Your kid might be the one with alfalfa hanging out of his lunch box, or the one in handmade clothes. Your house might be the one painted tangerine, and you might have a belly dancer instead of a clown at your son's second birthday party. Following your own mothering bliss means being ahead of the curve or feeling old-fashioned or out of step.

Yet questioning, avoiding, or openly rejecting certain mothering norms and trends is solely within your domain, as is your right to start totally new ones. I read an Indian mothering website that recommended one hour of total nudity for babies and children in sunlight every day, with a sunhat and sunscreen, of course. I added to this concept by being nude myself—and dancing before breakfast every day. Genius! And deliciously primal.

Some Highly Intelligent Natural Mothering Websites and Resources

www.kindredmagazine.com.au
www.motheringmagazine.com
www.childrensneeds.com (for slings and things)
www.naturalchild.com
www.taylormadeslings.com

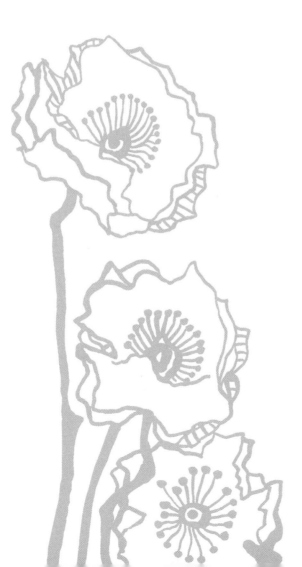

14. PALE, TIRED, AND SHAPED LIKE AN EGGPLANT

How to Dress the In-between Body

There is a clear-cut category known as maternity wear, but there is no such thing as just-had-a-baby fashion. Designers have great fun with the gravid belly, glorifying the changes of each trimester, but then they dump new mothers on the other side: that formless void of cotton-Lycra maxi-T-shirts and gathered skirts. Shortly after birth and in the months that follow, our bodies vary wildly from a small, manageable paunch to lumps, bumps, and extra bits we hadn't banked on. It's a rough time to improvise a good look.

A full year and a half after my son was born, I was still rounded like a Fuji apple; where my breasts ended, my hips began. I felt like a giant zeppoli cast in bronze, or a dense Picasso nude run amok in an Alberto Giacometti landscape of stick figures in short shorts. Having no waist is like losing one's compass—suddenly there is no line that demarcates north from south. As one rather blunt husband told me, "Pregnant women can wear anything and look stupendous because all eyes are on the prized belly. But then afterward the reverse becomes true, and a woman would rather die than wear a dress that wedges a big pink bow at the top of her midriff." Wise, if very unwelcome, words.

The trek from plus-size paradise to nonplussed confusion is swift. Flicking through catalogs and magazines in search of basics seemed pointless to me. The chic mainstays that had worked for twenty years—the thin-knit cardigan, the pencil skirt, even the little black dress—all looked faintly apologetic now or just clumsily tight in a Bridget Jones sort of way. The yearning to get back into normal gear generates very specific brands of style psychosis: Denim mania is the desire to wear jeans that do not make your rump look like a tightly up-holstered eggplant. Midriff phobia is a fear of any garment that dares to bare any part of the belly or hip. My personal fashion neurosis was focused on breasts. Squashed into pre-pregnant blouses and jackets, I felt someone had stuffed two loaves of sourdough down my bra. Suddenly I was in the dowager league of Margaret Thatcher and Queen Elizabeth. Striped T-shirts, polo-necks, and double-breasted blazers were *out*.

After a year of blunders, I arrived at the point where I dressed the body I had and not the one I wished would emerge from all my custard damage. Clearly delusional, I had pictured that my ribs and hips would swiftly snap back into place and that I would once again frolic in Earl Jeans and silver high heels. I still have the heels, but my bones ain't moving, and so in good stead I have developed a whole new bag of tricks. . . .

Golden Rules for a Glorious In-between Body

- Size matters, but proportion matters more. Flattering the in-between body is a matter of working with what you've got, and just that. It's never just about pounds gained. One must make a completely honest, highly personal reappraisal of exact proportions and not merely take a mechanical leap in dress sizes (especially if you have changed shape in an unlikely spot).

- Flatter your perceived assets: You might have fine legs and heavier upper arms, a developed derriere and a surprisingly meager bosom from sudden weaning, or a belly that is rebellious at best. It sounds old-fashioned, but ankles and wrists have plenty of charm if they are accented properly. Love a lace collar and cuffs (circa 1965 Julie Christie in *Darling*) that accentuate a well-kept manicure and shiny pumps. Adore a set of strong knees peeping out from beneath a tweed skirt, and let that clever trench coat deal with your suddenly vast torso and bosom.

- This is the moment to consider every detail afresh; elements such as the shape of sleeve, a skirt length, the cut of a bodice, and the depth of a neckline are critical.

- Play with new shapes and new styles. Kimono sleeves, 1970s princess-line dresses, capelets, ponchos, dropped-waist flapper dresses, and classic A-line skirts will all help you through an attack of the chubs as well as diversify your style.

- Stop heartbreaking about just how much of your old wardrobe doesn't fit (especially milestone outfits like wedding dresses, favorite jeans, and so on) and move all temporarily unwearable items to a suitcase under the bed. Fussy, flimsy, short, or backless pieces get retired indefinitely—unless you are in fact a ballroom dancer or a burlesque starlet.

- Salvage key pieces from your maternity wardrobe that can be transformed with clever use of accessories and separates. A wide belt worn on the hip, a cropped jacket with dramatically shortened sleeves, a long, trailing knitted silk scarf (I'm thinking Missoni), a lovely sequined beret, or some dancer's layers such as footless tights and ballet wrap tops take a simple Empire-line dress and make it look more pulled together.

- Be penny-wise about buying new clothes, since when your metabolism and exercise return, you could be dropping dress sizes more rapidly than expected. For this reason, invest in clothes with flexible cuts and non-size-specific (nontailored) waist- and bustlines.

- Prepare to invest in one good dress that is well cut and made with a "giving" fabric such as rayon knit, silk, or cotton jersey. Many new mamas opt for a Diane von Furstenberg wrap dress, wearing it with some coverage (a leotard or blazer) at first and then gradually showing more skin. The key advantage of the classic wrap is that you can easily nurse in one. Thank you, hot mama Diane.

- Play with proportion. While shaped like a yam, I wore Edwardian-style men's shirts with waistcoats, short opera coats, and even maternity dresses converted into blouses over knee-length breeches and low stacked-heel boots. This reversal in proportion stressed the bulk on top and lengthened my already short, very stocky legs, and the outfits were both comfortable and flattering. Flashing a bit of calf detracted from my solid knees and thighs, and broke the visual line in just the right place. In essence, I dressed as if I had legs to spare, when in fact I am five foot four and shaped like a bowling pin.

- Don't ignore an accessory, cut, or color that is overly trendy if it reflects your true style. Necklaces are an easy and often inexpensive style fix!

- Don't bag out! Many concealing clothes look like just that: a hideout. By dressing closer to your true form (but never too tightly), you reduce the illusion that you are in fact a human blueberry, and, yes, you still have legs, arms, and somewhere down there . . . a waist.

- Go for color instead of the traditionally dark, figure-shrinking shades of chocolate and black. You are celebrating a new baby, not mourning a lost dress size! Jewel tones such as purple, magenta, turquoise, and aqua blue make a vivid impression and actually give you energy. Wear pastel shades, and you run the risk of merging into the nursery, and we don't want that.

- Big, milky breasts the size of your skull can make you look like a Smurf if you don't dress for them. Avoid ribbed, shiny, or overly tight items, and especially reject high necklines. Every inch of fabric that covers you above your breasts doubles their sense of scale. Favor a modest V or sweetheart neckline. Find a maternity bra that isn't cut too high between the breasts and avoid T-shirts that are pale or flesh colored.

PS: Note to Sleep-deprived Mummies:

Fling one outfit that works onto a hanger each night, and hang it on the back of your bedroom door. Cluster accessories together with clothes and color block your wardrobe even if you don't have many pieces. That way, when you stagger in there to escape your pajamas, you can think in terms of chic ideas and know what's clean.

15. COMMON FASHION SINS OF THE MOTHER

Why Mommy Clothes Don't Work

Bad taste is environmental. If you live in a suburban area with a large concentration of mothers, you are likely to be offered very bland styles: shopwindows full of sneakers, quilted coats, pastel cashmere cardigans, knee-length Jackie O.–style sleeveless shift dresses, and bulletproof padded bras. Over time, even the most adventurous, fashion-passionate mama might capitulate to ecru cargo pants if that is all she can find. But Gap models never quite look like real women. The truth is, you need an expensively pampered body to wear cheap clothes well and a lot of character to wear simple classics with any distinction at all. On Anjelica Huston or Lauren Hutton, a plain white shirt is magic, and on me it's just, well, plain.

As a case in point, a new store opened in my area, a neighborhood flooded with stroller-pushing, window-shopping young mothers. The first week, it thrust its brightest pieces in the window; sundresses and handbags that looked like origami birds. The next week, everything went beige. Not even beige, but *greige,* that hideous, insipid infusion of two tones that are noncolors in the first place. My soul died a little. How are mothers supposed to be themselves if they are dressed like everybody else? How are they supposed to "keep the marriage alive" dressed in knitwear the color of an undercooked pancake?

The same deflation often happens in a conventional department store where merchandise is arranged chronologically to age (and weight). First floor: young contemporary fashion (denim, corsetry, message T-shirts, and Paris Hilton's old hot pants). Second floor: shoes, handbags, designer office clothes (remember the perky, faintly tailored classics you wore when you had a career?). Third floor: smart casuals (the dreaded stretch-cotton Made-in-China mom-wear ghetto). And fourth floor: plus size, where bad girls go if they eat too much kugelhopf! And where Grandma goes when she's done with Juicy Couture sweats.

When shopping in a mall, an independent boutique, or even a designer discount barn, I have to keep vigil not to be herded into my "supposed" demographic: the toddler mum cardigan zone. When meeting a hairdresser for the first time, I carry images in my handbag of women over forty who do not have bobs, and at the makeup counter, I demand the loudest red lip gloss they have. If plunged into an environment that is simply not you—and that could be downtown USA or anywhere when you're pioneering with a young family—a woman needs signposts and internal reminders not to lose her way. It's better to risk shopping vintage on the Internet than give your body over to a faceless chain. Forget fighting the visible signs of aging and instead battle against the suffocation of smart casuals. That mock Burberry raincoat and sensible chocolate handbag are going to add twenty years straight up.

Stylish women steal ideas but never translate them literally. Kate

Spade doesn't look one scrap like Audrey Hepburn, but she has built an empire on her streamlined sensibility. Clearly you don't need a squillion dollars to forge your signature style. I know one very Yummy Mummy of four famous for her bare Roman sandals and always beautifully kept feet. I know another who layers vintage slips dyed in outrageous colors and wears them as dresses through the summer. My own trick for throwing any "normal" outfit off kilter is a huge pair of sunglasses and a long, trailing scarf: sort of Isadora Duncan meets *Henry & June.* Whatever works.

I once peeked inside the French designer Catherine Malandrino's closet and found that she had lined up rough photocopies of all her style icons on the paneling inside the doors. At first the effect seemed almost adolescent, the teen pinup wall. But upon second inspection, I saw the psychology at work. Sophia Loren and Julie Christie give Malandrino her edge. They were her daily dose of self-imposed glamor boot camp. With all those pussycat eyes glaring back at her, there is no way she'll be settling for jeans, a white T-shirt, and a chunky cardigan. Paris is in her soul, so she invariably reaches for the art deco bracelets, the bold bag, the dress with the waistline, and the heel with a kick. Without half as much clothing or even the smoky French accent, you can too.

The Seven Sins of Maternal Style

1. *The Anchorwoman Bob.* News flash: Bobs didn't look so hot the first time round. Only Louise Brooks and Peter Pan did them justice. The truth is, no matter how thin or fragile your hair, it is often better to wear it very short (Mia Farrow in *Rosemary's Baby*) or quite long (Liv Tyler), but avoid all the dreary styles in between. Shoulder-length hair looks high maintenance (almost luxuriously so), but being able to wear it up most of the time is a great asset to have on reserve. Bobs, layered or otherwise, are considered easy but are actually inflexible and oddly noncommittal.

Bobs with bangs tend to compress the face and look weirdly girl-ish with work clothes or sleek evening wear. It is no coincidence that movie stars rarely wear bobs. Looking "nice" instead of sensual is box office poison.

2. *The Cardigan.* A cardigan is an important element that too soon becomes a habit of dress. Worn too often, it quickly looks more like camouflage than clever style. For best results, reverse the order of things. Wear a really spangly, beaded vintage evening cardigan for day and a brightly colored chunky Aran Isle or cable-knit with a flimsy flapper dress for night. Even the most subtle jolts in context make standards sing rather than just hum along.

3. *The Sensible Shoe.* Slip into a favorite loafer, ballet flat, or Birken-stock after baby, and you might be wearing the same shoe for the next five years. Give yourself an inch (or two) in the form of a plat-form or slightly stacked wedge heel, and you can go the extra mile in terms of both line and sass. Completely flat shoes look good only with very minimal, well-cut clothes and a rather slim body.

4. *The Over-functioning Handbag.* Mama's bag has a tough life. The many needs of baby spill over into its heart, and domestic rounds leave their heavy-duty stamp. It's tempting to invest in one big bag, but that choice is usually so conservative (navy blue, choco-late, or black) that, despite the price tag, this accessory simply doesn't travel well. Instead of lumbering around with one heavy-hitting big-label bag, I have fun with younger, less serious styles that do the same job. A white pleather satchel one summer, a tar-tan wool library style for the fall, and a vintage black-patent top-handled "lady" bag for the winter keep my wardrobe fresh. It makes more sense to own the serious-investment bag once the kids are in preschool and off your lap. There will be no diapers in my Birkin! Until then it's much more youthful and fun to mix it all up on the cheap.

5. *The Neutral Palette. Repeat after me: Earth tones do not make me a more sensitive parent, they simply make me look mousy!* With apologies to the great works of Woody Allen, more than one mid-tone or neutral shade on a woman makes her look like a field mushroom in a brown paper bag. If you love honey and eau de Nil and all that, then please break it up with something savagely bright: Palm Beach lime or Beverly Hills tangerine. It's the clash that confers the class. And the same rule applies to wearing too much black as well.

6. *The Cargo Pant.* We buy cargo pants in the vain hope that we will look luxe and loose like Gisele Bündchen fresh off the yoga mat, with that little bit of taut, tan belly poking through and the side pockets sitting just so on lean hips and legs. In reality, this style makes most ordinary butts look flat and wide. Try cargo pants in a bright, unexpected shade or in an unusual fabric like silk or floral cambric. Unlike jeans, these trousers don't work to sculpt you, so consider a more tailored Capri, a tuxedo-style trouser, or even a buttoned-up sailor style.

    Trousers bisect the body, so they need to flatter on all fronts. They are ubiquitous to a mother's wardrobe, and for this reason need to be chosen with the most care and research and often worn a half size too big, grazing your curves rather than munching into them.

7. *The Crew Neck.* When a neckline cuts straight across and high above the collarbone, it shortens the throat, broadens the bust, narrows the shoulder, and emphasizes the midriff. In a word: *frump.* T-shirts that have just slightly different tailoring—a flaring sleeve, an unusual neckline, a nicer fabric—work harder for you. If you are stuck with a big collection of crew-neck mommy T's, consider customizing them; it's a fun and inexpensive way to enliven a critical basic.

Ten Ways to Look Ten Years Younger

1. *Apply soft textures in every outfit.* Not only do they add contrast, they double your kittenish sensuality. Try a long, fluttery skirt with a tailored jacket, angora/cashmere/silk cardigan with a pencil skirt, a soft, loosely knitted mohair beanie with a leather coat. Women look younger when they look tactile. Attraction is ruled by sensuality; there's no point smelling like a vanilla sponge cake and looking as harsh as a Brillo pad.

2. *Soften the colors you wear near your face.* Ice blue, lilac, mint green, and peach all flatter. But contrast them with brights or black so that you don't melt into an Impressionist blur.

3. *Indulge in sexy accessories* that frame your face, décolletage, and shoulders. I love the very thin, little wisp of a chiffon scarf or a long, artsy ethnic piece of sarong or extralong men's knitted tie. Anything that draws attention to your throat is sexy, except turtlenecks!

4. *Wear your hair as naturally as possible.* Avoid tight ponytails, hardening hairsprays, or poker-straight blowouts; for a brunette, this is the equivalent of hanging thick black velvet curtains on either side of your face and playing "count the wrinkles."

5. *Mismatch a little.* Wear a patterned coat with a striped bag; a pink velvet skirt with a chartreuse cashmere T-shirt. A flash of eccentricity gives you a pulse.

6. *Always wear your shirts three buttons undone,* and if your toddler tends to tug them open, let him! Underneath, flash a very

beautiful French bra, a vintage camisole, or a brightly colored dancer's leotard.

7. *Try one new trend every season*—just one. It can be a small statement like a slightly puffed sleeve on a denim jacket, or wearing a long silk scarf as a belt, or something radical like brocade boots. Every girl needs one wardrobe item that shocks her own soul and especially her family just a little.

8. *Change your bra.* This is often the last thing we make over, and we travel through decades with a uniform bustline. Stiff, symmetrical-looking mounds for breasts are the result of bras made of too much foam and too much wire. Risk a slightly more natural look; it's *way* less matronly.

9. *Wear a loose, floppy handbag day to day* and save the Kelly for the power meeting. Structured, top-handled bags look terribly uptight.

10. *Flirt with a ruffle here or there:* on the edge of a slip, the cuff of a linen shirt, or the hem of your evening dress. And toss a silk flower into the mix. Romance is ageless, so let it kiss your style.

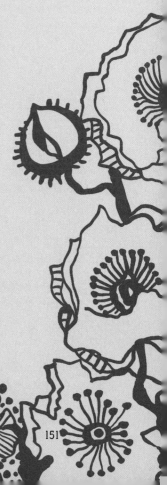

Ten Ways to Look Ten Years Older

1. *Turtlenecks* or any sort of style that looks like you are hiding something.

2. *Dark colors worn in clusters:* chocolate, wine, plum, and the dreaded navy blue!

3. *Wearing something because you think it is age appropriate.* If you've never worn golf shoes, a crocodile handbag, a tweed hunting jacket, or an argyle cardigan, don't start now!

4. *Heavy, clunky heels, lace-up shoes, sensible loafers, and anything orthopedic has to go!* Yummy Mummy red alert: Beware of too much comfort in clothing and too much chunk in your heels. Running around in shoes like Crocs and slip-on penny loafers can make you a blob woman before your time. Remember the close-up of Kathy Bates's loafers in *Misery*? Terrifying!

5. *Flesh-colored lingerie.* Anything flesh colored *is not lingerie.*

6. *Dressing to unwittingly match your husband or, worse, your kids.* Fly-fishing jackets, overalls, gum boots, denim top and bottom, flannel shirts, and even his old rugby sweater make you chummy but clumsy.

7. *Skirts worn midcalf.* Make it to the knee or wild and gypsy to the ankle, but nothing in between. Some freaks of nature can rock a mini—bonne chance!

8. *Too many layers:* pashmina, jacket, overcoat. No matter what shape you're in, don't obscure it.

9. *Too much coordination.* Matching bags and shoes, and gloves and lipstick say air hostess or suburban priestess of starch.

10. *Too much black.* Limit yourself to two items and diligently break them up, keeping bright, clear color near the face. I'm a broken record on this subject because Manhattan is a monochrome sea of ink, and everyone looks more tired, not more elegant.

16. THE SEX QUESTION

Love Is a Perennial, but Desire Has Its Own Season

Several months after my son was born, I bought a pair of leopard-skin knickers trimmed with lime green lace. Until I bought those knickers, I had been living in an asexual blur, focused utterly on the persistent needs of my son. Oblivious. That's the only word that can describe a tired mother who can pull out her breast anywhere without a second thought to silence a screaming little mouth. I had appalled diners at Dean & DeLuca, puzzled many guards at the Metropolitan Museum of Art, and mesmerized an old man on an airplane with my blithe boob-flashing ways. Profoundly insensitive. That's surely how I appeared to my husband in the face of his gnawing sexual frustration. Six months. That's how long it took me to even walk into a lingerie shop.

Not dead, but dormant, like a rose garden buried in snow. That's how I like to look at the desire that becomes so readily subsumed by

one's first stab at mothering. At six months, if my son was not suckling, he was cuddling, and when he wasn't hanging out on my lap like a Pomeranian, he was literally hanging off my torso, dangling in his BabyBjörn as I vacuumed, stirred hot porridge, and attempted to read British *Vogue* while he clawed at the pages. Breast-feeding stops one flow to create another, and, personally, without my monthly cycle, I fell out of the ebb and rush of sexual love. And nursing takes a very different sort of energy; as a baby's hunger and thirst are perpetual, the body has no real respite, no hiding place.

The dip in estrogen also has a nasty way of drying one's vital juices. With less of this elixir, my hip bones literally creaked, and my "honeypot" was as arid as the Mojave at midday. With less moisture, the walls of the vagina become thin and fragile. The resulting pain during intercourse felt awkward and was a strange reversal of all the visualizations I had studied for a natural birth: open like a flower, flow like a river; when, truly, I wanted to shut my legs like a clam and just rest.

Much is made of getting your body back after a baby, but really feeling safe and whole after a birth is probably more important. Motherhood gives you strength and fortitude you never knew, but it can also make you feel oddly fragile and profoundly sensitive. Sleep, and the lack of it, also hits the libido like an ax. A senseless comment about your shape can bruise your delicate self-image for days. And pressure of any kind, especially the intimate kind, makes you feel cranky, not lusty.

Those fallow months straight after a birth are also a good time to heal. For me there were no gruesome tears or crazy stitches, but my C-section had its own traumas. I had to feel completely healed before I was ready to open up. Physically and emotionally. Coming back into your sexuality after a birth is wed pretty tightly to coming back into your power. I wasn't allowed to lift Marcello, drive a car, exercise, or have intercourse for six weeks. For any woman who has had a rough birth, "six weeks" sounds like an astounding clinical understatement.

The day you can throw your baby in the air and laugh really hard without popping a stitch is the day you're ready to even look at your partner, and not a second sooner. In the meantime, there are about a million puzzle pieces of the self that need to fit back together.

In the first blind months of maternal responsibility, my body seemed to belong to no one *but* my child. The shock of a new baby makes every little thing feel like an emergency. Time becomes both horribly condensed and bizarrely stretched out, and there's no time at all for old habits of the mind such as worrying about that extra five pounds. Lord, no! Each breast now weighs five pounds. Oh yes, new mothers are blissfully absentminded about their allure. Or lack of it. For months on end, I sat bare-bottomed on the sofa in bed socks and an open kimono, working my breast pump and singing Bob Marley at the top of my lungs. Quite a vision. I wore unbuttoned Indian pajamas if I bothered to put clothes on at all, despite the fact that my breasts had now trekked a good three inches down my chest.

Because I breast-fed for a very long time (almost two years), it became something of a double-edged sword. On the one hand, it made me feel sensually powerful, taking a fierce pride in the life force my flesh affords. On the other hand, it was, quite simply, exhausting—and my husband did not savor the salty taste! In many ways and on many occasions, I felt divided. Nursing made me a woman and an ecosystem. Focused on vitamins and fluids and adequate rest to keep the whole food chain going, the first blazing obligation is to sleep. Not to have mad sex. Damn. Sorry, can't be helped. In this truly rough patch of mothering, I also feel that nature gives us an even break from reproduction and the twitchy desire that goes with it. How else could we pour all our passion, attention, warmth, and nourishment into a new being? Happily, I never had to explain to my man that I was not the sacrificial stump in *The Giving Tree* or the Energizer bunny. Indeed, in those first heady months, he probably just felt happy if I wasn't throwing a chair at his head.

Sleep deprivation made me a nudist, but solid foods saved my sex

life. My return to the marital bed coincided quite naturally with the gradual detachment from breast-feeding. As my son slowly drifted away from the breast, I gained a sense of my body returning to adult ways, on a number of levels. Unconsciously, perhaps, I knew that my son could now safely be sustained by stewed apples and survive (if not thrive) without my milk. The shift this knowledge creates comes as a profound relief. It makes the physical relationship with a baby less urgent, something closer to pleasure than mortality. Finally, with a robust and healthy baby in your arms, you can breathe out, feel playful, and relax a little. Until that moment, you simply aren't free. And freedom and leopard-skin panties go hand in hand.

I think a woman needs that slowly unfolding independence from her child, that latent sense of liberty, to make her way back to intimacy with her partner. It's less a matter of feeling "touched out" at the end of a nursing day than simply being burned out. If you haven't been for a walk completely alone or spent twenty minutes drinking a caffe latte and staring into space, you are probably not ready to abandon yourself to lust. It helps to feel human first.

Many times I would look at my husband's face and read the thought bubble that hung like a black cloud above his head: *Oh my God! Babies mean we are never going to have sex again.* I tried my best to amuse and distract my patient husband with affectionate, flirty banter, but for me, bed was a battleground of congealed milk and shattered sleep cycles. I didn't want to have brief mechanical unions just to prove we could. I wanted to feel *hot* again, not lukewarm, like reheated expressed milk. By seven months, the father of my child probably did have an out-and-out complex, but he kept bringing home bottles of red and being charming and optimistic. That worked. What I learned from our lumpy, bumpy road back to the boudoir is that even the smallest display of patience will rebuild the intimacy that a baby so rudely—if innocently—interrupts. Partners of new mothers need to be delicate not whiny, playful but not pushy, and for heaven's sake, no guilt-tripping! The question of how to be lovers as well as parents is just another riff on how to keep a marriage sizzling. It takes a lot of empathy, trust, humor, and tenacity. And sometimes it just takes something small and silly to reconnect, like a pair of tacky, delicious leopard-skin panties trimmed in lime green lace.

The day I bought the fateful knickers felt like the first spring bud, but I had been prodding the frozen earth for quite some time. Just because a new mother doesn't feel specifically or spontaneously sexual does not mean she is sensually numb. Erotic twinges, a welcome liberation from self-consciousness (the nudism!), a feeling of solidity within your burgeoning body, and the simple satisfaction of fertility fulfilled create a new sort of sexy. Yet few of these feelings or revelations fall into place all at once. Desire doesn't return mechanically when "the weight comes off" or the baby "comes off" the breast; instead, it grows like a quietly sprouting seed, blossoming slowly inside a recovering body.

Taking a little time to resume the raunch also has its advantages. When I finally welcomed my husband back into my skin, it was with a whole new layer of depth and experience. I felt fuller, more substantial, but holy as hell, like some sort of champion from an ancient myth. Having a baby changes the body in obvious but also very subtle ways. Right now I've got hips like a flamenco guitar, and with them I can play some new notes—lower, fruitier, earthier notes no green girl would know.

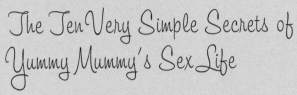

The Ten Very Simple Secrets of Yummy Mummy's Sex Life

1. *Understand this:* Intimacy between parents is not taken as much as stolen. This might be your moment to break out a completely new erotic persona and become a morning sex person, a quickie person, or a "standing up and doing it with most of your clothes on in the middle of the kitchen" person. Be prepared to shock yourself in order to rock yourself.

2. *Time is not the issue.* It takes longer to lie in bed worrying about a stalled sex life than it does to actually make love of any kind.

3. *Never compare.* There is no normal time to return to desire, and other couples always seem to be "at it" when your relationship is at its most fallow, volatile, or fragile. Concentrate on creating your own scenes, as no one else shares your story.

4. *Talk your way back to bed.* When sex grinds to a halt in a relationship, it is usually deeper than tiredness, business, or laziness. Some couples need a screaming fight to clear the air, others need popcorn and Jack Black acting ridiculous in *Nacho Libre,* and others simply need time to forget the kid and just look at each other across a candlelit table.

5. *Reanimate your body.* New mothers feel the constant drain on their arms, back, and breasts. For this reason, it's vital to bust some moves that engage the whole body in a graceful flow.

6. *Revisit your own erotic library.* I reread *Lady Chatterley's Lover* sixteen months after my son was born, and delighted in the utter selfishness and famished absorption of the lovers. It forced me to

remember my body as a map of desire and not just a cradle and service station. It's useless to think that something as static as a weekly "date night" is going to make you feel hot again. You need to light the fires deep inside your sensual imagination, and evocative, spicy prose always helps, be it Anaïs Nin or Jilly Cooper.

7. *Make a sexy picnic and share it in bed* or on a vast old blanket on the floor. Raw fruit, baked chicken, green olives, cherry tomatoes, chocolate mousse in tiny cups, icy champagne. Stodgy comfort food leads the mind to pajamas. Tingly, fresh, exotic food leads the mind to deep, tingly, fresh . . . activities.

8. *Book an hour-long massage* to reawaken the sense of being touched. Often it's hard to give pleasure if you feel you haven't received it in a long time. The skin is like a field of memories, and many emotions get stuck in the places where we are rarely caressed. Warm oil and sweeping hands on the small of your back or skimming down the side of your waist will get the energy and the desire moving again.

9. *Find an oil or perfume* that will be worn only for your love. Make it the darkest, juiciest, most mysterious scent you can find. And if you are worried about suffocating the baby, wear it behind your knees!

10. *Forget perfection.* If, before the baby, feeling sexy for you was all wrapped up in feeling toned or slim or thick-maned or glossy skinned, it's time to let all that go now. Make love in a silk caftan with great slits up the side or fling on a black push-up bra if you're worried about leaking breasts, but for heaven's sake jump back in, baby fat and all. Nothing is better for body issues than having pleasure with the body you have.

17. STICKS AND STONES
How to Fight Fair

It seems easy in the early stages of parenting to have the same argument with your husband every day . . . for a year. The smallest things can set off a terrible fight. A stolen half hour of sleep for one partner and not the other. A look from the doorway. A sarcastic remark. And worst of all, a criticism. New mothers don't "do" criticism. Possibly because they are plagued with so much built-in self-criticism to start with. The trouble with communication once a baby comes is not so much what we say to each other, but how and when we choose to say it. When we're feeling vulnerable, angry, and reactive, the context and tone of our words become critical. When the fighting begins—and won't stop—we desperately search outside ourselves for a solution. I went through a long phase of reading pop psychology and inspirational books in the bathtub—my marital peacekeeping headquarters and unofficial emotional think tank. "Help us," I chanted in

the tepid depths. "Help us . . . Saint Francis . . . Emily Post . . . Linda Goodman . . . Oprah!"

But so many of the books specifically about marriage often made me laugh out loud. Even the very best of them put the onus on the woman to be the peacemaker, no matter how exhausted, provoked, overwhelmed, or depleted she might be feeling. *Mother Nurture* (Rick Hanson, Jan Hanson, and Ricki Pollycove), one of my very favorite books for maternal well-being, is a magnificently attentive guide to everything from nutrition to erotic intimacy. Yet in the chapter devoted to communication and conflict, the authors suggest a balanced verbal tone, a level of civility, and a clear head, which I find nigh impossible to achieve in the middle of a raging marital battle. In the face of a volatile exchange, they suggest: "Let his words move through you like wind rustling the leaves on a tree." But what if Daddy is raging like a hurricane? Is it enough to bend like a willow, or will you simply snap? And when does bending become submission?

Buddhism teaches us that anger begets anger and that the compassionate heart breaks the chain of rage and spite by holding up a mild and knowing hand to any onslaught of negative emotion. How I would love to be Gautama the housewife during our arguments. As my husband stewed and spat venom, I'd watch him calmly, as if he were a distant storm at sea, then say sweetly, "Come to me, my husband, and accept the love I have for you; life is but a bubble in time." No, no, no, *no*! Much more often I find myself in a reactive hell: swearing (and really meaning it), slamming doors (that old chestnut), and once (mea culpa), throwing a deck chair across a patio. Not terribly constructive. Not nice. But very normal.

It's hard to fight with grace, and it's hard to be honest enough to fight fair; to resist name-calling, shaming, and blaming—the fun but extra-hurtful stuff. It's hard to be constructive and get your point across when you are too deep inside the battle to rationalize, and it's hardest still to contain an anger that feels bottomless. And, believe me, maternal anger is constantly being replenished by the challenges of the job.

Most arguments explode along a fault line of what is left unsaid. It took a long time to learn how to ask for things *in bright red letters* rather than insinuate their absence. It is something of an art to point out the need for more help or support without pointing the finger at your partner, especially if that help is hard won or given begrudgingly. For a mother who is home all day, so many small frustrations accumulate by the time her partner walks in the door that it is very hard indeed to be upbeat and gracious about her needs. It seems more tempting instead to thrust the kid into his arms, leap into the tub, and bolt the bathroom door. Or for the first words to fall out of your mouth to be verbal snakebites. For a mother who works, it is very easy to grow steadily more anxious as the day passes and return home deeply sensitive to a house full of faults and obstacles.

Perhaps the easiest way to stop fights is to calm yourself in the moments before reuniting on the home front. To literally stop and breathe while you are putting your key in the door, and visualize an equal but very different level of stress in your partner's day; to imagine love instead of conflict; and (this is the toughie) to let the first thing you say not be a complaint or a request. Sometimes, when I'm feeling as mature as an oak tree, I greet my husband after a long day and simply say hi. Then I smile and quietly get on with my thing, giving him the chance to land in my world and find his feet. I know how to nag, but that is not the way I want to be heard—or felt.

So much of getting what you want is a matter of timing and tone, and having the subtle skills of knowing how to ask. Being naturally pugnacious, I have had to work hard on my own opening gambits and find clever ways to diffuse hot topics with humor or a sense of camaraderie. If a sentence begins with the words "Why can't you . . ." or "Why do you always . . . ," a defensive reply is almost guaranteed. If a request comes after a criticism, you will hit deaf ears. If it is delivered in a sickly sweet tone, it could be construed as passive-aggressive, and if it is accompanied by flying objects, you can expect resounding defeat. Cooperation flows instead from thinking communally, from working as a team—even if the team is not yet in place. Sometimes it

is as simple as dropping a plural pronoun into a problem: How can *we* budget better? How can *we* keep this house clean? How should *we* get the baby to sleep? What can *we* do to feel more connected/intimate/free spirited?

Another crucial aspect to having civilized conversations rather than slinging matches is clean language. Name-calling and swearing make any discussion degenerate into an emotionally violent place. I made a rule of avoiding words that end in k . . . jerk, freak, prick, and worse. I never realized how much swearing hurt my case (and his pride) until the really terrible fights, which are also a very ugly thing for your baby to witness.

Wit, rather than sarcasm, is a vital commodity for resolving conflict. Yet, I noticed a complete hemorrhage of my humor in the first year of mothering. Nothing said about me or my baby made me laugh; in fact, any good-natured joke at our expense made me wince. I was just trying too hard to run a house and mothering way too intensely to allow for gentle teasing of any kind. The patience and concentration needed with a new baby have the power to make a mother a righteous prude and—I hate to admit this—a bit of a moralistic bore. As a rookie mum, it's easy to get stuck in an almost fundamentalist state of zeal and focus. And it becomes very, very hard to loosen up. Play, that flexible, spontaneous, magical mind-set we apply to children every day, is in short supply between warring couples, yet it is the one skill that can defuse the fury and rebuild desperately needed neutral ground.

What every warring woman needs to realize about arguing is that the conflict is not usually the fruit of that exact moment but rather an outburst that has been brewing for weeks, months, or, in the case of unresolved emotional and childhood issues, decades. Tsunamis begin far out at sea and build as they move toward the shore. Fights build in much the same way, so that the cumulative force of many small irritants grows into one large ball of loathing over time. Resentment is often optimism turned toxic, fear turned inward, and loving expectation that has been disappointed or bruised. The more you expect from your partner, the greater the potential is to deeply resent him when he misses the mark. And marriage is fraught with heavy gaps between the real and the ideal. The growing fissure between what we dream our marriage will be with children and the reality of what it actually becomes is where the discord thrives. And where the really deep learning begins.

Before my child, I imagined that my husband and I would share the caring, cooking, and cleaning evenly and fall into bed to make love, laughing at the end of each complicated day. Unbelievably, we have actually experienced days like that, but only after months of painful experimentation and heated negotiation.

Learning how to strike a delicate balance between duty and generosity has been humbling for both of us, as everyone has his or her bizarre household blind spots. The details of our very human habits are boring, no doubt, but to make a life with children work, they have to be faced, refined, and oftentimes purged. I think the core of a happy marriage with kids dwells in resolving or at least facing several issues. Money is probably the first; sex, spiritual beliefs, and value systems the second; and housework is the third. Run dry on or run foul of any of these vital resources, and the fighting will begin. Once locked into a combative relationship, scoring points becomes more critical than actually hearing each other.

My son's godmother once said to me, "Do what you've always done, and you'll get what you've always gotten." If you apply this advice to communication, it is an open invitation to shift the goalposts, change the rules, and experiment with your own responses and arguing style. As hard as it is to be the mature one, the cool one, or the laughing one, I find that any response that is deliberately different stops my husband in his tracks. He banks on my anger to fuel his own, and when I don't play along—when I smile, or drift into another room, or ask for a minute to simply jump into the shower to think about his accusations—he has time to calm down and tell me what he's really thinking, to find the original thought under the pile of incoherent rage.

Toddlers have tantrums because they feel powerless, overwhelmed, and can't achieve what they desire so badly. I think adults are very sim-

ilar. When we can't effect change in our own lives, we impose extreme demands and criticisms on those closest to us. At the heart of most really awful fights between parents is the same challenge ripping at both the mother and the father but often in different forms. Yet how easy it is to forget that divided we fall. After some truly rough times, times when I wanted to simply walk away, I still found the strength to remind my husband of my favorite family battle cry. Embracing him with stiff limbs, weak with pride and remorse, I'd say, "Remember, babe, it's us against the world, not us against each other." If love was easy, it wouldn't be love, it would just be romance.

MARRIAGE TROUBLESHOOTING

Housework: The Big Fat Question of Who Does What

Motherhood does not instantly confer housekeeping skills; in fact, for most women it implodes them. Once our baby came, the housework tripled, and I wondered how to wedge or seductively wriggle myself out of a 1956 housewife's horrific workload. Three months in, and I was ready to burn effigies of June Cleaver and Julia Child outside the nearest Barnes & Noble. Small errands that were once a delightful distraction (shopping for fresh ingredients, scampering to the post office, hand washing a business shirt) become purgatory with a child attached.

I think domestic inequity lies at the core of most marital strain. Because a woman truly does not know just how much she does until she adds a baby to the equation. Housework is drab, but it is especially grating (and soul wasting) if left solely to one person to complete. Who the hell wants to wipe down the same kitchen counter for eighteen years? When I broached a fairer division of labor in our home, I had to stomach long huffy lectures while my husband cleaned. "This," he said with a flourish of the Swiffer, "is how it's *done*!" "Right on!" I cheered dumbly as I calculated in my head the hours of freedom gained. It seems an awful truth that first house training a man to help you tackle the house can simply feel like double the work.

I do not mind sticking my tongue in a man's ear if it will make him listen. I used humor, bribery, lists, loud groovy music, and the promise of a great lunch to get our mutual Sunday morning cleanup sessions in place. Once you reach the glorious point where you have jobs you can share, you also need to delegate the jobs that neither of you can face. Like a budget or the grocery list, every couple should have a household list, and from that list each can choose the jobs he/she wants to do. Changing the routine as they see fit. I think it's brilliant to clean together in the same time frame. How else is a man who is never home going to gauge how much it takes to keep a house running? And how else are you really going to share the drudgery without facing it together?

Clearly, though, running a home takes more than two hours on a Sunday morning. Especially if both parents are holding down full-time jobs and needing family time.

I think it's sensible to ask for a weekly cleaner for Christmas instead of a mile of expensive shoes. Come New Year's Eve, you want to smell of Chanel No.19, not dish-washing liquid.

Money

The question of money in a marriage could fill a whole series of books. Few issues break relationships asunder as this one. But whatever your spending, saving, or earning style, it is crucial to get on the same page with money when a child comes along. Before my son, I had no budget. I could rationalize a $400 handbag splurge in any language. Now, with a strict budget, I have a safety net for emergencies, sickness, or the very basics. After Marcello came, I simply stopped buying fashion shoes and hiding shopping bags under the bed. Motherhood cleaned up my money act. It also brought my husband a deeper appreciation of the contribution I had made financially before being a

mother sliced my time and income in half. When the burden fell on him to make our rent, I had to concede to my own excesses and become moderate, almost spartan. When I stopped overshopping, the fighting stopped. My husband saw my newfound frugality as a sign of respect. And responsibility. I bit my tongue but felt secretly relieved to shift my priorities. We shared a common goal.

To save heartache and miscommunication, I urge all first-time parents to see a financial planner or even an empathetic bank manager to map out a budgeting plan for the first year. Knowing exactly what food, entertainment, insurance, child care, toys, and travel should cost is critical. Though most Americans live with the burden of debt, following a financial plan that fits your means creates emotional security. To honestly know what you have (and don't have) materially is the most liberating starting point for a young family. It is the basis of teamwork, survival, and, in time, abundance for everyone. A little scrimping is inevitable when baby arrives—there will always be the Barneys sale next year.

Value Systems and Beliefs

I don't believe in cutting a baby's hair or making him wear shoes till he can walk. My husband didn't feel comfortable with prolonged breastfeeding. I love to watch our son make art with spaghetti sauce and feathers. His daddy likes to see him in ironed, bleached clothes and shining shoes. To strike a balance between our very different beliefs, I actively ask my man to read or even just skim through books about child development, education theory, vaccination, spirituality, and even discipline, to think about where he stands and to evolve a shared philosophy for the way we are raising our child. Nothing about parenting is passive or arbitrary; every choice has deep ramifications. It pays to make very important decisions about health, religion, moral action, and education with many hours of conversation backing up your choices.

I often make my husband choke in the middle of lunch on big

loaded questions about God, sex, and politics. I especially love hypothetical scenarios such as "What if our son is gay?/wants to be a Hindu priest or join the army?" It is precisely the what-ifs of life that make real conversations and make our minds—and hearts—more flexible. The most important thing about having values is to appreciate those you do not share with a measure of respect and curiosity. My parents get irritated when I deviate from their point of view. Many husbands are disappointingly similar. Independent thinking can resemble a betrayal or a bolt from the blue. To avoid such serious rifts, try to reach agreement on the very big decisions in your family well in advance and with mutual respect. This will take many, many weird and wired dinner conversations, but it's worth it.

Sex

I know I have devoted whole chapters to this subject, but just in case the gentle mother has forgotten . . . men need to shag. Quite a lot. Whatever you might believe about gender roles, emotional differences, destiny, and biology, the libido of men does not appear to collapse under stress but rather, quite horribly, intensifies. It's a hard pill to swallow that making love more often decreases arguments. Especially when fighting shrinks your loins and fires your heart with spiteful castrating revenge fantasies. When truly despising one's husband, sex can feel like an extension of housework; another repetitive ritual performed while kneeling. But making love, like laughing, relaxes two partners enough to let several guards down at once. It reminds you that you are man and woman, and not just Mum and Dad. I won't bang on about getting it on, nor shall I promote the emotional Band-Aid known as make-up sex. If you have very serious problems, regular intercourse is not going to mechanically fix the fighting. However, if somewhere inside the nudity and the contact you can reconnect with intimacy, fantasy, and a sense of play, you might just find the flame that fueled your love in the first place. As my very pragmatic friend (and mother of three) Sally would say, it takes longer to fight than it does to fellate.

18. MIND-SET, MOTIVATION, AND INTEGRAL MOVEMENT

Fitness and Easy Wellness after Baby

The days and weeks that follow having a baby are a very vulnerable and intensely private period in the life of a woman's body. There are few if any social rituals to honor all that the body has yielded and accomplished by giving birth, and emphasis falls almost arbitrarily on "losing the baby weight," a goal that hardly takes into account the shock of transition from a single entity to a double entity. One day we are replete and secure, a planet on legs, and the next day we still feel vast but strangely unmanned, like a battleship with her heroic sails deflated. Everything felt extra in the weeks after I gave birth. My breasts felt like two down pillows on fire. And as I ran my hands over thick hips, I wondered if I could excavate my bones again from beneath this heavy temple of flesh.

After giving birth, the taut pregnant belly is replaced by the fragile bloat of a slowly deflating uterus. A thickly stubborn layer of fat lingers on arms, hips, belly, and legs. Breasts are veiny, skin can still look blotchy, and firmness and fitness seem far, so far away. Experts comfort us with the advice that baby weight is gained gradually and needs to be lost just as gradually, but that feels very hard to believe in the first weeks. And we expect the return of our prepregnant body so much sooner. Like, in weeks. Instead, the radical yet incremental changes such as stretched ligaments and expanded ribs and hips make many mothers feel like they have been stitched into a softly cushioned bodysuit like a satin doll.

Of course, the return back to what you sense as your own body is not simply a mere question of weight and form; it's also a matter of movement and energy. We are bigger but often not stronger in the early days of motherhood. The depletion of muscle tone, loss of agility, and dull weight of new-mother exhaustion pin us down. I had so wanted to be brisk and agile in the early weeks with my son, but the energy simply wasn't there, and my thighs seemed to have bonded and formed their own republic.

It becomes hard to judge what is a safe, reasonable, or even normal expectation for weight loss, regained fitness, or energy levels, both immediately postpartum and for a year or more into mothering. Some smug Yummies are out jogging with a three-wheeler and squeezing into prepregnancy jeans a few months after giving birth, but for most women the road back to even finding some semblance of a waistline is a longer one. Much longer. Mine was twenty months and seven hundred chocolate biscuits long. I knew how to slim down in a healthy, gradual way, but it took a full year and a half before I could face the simple disciplines of cutting carbs after dusk, flipping on a yoga DVD while Marcello slept, and doing three sessions of cardio a week. But I failed to do even the bare minimum, and openly despised the women who began working out straight after birth and looked hot in a wrap dress and footless tights at their baby's first birthday party. But, of course, this was not a new problem. I was born with a rattan chair welded to my bottom, and the baby made the propensity for sitting faintly justified.

Lactation was to be my salvation. I rationalized that breast-feeding burned off five hundred calories a day and took the lazy, languid, and super-slow, long-seated approach (accompanied by a raging appetite). Of course, I didn't really transform at all but simply hovered, with a set of Botero hips, in a holding position. Not gaining, not losing. Heavy and replete. For every calorie that left my body in mother's milk, I would put back ten more in toasted fried egg sandwiches and steaming hot cocoa. Like many, many new mothers, dieting was not a realistic avenue for me because I had decided to nurse indefinitely, and without substantial meals I would simply keel over.

A huge factor for appetite is also exhaustion. The less we sleep, the hungrier we are. And the less rest a body receives, the slower it metabolizes energy. It's the biology of survival. Given this fact, the best avenue for slimming down and firming up can only be exercise. Terribly sorry, but it's true. Those who only diet look somewhat desiccated over time (especially older mothers), and new mums can't afford to diet if they are to have optimum nutrition both for themselves and their breast milk. These stark facts put all of us on the same gangplank, and it leads to the gym, the park, or even the front step, skipping rope in hand. Having a baby forced me into a fitness corner, and I came out swinging in a pair of red boxing gloves, finally active at forty-one! I am happy to say I have a better figure after giving birth than before, probably because I don't take anything for granted, and there is a fierce desire to be one's strongest and healthiest in order to protect your young and possibly have a few more. Even a hippo can become a lioness—if she has the will.

Of course, the benefits of movement are not just cosmetic, though this is the main selling point. When a mother starts to move, she doesn't just reverse the atrophy of muscle, she also regains mental clarity; sheds stress; kick-starts her libido; clears her skin; produces endorphins, neurotransmitters that actively combat depression; and enjoys respite that does not involve chocolate or shopping. Working out is the

ultimate alone time because it is so constructive and so concentrated. It might be the one time in your day when you do not feel dispersed. And exercise rebuilds self-esteem from the inside out. If I can feel my muscles, then I know sometime soon I'll actually unearth them from the incarcerating layers of flesh. And when a woman can gradually top her personal bests, she replaces the guilt of being sedentary with the passion of breathing deeply and sweating out blues, mental blocks, and fears.

Fitness is a mind-set that many women lose during pregnancy—especially late pregnancy, when back pain and the sheer weight of the baby make leaping about or even getting to a pool impractical. Some women are sporty till they labor, many more are not. While others were lumbering away at pregnant Pilates, I hoarded sleep like a grizzly bear and then spent it all in one extraordinary night laboring naturally for twenty hours straight. Birth, in some ways, is the call for the body to wake again and to work like it has never worked before. Fitness after birth is like the second wave of that fighting spirit. Movement creates strength, spiritually and physically. In the words of Led Zeppelin, "When the levee breaks, Mama, you've got to move!"

The following basic principles for getting your confidence and energy up and some semblance of waistline back are honed from a very lazy woman's experience. Read on if you have never run a marathon, or if mothering is starting to feel like one.

ACCEPT YOUR STARTING POINT

You might start at three weeks or—shock! horror!—three years after baby, but cut the guilt, shelve the body shame, and pocket your doubt. Even if you join a gym and don't get there immediately you are enroute to fitness. Give yourself a deadline to begin and find a way to diffuse your excuses if you find yourself backing out. The only time is NOW.

KNOW WHAT YOUR BODY CAN DO

If you've had a Cesarean, the mandatory healing period before lifting or exercise is six weeks. And if you've had a difficult vaginal birth, you might also like to slow things down. Before starting any exercise regimen, have your doctor check your blood pressure, blood sugar level, breathing, and general fitness levels. Mums who are obese need specially tailored programs to sustain the energy needed to nurse, care for baby, and exercise, though certainly it's the heavier mothers who need fitness most to balance their lives and redefine their appetites to a more wholesome routine. If you're a larger mum, don't lose heart; motherhood is the best time to get your health on track, especially before your *child* turns two and really challenges your mobility and endurance. Use this time to seriously eat for nutrition and move for pleasure.

Once safety and health concerns are out of the way, anytime you start a fitness program is the right time. Some mothers are deeply exhausted, emotionally unready, healing, or just sort of stunned at the beginning of their journey. You might need to feel desperate to get started, and that's OK. Forgive yourself for the millionth evasive excuse, and then push yourself to act. What we all need to know to get started is that exercise will give us energy rather than just burn it up. This really helps with all of the bone weariness of mothering and instills a sense of balance and peace in a life that is only going to get more chaotic.

CHOOSE YOUR MANTRA

Positive self-talk is everything. It will get you out of pajamas and into your trainers and out into the fresh morning air. En route to my Baby Boot Camp class, I would chant inside my head, Movement is for life! I'm alive! I'm alive! Even though I usually felt (and looked) half dead. Then after an amazing forty minutes of running, jumping, and stretching, with two or three other new mothers, we would lie under a vast budding oak, staring at the clouds and *really* feeling alive. Getting there was a trick of the mind. Find your own mantra and chant it. When the mind is convinced, the body will follow.

CARVE OUT THE TIME

The compromise we all strike with exercise, diet, maintenance, and well-being after baby is between time and energy. The diet traps include eating baby's food scraps; eating high-fat, high-sugar, or high-caffeine snacks to keep going; skipping meals and then hoarding food at one sitting; and relying on food as a sleep substitute for energy. The inertia trap is fed by a sugar- and carb-heavy diet draining the body of nutrients and energy, an obvious sleep deficit, and the fact that the less we exercise, the less oxygen we pump around our bodies, and the more sluggish we feel. Given the choice between sleep and a yoga video, it's tempting to believe that rest creates energy and relaxation, but gentle exercise can actually yield more. For the first year, I blamed breastfeeding for the energy drain, but by the middle of the second year, I knew it was not long nursing that was so debilitating but simply a radical lack of balance. I mooched by on health food, early nights, and very little alcohol, but my thighs didn't care. They collapsed anyway.

The longer we wait to start moving again, the longer it's going to take to feel well and look better. The first and only step to actually, really, finally exercising is to carve it into your life like sleeping, eating, or bathing. You literally have to force the ritual until it becomes habit. And be honest about how your time is spent. Everyone can find twenty minutes in a day—where're yours hiding?

- Start by walking: In the early part of your postnatal exercise plan, walking is great because it has virtually zero impact on your joints when your body is still "loose" and trying to recover from the stresses of birth.

- If you take a daily hour-long nap, steal the first fifteen minutes to do a stretching routine. Over time, the stretch might replace the snooze.

GET SUPPORT

If you can exercise two to three days a week for a month, you can forge a healthy addiction to exercise. The trick is doing it long enough for it to take hold and become a physical desire. See if several family members (husband, partner, sister, grandparents) can each cover you for about an hour and a half. Draw up a roster and be really strict about your appointment with fitness. Some say that exercising at home with a DVD works, but if the wail of your newborn throws you off track, try to get to a postnatal class instead. Start with fairly gentle movement that builds your confidence and stamina, and let everyone know what a gift they are giving you in these small blocks of time. Also, if others know your routine, they can push you when you start to slide.

TRACK YOUR ENERGY CURVE

Metabolically speaking, the optimum time for fat-burning exercise is morning. Afternoon and evening workouts promote deeper sleep, but because you need to refuel with dinner, this is not ideal for trying to rev up a sluggish postpartum metabolism. These facts aside, you have to find the highest energy point in your day and try to move then. Timing it all with baby's nap is tough, but as the baby settles into a routine of predictable rest over time, you can make appointments with yourself and stick to them. Don't worry if you are out skipping when everyone else is watching the evening news. Babies teach us to do everything in an upside-down, spontaneous way.

GET THE RIGHT GEAR

It's not at all superficial to feel that the right hoodie will get you to the gym. If I go to work out dressed like a roadie for Neil Young, I rarely get results. I do yoga in old silk Vietnamese pajama bottoms because I am not at ease doing the downward dog pose in nothing but tights and a smile in front of some dude. It just seems impolite. You have to feel comfortable and confident when you get started, so choose your outfit well. I would have loved a message T-shirt that read "I'm Not Fat, I'm Fertile" and perhaps some shorts that read "Kiss My Assets" across the butt. Maybe for the next baby. Get the best sports shoes you can afford; your back and posture need plenty of protection now. And think about how much you would use a three-wheeler multi-terrain baby jogger. You might find that if you share it with a neighboring mum, you may be more motivated to actually run with it.

FIND A MOTHER MENTOR OR BECOME ONE

The first trainer I was willing to follow had a baby strapped to her chest and had us motley mothers madly high kicking behind our strollers. It was much better than sitting in a circle talking about solids and sleep. I was cynical about exercising with my baby in tow (how L.A.!) but found that he actually loved yoga and running and rolling on grass, watching me groan. Sloth moms need to seek out action-packed friends who walk a little faster, and find ways to watch fitness DVDs together if you can't afford a formal course. For those slim sisters and manic mothers who are natural jocks, please lead your mother groups outdoors while barking orders, sharing moves, and breaking sweats. When it comes to finding their body and soul strength, new mothers need one another.

MAKE MOVEMENT INTEGRAL TO LIFE

Most trainers will tell you that everyday activities from gardening to shopping and even housework present opportunities for fitness and exercise. Its called incidental exercise, and it's actually what everyone did before cars and TV ate up our lives. Certainly lifting your baby (safely, with a straight back and bent knees shoulder-width apart) repetitively over time will build up your arms. But you can easily work squats and lunges into your stroller park visits (dumb as it looks!), walk a little faster and a little longer each day to get yourself up to one hour of walking a day (that's seven hours a week!), and pick up speed and put grunt into the activities you usually do in slow motion. Set yourself a bare minimum (twenty minutes of walking or physical play) and a tolerable maximum (an hour of cardio, a heavy salsa, or even a sex session). An hour of fast salsa dancing for a 150-pound woman burns up to 450 calories. So cha-cha to that and accept every variation of movement in between. If you even clean the house with The Arctic Monkeys amped up and lots of dancing in between, you're moving and feeling better at day's end. The trick with exercise is to fool yourself into doing more without really feeling it.

MOVE LIKE A SKINNY CHICK

Slim, vibrant women, I have noticed, are always moving. They squat instead of bending, they do more things standing, they walk instead of hailing a cab, they always take the stairs, and they seem to be out in all sorts of weather. They annoy me terribly, but these hale and hearty specimens put a little bit of locomotion into every gesture. And it's actually much easier to integrate movement into your life organically than to have to factor it into the form of classes and workouts. To see how you fare with becoming more physical, keep a movement journal for two weeks. Each day, see what new activity (no matter how subtle) you can factor in and, most important, note how you feel. I see the difference when I clean playing *Scorpion* by Eve; I move like a gladiator, and the kitchen cleans itself.

THE BARE MINIMUM AND THE TRUTH

Gentle exercise is OK if you want gentle results. So, even if you hate "huffy puffy" exercise, this is the one and only thing that will sculpt muscle and burn fat quickly. You need to sweat out the calories and breathe hard and fast, and there are no real substitutes for this. If you do thirty minutes of cardio, and your shirt isn't glued to your chest, you're faking it and cheating yourself of results. Plan to do two to three really sweaty sessions a week and find the ones that are easiest. In terms of motivation, group classes can be better than machines or solitary circuits, because you will be pushed to keep up. Lose yourself in each class and don't waste time worrying if you are the slowest. Everybody's personal best improves over time. Face the truth about what you need to improve your well-being, and commit to balancing the hard stuff with the kinder stuff. Over time, pride in your transformation will replace dejection about feeling stuck. Or still chubby.

FOODS THAT WORK OUT WITH YOU

Most trainers encourage their clients to eat five small meals a day, each including a protein and a whole-food carb. They stress the importance of drinking a gallon of water a day. Other principles to follow include: reaching for high-energy, high-nutrient snacks such as whole fruit and nuts; avoiding carbs after five o'clock; and, finally, staying away from white sugar, fatty or fried foods, and bleached flour. To eat like a movie star, you need to be very organized. You need to stock the fridge, the pantry, the car, and the handbag with good, healthy fuel. Slug down water, herbal tea, and fresh juices on the hour. And choose foods that love you back.

I really love the "jock" approach to eating because it signals the end of calorie counting and appetite. When you are exercising enough, eating what you want within reason really becomes deep and well earned. It's a wonderful thing to move more. But do not fall into the trap of overcompensating a workout with food. For example, the "I did it!" post-aerobic chocolate sundae. Or the "I'm Rocky Balboa!" massive steak sandwich after a single boxing class. When it comes to food, you need to remain starkly real. A faster metabolism wed to eating more food will only maintain weight, not help shed it.

TAKE IT SLOW, TAKE IT FAST, MIX IT UP

If you want red-carpet results in no time, you need to work out like a freak in a rigorous routine, often with supervision. But, like more ordinary mothers, if you are happy to embrace more gradual change, you can do much slower, much gentler exercise and simply mix it up to keep the flow going. The trick for keeping fitness interesting is to diversify your moves every day. A little mat action, a little outdoors time, a little solitary skipping, a little social dancing, a little rigorous climbing, a little silly toddler running and jumping all work—especially to music.

FIND YOUR INNER TRAINER

I hired a twenty-three-year-old six-foot-two-inch trainer with arctic blue eyes, muscled honey skin, and relatively little mercy, for five sessions. Oh, *Alex!* He had a gentle way of always getting me to do more. He smiled as he cracked the whip, and his approach was very light-hearted and accepting. By saying some beautiful lie like "You're not

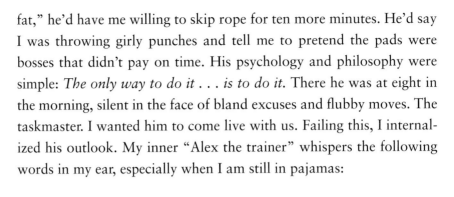

fat," he'd have me willing to skip rope for ten more minutes. He'd say I was throwing girly punches and tell me to pretend the pads were bosses that didn't pay on time. His psychology and philosophy were simple: *The only way to do it . . . is to do it.* There he was at eight in the morning, silent in the face of bland excuses and flubby moves. The taskmaster. I wanted him to come live with us. Failing this, I internalized his outlook. My inner "Alex the trainer" whispers the following words in my ear, especially when I am still in pajamas:

- No matter how tired you are, exercise will clear your head, boost your immune system, and oxygenate your whole body. *So get outta bed!*

- Everybody has twenty minutes a day to exercise. Don't spend those minutes thinking about it . . . *move!* Use these blocks for a simple routine, walking, dancing to a whole White Stripes album, or making love.

- *Show up.* Getting into your gear and arriving at your workout (even if it's in front of the TV with the cat watching) is 80 percent of the challenge. *Congratulations . . . Now move.*

- *Never waste a workout pretending.* If you're here and ready, don't fake it. Put as much into your workout as you can, and you will get better results in less time.

- No *skipping the hard or boring moves.* Whatever you're resisting is probably what your body needs most!

- *Stretch yourself, Mama!* Take what you can do and push it just a little bit further each time. Work until you can feel your muscles.

- *Believe* in the deep, almost immeasurable benefits of exercise. Visualize not only a great figure while you move, but strong bones, happy organs, a powerful digestive system, better nerves, a healthy and vital old age, and vibrant well-being in all the years in between. Every time you move, you invest in the quality of your life on a profound level.

- At the end of each session, take a few minutes to congratulate yourself and give thanks for good health. By giving yourself the gift of a small pocket of time to move your body, you honor yourself, your family, and your child. *A happy mother is a healthy, vibrant mother. So, well done.*

PS: Don't Give Up!

As your babies grow, life gets more tangled, and it is tempting to cave in and lose your "dates" with the gym, dance class, and yoga. Skipping one or two appointments can lead to abandoning your commitment to fitness and wellness altogether. Ironically, it is the busiest mothers who need the release of working out the most. Keep a mood journal in your gym bag, and when you find yourself slipping, revisit your notes. Jog your memory about how vital and happy exercise makes you feel, and don't let personal setbacks, weight plateaus, or plain tiredness and loss of discipline slow your aims.

Movement, like eating well, is a plan for a life of well-being, not just a stopgap measure to keep your dress size down. Try to remember too that it doesn't matter when you stop moving as long as you start again and that everything gets better from that moment on. Burn your excuses and start building up your bone mass, stamina, muscles, nerve, and general gutsy outlook for decades to come. The happiest mother on the block is the one that can deal. And that takes tremendous energy.

19. NO MAMA IS AN ISLAND

De-isolating on Decaf

For a woman without children, time alone can be sweet solitude: a deep refreshing silence, a soulful respite, a chance for renewal that can come only with a remove from others. For a mother, being alone—but with children—can never truly be solitude; it can often become isolation.

I never imagined that I would suffer or feel crushingly cut off with a child. I thought loneliness was a fate reserved for women in remote suburbia or strictly structured societies that kept mothers chained to ovens and bedposts. Living in the youngest, trendiest, and most promiscuous neighborhood of Brooklyn, New York, I envisaged an instant inclusion into the throbbing vein of life: parenting set to disco. How foolish I was. In the local Thai restaurant, scrawny young couples sniffed at my bulky stroller as a waste of space: theirs. In the effete

bookstore, the neurotic poet behind the counter watched dispassion-ately as I pushed the glass door open with my behind. On the street, wearing a knee-length skirt, plain ponytail, and no tattoos, I was nearly invisible. And very few shopgirls or waitresses or young single women standing at bus stops wished to share the smallest of small talk. My strolls to the supermarket, set out with such optimism, soon shriv-eled to the maternal equivalent of a walk of shame. In the eyes of the groovy, I suppose I represented a life of sacrifice, navy blue raincoats, and insufferable boredom. A messenger for the Grim Reaper with a Bugaboo.

Despite my son's Ramones T-shirt and a cup of decaf in my pale hand, I was officially outside of the scene, and I felt quite desolate. The spontaneity of life had suddenly perished, and I felt as welcome as a duckling on a freeway. One afternoon, out of sheer defiance, I stormed into the bar below our building and ordered a ginger ale. It was right at dusk, and my grocery bags sagged around the foot of my bar stool. A gang of Irish construction workers were hard at their beers. My son smiled at them with his hands splayed across the bar, his fat legs dan-gling from the front pack strapped to my body. You could have heard a diaper pin drop. Utterly defeated at such a public display of social need, I slinked home to drink tea and think.

I had friends, but suddenly I never saw them. Most invitations that fell after sunset were beyond me. Brunch in a crowded Manhattan restaurant with a baby was possible, but not really fun. My single girl-friends still went to bars. My married childless girlfriends were still going to obscure art openings and silent yoga retreats and samples sales, places where a BabyBjörn made you feel like a cross between Shiva and a Martian. And my two bosom buddies with kids continued the same pattern of friendly visits that ended suddenly and sharply when our babies either set each other off on crying jags like screaming car alarms, or when magic struck, and one baby went down. Play-dates afford very little real quality time for the women involved, un-less the offspring are small enough to place in baskets on a brasserie floor, or another person is present to keep small toes and fingers out of danger.

Socially segregated by a strict sleeping routine for my son and a pretty obvious case of exhaustion, I looked to things I could do in the day that would afford adult conversation peppered with just enough mummy speak. In parks and in cafés, I found myself cruising for like-minded women with children. It was strangely similar to looking for love: an innocuous opening line, a shared joke, a smile, an offer of a phone number, and a hypothetical (but nonthreatening) allusion to a meeting in the fuzzy future. By week's end, I found a half dozen phone numbers scrunched in my spring coat pocket. Weirdly, I rarely phoned them. I worried, perhaps wrongly, that these other new mothers would be too busy, have their own established circle, or simply have no time to talk. Rejection and the fear of it loomed large. No one wants to follow rules to be accepted, and yet the terrain of motherhood is rife with them. Trying to find allies in other mothers is made more complex by the strange games, snap judgments, and unspoken rivalries that so riddle seemingly simple exchanges. In a bookstore, two mothers collide, and one asks the other which picture books her seven-year-old daughter is reading. Mother number two sniffs and says that her child is already into chapter books. Conversation over.

One clear memory stands out for me how loaded encounters between mothers can be, and how many obstacles to honest friendship block the way. One dreamy morning I was looking for toys in a secondhand store when I met a woman with a toddler and a three-month-old son. Sitting on the floor, blissfully thumbing through the board books, I asked her about her life with a second baby. "It's precious," she boomed and then, in a softer, more searing tone, added "I am *never* without him. Every second of his babyhood is so fleeting, I don't want to miss a minute." I felt, in that moment, like a cardboard effigy of a mother. My son, nine months old and equally precious, was far away with a sitter. Stabbed with guilt, I ran home through the rain, suddenly aware that despite the fact that I was shopping for him, I was not *with*

him. The words of a woman I would probably never see again had found the power to wound, and my sense of isolation grew that much deeper.

Women are naturally competitive. Women with children can be ferociously so. I can't tell you why this is. Perhaps because, unlike beauty or wealth, motherhood is a skill that is not explicit upon first glance. And, as insecure as we might be about our looks or our accomplishments as women, as mothers we need to know we are doing it right. In the first year, as you are finding your feet as a parent, the approval of other mothers becomes more important than the attention of men or even the acceptance of your own parents or society at large. Because of this need, I both craved the company of other mothers and feared it— almost resented the need for it.

In one last-stand grab for bonding and empathy, I took a drop-in class at an alternative Manhattan mothering center for the under-ones. It was simply called "Color and Movement." My rosy vision of an intimate little mummy coven—hair flowing, drums pounding, babies cavorting—roused my spirits. But when I showed up, I remembered where I was: New York City, 2005. There was a gridlock of expensive strollers outside the class, and the brightly lit room was crammed with about thirty-seven women, half of them very bored-looking nannies. Smiling, I found the coolest-looking mum in the room and sat close to her. Her son had electric blue eyes, and his name was Dov. That is almost the only detail I remember before the room exploded into a frenzy of frenetic movement and a spasmodic medley of horrible music. The lady leading the class was a mix between modern dance priestess and aerobic dominatrix. One minute we were thrusting our infants into the center of the room like crazed Satanists, and the next we were doing a do-si-do with the nearest leaping, bounding mother and child we could find.

No sooner would the music stop, than another bizarre move would be foisted upon the blinking, shocked babies. We had to wave their arms like miniature squid, then whirl in a circle, then boogie to blues, then lie on the floor and have a parachute descend upon our heads like a vast, suffocating petticoat falling from the sky. Very few women were smiling; instead they burned with zeal and intense concentration. One mother boasted of her two-month-old son, "This is the first time he hasn't cried; he's obviously getting socialized." Another kept madly gyrating her babe in arms long after the music had stopped. The color. The movement. The coldness of competitive mothering. It all made me want to cry.

Wheeling my sweaty little son onto the pavement, I felt a sudden relief to be alone and wondered if isolation was simply easier than trying to join in: if indeed it was part of the key to my own intimacy with Marcello, who clearly had no concept of connection or disconnection—only a very deep desire to be close to the breath and body of his mother. In the months that followed, the worst moments of lonely mothering became my hardest lessons: the nights when my husband staggered home to tell me about his concerts and parties, the days when the cold wind and dejected people on the subway blew straight through my soul. The afternoons when I would have killed to have another woman to shamelessly quiz about sticky but specific subjects like mastitis. The mornings when I turned to blogs and Google searches for answers to questions that had plagued me through the dawn. But all these moments helped me grow wiser. More sturdy and more selective.

One comes to realize that a certain reserve holds a new mother in good stead. Other than my husband, I had no family in my son's first year. If I had been lucky enough to live on the same street or even the same city as my own mother and a dozen other close friends with babies my age, I would have had instant relief but also endless external advice. And advice can blunt the second sense. Left alone, I was left utterly to my own devices, and the person I listened most closely to—without choice—was my child. After about eight moths, I didn't have to second-guess my hunches. I knew my kid. After ten months, I stopped caring what the bright young things on the street thought of my style or lack of it. At eleven months, I knew at forty paces which mothers to trust and which to leave for dust in the playground. At one year, I celebrated by starting my own mothers group, the Crazy Mothers of Brooklyn, and I did so in complete communion with Groucho Marx's philosophy: Groucho didn't want to join any club that would have him as a member.

I refuse to see motherhood as something neat enough to fit into the confines of a club. But I believe there is strength in unity. And the next time I walked into a bar at dusk with my baby on one hip and my groceries on the other, I did it with five other mothers by my side. We ordered a jug of sangria and didn't notice if the room fell silent or not. The women and their offspring were making all the noise, and the music was good old-fashioned jukebox rock and roll.

20. TRACKING THE JOURNEY

Love in a Shoe Box and Other Aids to Memory

To commemorate the fleeting span of early childhood, the Victorians fashioned jewelry from human hair, commissioned tiny keepsake portraits for lockets, and had delicate marble sculptures modeled after pudgy hands and feet. The notion of some tiny creature of perpetual motion being frozen in time is unappealing to most people—until they have a tiny creature of their own, and every little trace of their being becomes charged with emotion. Now that I scrub two tiny palms each day, I wish I knew where I could find a cut-rate Canova to sculpt not just my baby's hands but his tiny Converse sneakers and outgrown overalls as well. Keepsake mania starts with the hospital ID bracelet and culminates with those time-capsule children's rooms that are kept intact, like Proust's boudoir, long after Snookums has split for college. I don't want my offspring's life sealed up in a wallpapered bell jar, but nor can I simply settle for a library of undated photographs on my laptop. I'd like to be thoughtful enough to keep the things that will make him laugh (or wince) when he's forty.

Tracking the journey of a child's early years takes more than ingenuity; it takes presence of mind, which is hopelessly missing in the first year. I think it's perfectly respectable to tackle a scrapbook when your child is eighteen months old. But without dates scribbled on the back of photos or first-solid-food descriptions scratched into the corners of your Filofax, milestones melt into one big, indistinct blob. And it's not the dates that really matter, it's the moment. The day my son first stood up by himself, we were in a café where the owner had a Polaroid at hand. Serendipity! But a mad sketch of the event scribbled on a paper napkin with a shaky Biro would be just as memorable. Anyplace (laptop, notebook, chalkboard, drawing album) is a good place to catch a small reflection or a three-word mothering epiphany. *Today he smiled.*

The corny baby-blue and rose-pink albums that grandparents give are excellent places to write down conventional milestones (first word, first wave, first laugh), and they're even better places to put more less-lovable observations (first monster poo, first spectacular tantrum, first bite on the playground). The irritating quality of mass-produced baby brag books is their repetitious structure and fuzzy, rhymey prose style: the things you say, the holidays, the funny little games we play . . . All that laminated pastel gingham has a way of neutralizing the drama and the passion of a child's first years, especially if the kid wears purple tie-dye and sleeps in a hammock. OK, I confess to owning a chintz-covered illustrated diary called *Moments of Childhood: The First Five Years,* but the glory of this book is that it is completely illustrated with watercolors, poems, and etchings from the 1900s. Secondhand sentimentality is about all a modern mummy can take.

IDEAS FROM THE YUMMY ARCHIVE

Relics

0 TO 12 MONTHS

What to keep or commemorate the first year is a subjective matter. Shoes and booties are usually a favorite because babies rarely wear them, and so many relatives give such expensive ones. And as for clothes, try to limit yourself to one standout item from each category: one dress, one singlet, one amazing sweater, one novelty message one-sie, and perhaps something from the first Christmas or first birthday. Toys from the first year are often ignored completely by the baby but chosen with great care by you. Keep one or two that look lovely on a mantelpiece or evoke personal memories. If they were never drooled on, consider that a blessing. Soft hearts will want the candle from the first birthday cake, a christening memento, and maybe a corner cut from a favorite Lovie or simple flannel wrap. Why not cut them in an unusual shape such as a star, a little hand, or a whale, and use pinking shears to boot?

12 TO 24 MONTHS

The shoes your baby first walked in are a must-keep, but usually this quantum leap happens barefoot. The first markings of crayon on paper are usually fainter than spider's urine, but firsts are firsts. The first time Marcello used paints, I kept the originals and then bought some small, blank framed canvases for him to work on. His maternal grandfather is a painter, so it made a lovely gift. Advanced tots might create something we'd like to think is art: a primordial lump of clay, a Play-Doh cup and saucer, a scrap of paper with a feather stuck to it. Clear Per-spex boxes make baby art last, and make these relics look like very fancy love-junk. Birthday cards written *to* your child are nice, but even better is a small book passed around on each successive birthday to be

filled with messages, sketches, notes, and loving thoughts written on the day. Good places to store memorabilia are in stacking boxes that match (splurge, or find one for each year), in proper archive boxes, in clear plastic or wooden glass-front frames, or in a hatbox protected by plenty of tissue and tight ribbon to keep small hunter-gatherers at bay. If you want to make a collage box of different baby items, for inspiration look to antique keepsake boxes that used ribbons and silver pins or to the box-art collage and sculpture of Joseph Cornell and Max Ernst.

3 TO 5 YEARS

Memories start to take the shape of institutional creativity when children start preschool and then kindergarten. What could be worse than a grown-up writing a kid's name neatly and authoritatively in the corner of his completely abstract drawing? To make things more memorable for yourself, be sure to keep plenty of the art and writing created on rainy days at home as well as at school. Think about making your own relics with your kids. For example, let your daughter draw or paint directly onto a favorite dress she has outgrown, or have your son do your portrait while you do his. Expertise not necessary—in fact it would just get in the way of a really good time. Take a trip to a big museum and let your mini Matisse scrawl his own version of a masterpiece, or note his responses on the back of a postcard of the work he reviews. How else would you remember all that detail? As children get older, they have their own ideas about the most important days in their short lives. Ask them what they'd grab if they were allowed only three items, and keep these three for posterity. Yes, jars of marbles and fairy wands are historically relevant.

Journaling

0 TO 12 MONTHS

Sometime after eight months, you will be living in a warp-speed world where every other move your baby makes is a milestone. The leisure with which you watched him unfurl his hands or learn to swipe for dangling objects is gone, as one day he is learning to stand and the next he is making wry, complex faces that you thought belonged only to Spencer Tracy. Building up to this point, I suggest using downtime (or insomniac time) or a very young baby's long naps to write as much as possible. When I was holed up in a tiny hotel room in Italy nursing my son through bronchiolitis, I wrote for many hours. It was that or stare at the wall, listen to his shallow breaths, and panic. You don't need to be a writer to capture your own thoughts. In crisis or in stasis with a baby (and they often feel the same), you have a rare chance to ac-knowledge all that you are learning or resisting or fumbling through. Keep your observations as simple and honest as you can.

Confess your worst emotions and the best ones, and don't try to glaze your days with pink icing. The bare rudiments of reporting weight and length and what was eaten at the first Christmas will not be the real stuff of your memory. Ask yourself instead what you did to stay awake while breast-feeding. How you felt when you got your first rush of mother love. How you coped on days when you felt ambivalent or hopeless or even dangerous. Nice images to put in a journal are your baby's handprints, simple collage elements such as a baby food label, an airplane ticket, a square of ribbon, a doctor's note, or a clothing label that strikes your fancy.

If you simply forget to write down anything in the first year, ask your close friends and family (well in advance) to keep a selection of your e-mails. A few months' worth, and you have your own mini motherhood blog.

12 TO 24 MONTHS

The rapid changes of the second year really demand a weekly if not monthly inventory. Good ways to note the rapid evolution that is happening on so many fronts is to reserve ten daily minutes (before bed is good) to write a sentence or two on the big happenings of the day. Imagine you are a war reporter dispatching headlines from the front lines, and you have only a few words to capture the color: *Eric puts asparagus up nose but eats straw . . . Lola chases sunset to water's edge . . . Viva declares peas illegal . . . Steig barks like dog.*

When you feel tired or uninspired, ask your husband or older siblings to track some entries or think about posting a guest book by the nursery door for special occasions, and don't edit anything. Better still, keep sketch pads or blank notebooks all over your house to scribble in when the mood strikes you—or when you have a hand free.

3 TO 5 YEARS

Once your kid can draw, why not create books together, with written words by you, and your little muse's stories and images? To track their growing imaginations, ask them to draw the same scene four different ways through the year following the change of the seasons. Ask a kid to draw a bouquet and press a flower from the same bunch. Visit a photo booth together and pull silly faces, and be sure to keep those first Mother's Day, birthday, and Christmas cards. The importance of what you note and keep now is not just for you but for the budding self-esteem and sense of discovery of your little autobiographer.

A QUICK NOTE ON PHOTOS
AND ACTION FOOTAGE

Unspoken convention often rules family snapshots, and so we end up with pictures of grandparents holding babies as if they were freshly caught fish. Instead, imagine your most intimate and sweetest moments as photos: baby finally asleep, you asleep with baby, baby swimming for the first time, baby in the bath with you, baby flying as Daddy throws him in the air, baby completely covered in food—then do your best to shoot them all. Use black-and-white film or very fast film for intense colors, and play with abstraction, cropped compositions, and close-ups.

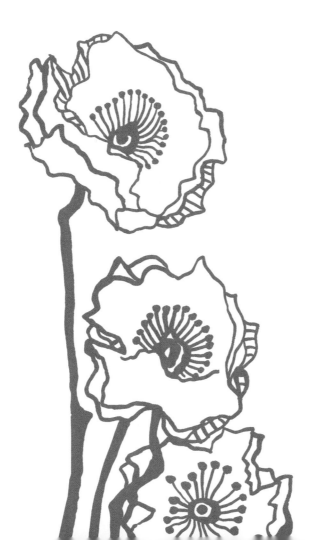

21. THE MOTHER WITHOUT A HEAD

How to Put Yourself Back in the Picture

When I became a mother, I lost my head. Literally. In the Christmas photos of our freshly hatched family, my son engulfs the whole frame and is plopped majestically on a set of rather fat white knees: mine. In the Mother's Day photos, the baby is on a blanket, attempting to stand for the first time. A pair of hands with chipped shell-pink nail polish steadies his waist, and somewhere above his domelike head is a square, pale chin: again, mine. There is a growing gallery of father and son photos on my laptop. There are hundreds of moody, masculine, almost heroic images, and sometimes, but very rarely, there is a pale, haggard woman in the background. She looks like a ghost in a Japanese horror movie, ever present but not quite in the picture. Like human mist. And that is one of the best

metaphors for motherhood I can find; it's a job that makes you both central and peripheral. More often than not, you find yourself behind the lens, behind the scenes, or behind the baby. Mummy as landscape. Mummy as wallpaper. Mummy as physical prop, a sort of human plinth, for the support of the star: her child.

I smiled in disbelief when my friend Charlotte, a spectacular French blond Yummy in her twenties, warned grimly, "Watch, people will be talking to your chest and not to your eyes for a whole year! It's the social guillotine, Madame! Suddenly you will be the woman without a head!" *Mais non? Mais oui!* If your child is pretty, it is also pretty likely that you will start to feel more like his publicist or a paparazzi bodyguard than a blood relation. On terrible days, I wear heavy chocolate brown mascara so that my eyelashes "match" my son's. This genetic paranoia arose after one very tactless woman looked at my son and blurted, "He's gorgeous, such long lashes!" and in the next breath, "He looks nothing like you." Of course, my depletion is the ticket to his infant glamour. If you are forty and have not slept for ten months, you don't glow. You glower.

Given the obvious disparity between how you might feel emotionally as a mother (spiritually rich, replete, gloriously touched) and how you often look (like roadkill with a ponytail), it's a hard moment to try to wedge yourself into the archive. Many new mothers become invisible by choice ("Not now, honey, I have avocado in my hair"). It's damn hard to be camera ready in the thick of parenting, and celebrity mothers drive the stake of self-consciousness even deeper. I was enormously relieved to read that Jackie Kennedy had squads of publicists orchestrate her family portraits, even the ones of her in a soft print dress, standing at an easel. This was the image of mothering poufed up with hot rollers and frozen in time with copious hairspray. And the 1960s First Lady look is still big for mother and child portraiture among the elite. Thinking about the composed portraits of New York socialites posing with their children in mansions in Maine and estates on the pampas, I look around my living room and laugh. Who on earth is ready for their close-up in the first year of mothering? Whatever we have that fits is often faintly stained. My favorite Issa dress still smells like milk.

So, it is easy to want to strangle those Amazon mamas bouncing on Italian sofas on the front cover of *Cookie* magazine when one has not worn an evening dress or plucked one's own eyebrows for almost a year. Yet despite the fact that none of us will ever look as smugly plush as Angelina Jolie, with her glossy mane and smoky eyes, caressing her newborn, it strikes me as a terrible mistake to constantly evade documentation on grounds of exhaustion . . . bad hair . . . food stains . . . or madness. First, it robs your kids of a chance to see you with them growing up, and, second, it robs you of your own memories. The first year of a baby's life is so intense moment to moment and yet so susceptible to dissolving in the mind's eye. Photos and footage are important; they capture details we can't replace or reconstruct later.

To put yourself back in the picture, you need to cherish the mother you are right now, not the one that means to lose ten pounds or get her roots done. Here are thirteen ways to get your head screwed back on to your body and give your grandkids a glimpse of how glorious improvised glamour can be.

Thirteen Ways to Shoot Mummy

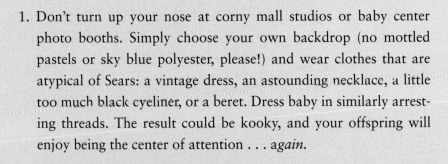

1. Don't turn up your nose at corny mall studios or baby center photo booths. Simply choose your own backdrop (no mottled pastels or sky blue polyester, please!) and wear clothes that are atypical of Sears: a vintage dress, an astounding necklace, a little too much black cyeliner, or a beret. Dress baby in similarly arresting threads. The result could be kooky, and your offspring will enjoy being the center of attention . . . ag*ain*.

2. Next time you get dressed up to go out, insist on taking a shot with your baby before you swing out the door. Nothing looks better than a woman in an evening dress holding a naked child: Just ask Helmut Newton.

3. For holiday family portraits, use a picture that is deliberately unposed. The family all lying on a big gingham picnic blanket shot from above looks better than sitting tensed up on the couch.

4. Choose complementary colors, but avoid clothes that match your child's too closely for family snaps—shades of Joan Crawford in *Mommy Dearest*.

5. Plan the times when you know you will be home fresh from the hairdresser or from a great holiday, when you know you'll have it together, and arrange an impromptu portrait session at home.

6. Always insist on natural light instead of using flash, and think of settings where you are especially relaxed with your children: in the bath, on the floor, under a sprawling tree, or elbow deep in cookie dough.

7. Consider investing in a professional portrait for a milestone occasion such as a first birthday or wedding anniversary. At the time, it seems costly, and yet in retrospect the irreplaceable moment becomes priceless. Photographers also know how to work the lighting to give you Jackie-glow. To get the result you want, take along images you particularly love, and don't be afraid to style the image in a romantic way. Why not wear a 1940s print dress or an Edwardian lace blouse instead of jeans? If you are paying for your domestic fantasy image, then leave the Juicy sweats at home. Style icons don't wear trainers.

8. Don't be afraid to have your silhouette done, your faces drawn in pastels, or even to have a sidewalk artist draw you with baby in tow (he'd better be fast). Formal portraits have a dreamy, timeless quality that photography lacks, and they quickly become heirlooms.

9. Try not to forget to get a snap of the whole family (both parents) at least four times a year.

10. Invest in a huge bouquet, a set of bright Marimekko curtains, or an amazing bedspread—all of these splashes of color help you avoid drab but typical photo settings such as the driveway, the TV room, the kiddie pool, and the inescapable kitchen table.

11. Carry lipstick, a bright silk scarf, and eye shadow in your diaper bag, and don't feel shy to stop cameras until you feel a bit spiffed up. When you work this hard at mothering, you get to call the shots about how, when, and where you're being snapped.

12. Have fun with silly props: Chinese parasols, old feathered hats, movie star sunglasses, carnival masks, and fairy nets. Children come to life if a portrait becomes a play.

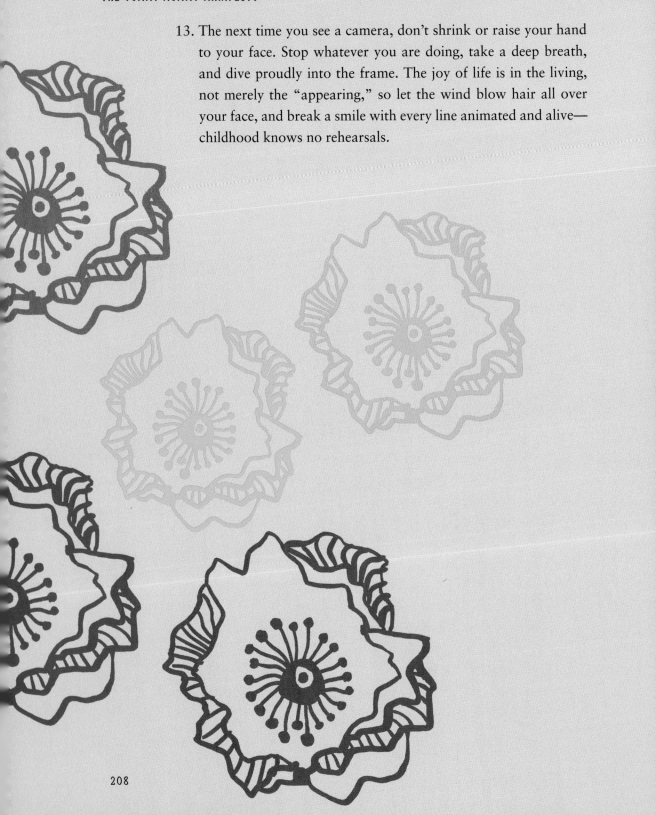

13. The next time you see a camera, don't shrink or raise your hand to your face. Stop whatever you are doing, take a deep breath, and dive proudly into the frame. The joy of life is in the living, not merely the "appearing," so let the wind blow hair all over your face, and break a smile with every line animated and alive— childhood knows no rehearsals.

22. MANUFACTURING BLISS
The Playful Joys of the Everyday

I have met many women who say they have no gift for play. They can structure a day constructively, choose brilliant outdoor classes and group activities, delegate household tasks, and even come to grips with crafts. But they do not enjoy trying to think like a child, or dream like one, or make life entertaining on purpose, looking for games where there are none. "I am not a get-down-on-the-playroom-floor kind of mum," a friend once told me briskly. My heart sank for her, because of course it's down on the floor that the best stuff is happening. That's where you can see where the rainbow-colored marble rolled to, why the drapes look like wizard robes from below, and how big Dad's shoes look walking through the door.

I confess to being obsessed with child perspective and logic. First, because I want to remember all my own buried magic rituals, and, second, because it's my son's chance to show me his tricks, ideas, and sin-

gular wisdom. It's hard to remember how big the world is, how fascinating and detailed life is, when you're rushing through it at adult speed, barely looking down, and stopping only for traffic lights and ringing telephones. I confess to breaking my son's first crib because I climbed inside it and sat peering through the slats to figure out what he could see. After that experiment in "method mothering," I gained a humility about the role parents play as guides and the delicate exchange that exists between our masterful proportion and their vulnerable need and powerful curiosity.

The view from inside the crib was a bit dreary: spines of books and piles of nubby sweaters lined the facing wall. I promptly placed a row of sailboats at eye level and made sure to kneel down and laugh through the slats every morning. To get through daily routines like bathing, dressing, tidying, and grooming I sing songs about each stage. Songs full of praise and mad detail. One starts off very shy singing to a newborn (almost an apologetic murmur) but ends up bellowing along with their toddlers a few years later. Know that your own voice is every bit as good as Grover's or Cookie Monster's from *Sesame Street* and that rhymes make routine a little changing-table cabaret. Trilling like Carol Burnett, I sing, "Diaper, diaper, big brown poo, wipe it up and clean it up, and feel all fresh and new. Pants, pants, they're filling up with ants, I'd run around all naked if you gave me half a chance! Tops, tops, flippity-flop, wriggle in each arm and let your head go pop. Shoes, shoes, they give me the blues. I can't get a handle on my sandals or my shoes."

On our full days at home, which can range from three to seven days a week, depending on family finances and work deadlines, I gave each day's play a very loose theme such as color, water, helping Mummy, things that grow, or the seasons. Water is the best theme for summer, as you help small ones with frequent water play and cooling off in a plastic inflatable pool or the bath. Engage them with ice cubes and food coloring in a simple old bucket of cold water or over the kitchen sink, and then see what water can do as you clean and cook. To get a grip on the elements, it's best to take the play outside. I never miss a rainstorm to get out in rubber boots and jump up and down in shallow puddles or stand under a huge tree and watch the dance of summer rain through the leaves and branches. If I were in the country, I'd do some body painting naked in the yard, but we live in Brooklyn, not Woodstock, so we trek fully clothed to the local park to poke around tree hollows and collect leaves to make shadow drawings, collages, and fall bonnets back on the kitchen table at home.

The beauty of keeping a daily theme in mind is that you can roll with the spontaneous nature of play but implement a lot of learning into the process. Concepts as simple as *up* and *down, open* and *close,* or *big* and *small* can occupy an entire morning, starting with familiar objects in the house and then moving out into the world. Some days you feel like a one-woman preschool, terribly constructive and focused, and other days you just want the time to go quickly. Sometimes the best plans for constructive play with nicely laid-out materials and clever games are rejected for something bizarrely basic. For three mornings in a row, my son has been slotting coins into a plastic piggy bank and emptying the contents on the floor, hooting, *"Money! Money! Money!"* It's my worst counterculture nightmare, but he loves the hot pink plastic and the cash.

A gift for creative, interactive, simply enjoyable play comes when you loosen your desire for speed and results and get a little lost in the process of things. Given a day or two of practice, even the most rational adult can speak in rhymes, draw spiders on misted bus windows, turn the front doorstep into a chalk gallery, and believe the broccoli stand at the supermarket is actually a forest from the island of Sodor (home to the beloved Thomas the Tank Engine). Imagination takes a little practice, but once reanimated from the depths of our memory, it becomes a gradually stronger habit of mind. A reflex for seeking the joy of the everyday.

Some might argue that play is a chance to teach, and much academic jargon lands on the things mothers do very naturally. Quite frankly, early-learning stores dry up my playful juices. All those laminated charts! It's very easy to see what your baby or child needs developmentally; they will play the games they are ready to play, and they will show which sounds, tastes, materials, and textures turn them on . . . or off. Games are best made up from what is at hand. Rolling a ball through an empty cardboard tube is actually a lesson in the laws of physics, but why get all heavy and stern about it? And as for toys, well, anything that has more than one function and does not harm the body can become one. A sock with buttons sewn on. A sealed plastic jar full of beans. A sequined mesh bag full of feathers and old ribbons.

Depending on manufactured toys to play with for more than a few hours of the day locks a small imagination into a dependence on products (brands, gimmicks, advertising, gender clichés, and so on) and puts undue pressure on Mum to keep up with every commercial whim. I select toys as I would clothes or vintage furniture. Some are well made and will last the years and earn their keep, and others—I'd say most—are just landfills waiting to happen. I give my child occasional toy pig-out sessions by taking him to playgroup where there are large mountains of lurid plastic toys and actual kids to interact with them, or let him ramble around the larger toy sections of local department stores. We use these huge stores like a sideshow alley, reading the type on the side of the boxes, pressing buttons that scream, *"Press Me I Sing!"* and looking at the brain-numbingly complex Lego installations. We always carry his own best toys, so he whines less for new purchases, and I save these expeditions for days of heavy weather and cold. The rest of the time, we try to be near trees, water, sunlight, amusing people, markets, animals, or live music. Right now I comb the city for free rehearsals, lunchtime public concerts, school band practices, or attend the orchestra in my kitchen comprised of wooden spoons, pans, and bean shakers.

In the course of each day, I also leave the kid to his own devices—sitting quite alone, singing, "reading" board books to himself, pushing engines along banisters up to his little room. Late at night, I might dip into a book such as *365 Games Toddlers Play* by Sheila Ellison or *Unplugged Pay* by Bobbi Conner, but the next day I am bound to forget even the most brilliant activities, lost instead in where my son leads me: releasing a single balloon into the pearl gray sky, crushing watermelon pulp onto a steaming sidewalk, skimming froth off the top of Mummy's decaf and painting faces on the table with the dregs, throwing petals into the bath, and blowing bubbles into the breeze. Lying on the bedroom floor with our feet in the air, singing along and wiggling our toes to "Starman" by David Bowie. Doing stuff that looks like nothing but contains the key to almost everything.

23. OUTRAGEOUS SIMPLICITY
Underspending for the Under-twos

When my son was five months old, each night at dusk I would wrap him in a long length of sari fabric and leave the house for an hour-long walk. No pacifier, no diapers, no wipes, just a thin length of silk and a strong set of arms. As I walked slowly, he could feel the rhythm of my steps vibrating up through my body. His small head bobbing like a sunflower, he could see the wind in the trees, peep into open doorways and curtained windows, and smile at the rushing faces coming home from work. It felt important, after so many months of anxious adjustment, to feel free with my baby and to show him that all he needed—for a short time, at least—was the strength of my body. By the end of that walk, my arms would ache a little, but we would always feel calmed. We'd sit at a table at an outside café owned by a friend and talk a little. Then home to bed.

Almost a year later, we were standing in a toy store in New York City. A pale, quiet little girl who looked about eighteen months old pulled up in a stroller being pushed by her mother. The stroller had a stereo fitted into the headboard, a beverage holder wedged between the handles (with enough room for three large cappuccinos and a water bottle), a full diaper bag hanging at the rear, a plastic faux dashboard with educational bells and whistles, and one shallow bowl of raisins on the left and a mound of Cheerios on the right of the front tray. Several new child-related purchases were stuffed into the shopping net below, and then, almost as if the carriage were a deluxe Harley, two side-buckled saddlebags hung below. "For her other needs," the mother told me, beaming.

"What else could she possibly need?" I asked.

"Well," came the proud reply, "Emily has a very low boredom threshold. She needs her things, so we've got a nursery on wheels." It looked like hell on wheels to me.

Where did we get the habit to load up our babies for the apocalypse for every outing? Many mothers carry their world in the dashboard of their car, so perhaps this is an extension of our culture of highly functioning mobility. Yet the impulse to confuse organization with hoarding, and intrepid creativity with mad consumerism, is driven by yet another strain of mother guilt: the good-camel complex. Our diaper bags weigh more than our kids! And the "better mothers" have a bottomless supply of long-lost favorite toys, thermometers, and snacks in Ziploc bags. Bad mothers, by contrast, bum wipes off the nannies in the playground. Yet on the days when we pack too many snacks, too many books, or too many very small hard-to-reach objects, we become imprisoned by the whining demands for their retrieval, and our capability becomes a bear trap, serving toxic levels of artificial need.

Even the smallest child learns how to milk his endless appetites, growing to expect his mother to provide sensation, entertainment, distraction, and appeasement. I make my son think the sun rises and sets because of grapes. Not crackers, Cheerios, raisins, or wing-doodle kid food—organic grapes. I feed them to him one by one when I'm feeling playful or dump them in a pile between his knees when I'm feeling lazy, and he's happy.

When we travel, we pack a half dozen skinny travel-size books and several small wooden trains and trucks, as well as discount-store treasures (hand mirrors, little puzzles, kaleidoscopes, flip books) wrapped in old Christmas paper to delight in long lines and stopovers. Other than wipes, Band-Aids, pacifiers, and liquid vitamin C, we don't haul much else. Our diaper bag can be any kind of bag; I like good, deep pockets and a set of good, strong straps that balances well off the stroller's handles. Yet if what I am using is really *nothing like* a diaper bag, the absence of internal compartments is solved by the inclusion of a trio of zipped bags for special items. I also find that a large clear plastic pencil case works perfectly for small but critical items like pacifiers and favorite cookies.

Then there's Dad. To foster a stronger sense of shared responsibility in a family, I think a contingency pack of pacifier, diaper, or wipes should be carried by your parenting partner. Men especially love to stand there looking passive and useless when the baby is screaming for something small but vital, like a sippy cup. Somehow their absence of lactating breasts seems to make them abnegate baby-carrying duties, but it would make sense to make them transport some of the vitals, since Mum is already so heavily loaded.

In my ongoing quest for simplicity, I have rules. No favorite toys trek to the playground. One small plastic box containing amusements for the car—no free-for-all nursery on the backseat. One baby-carrying backpack per parent for short errands that do not require a stroller (my super-simple Ergo carrier is going strong in its second year). Clothes that layer, with as few buttons and zips as possible. In terms of gizmos for baby, my rule is that if it sings, vibrates, or recites the alphabet, it doesn't get through the front door. Mechanized high chairs, baby rockers, papasans, and swings simply take up space, and the horrific spectacle of a baby stuck inside an ExerSaucer crying to be released is something to be avoided. When you put a ban on plastic for children under two, and you spread the word to all who visit you with gifts, you'll be amazed by how much space you can retain in the nursery and common areas of your home. Conversely, when you turn up at a day care or nursery where plastic toys (kitchen sets, vacuum cleaners, cars, and a virtual landfill of trucks, dolls, and trains) are plentiful, you will be truly shocked by the ugliness of commercial playthings. Soft toys also have a way of breeding like velveteen rabbits. Blink, and you will be in a jungle of plush. I regifted almost every second soft toy my son had and still had plenty. And to satisfy his terrible, unquenchable book lust, I comprised our collection of half from the library; one-third smaller, travel-sized books; and the rest large-scale hardbacks. I truly cherish the handful of books that he has read from three weeks old to three years and do not object to amassing the collected works of favorite authors from Dr. Seuss to Richard Scarry and Eric Carle.

At three-month intervals, I would make a loose inventory of the toys, books, and clothes my son had outgrown and give them all (except for favorites) to charity and friends. Streamlining my son's possessions made him cherish them more. Keeping his nursery clear and tidy for each new day meant that he never suffered from the weary visual exhaustion of the hyperstimulated child.

Now that he's nearly three, I face the challenge of my child becoming a mini consumer himself, a little creature with shifting needs and obsessive wants. He doesn't just want Thomas; he wants Limited Edition Gold Thomas (the idea of him constructing an entire Thomas republic from cast-metal trains and accessories makes me feel ill). He has friends whose bedrooms, fueled by eager grandparents and rival toddler toy lords, look like recycling centers. And so, to keep the demands for weird food and expensive, ugly toys at bay, the TV has a silk sari flung over it with a large vase of flowers holding it in place. DVDs are strictly controlled by Mummy, with a rigid deletion of all other advertised trailers. Right now I don't mind playing Big Brother and strictly editing his media diet. I know, this is just a wistful utopia while he's small, but while it lasts, we live simply, and we eat lots and lots of grapes.

Part 3

TODDLERS, TIARAS, AND EVERYDAY TRANSGRESSIONS

24. HOW OLD IS A YOUNG MOTHER?

The Knees Are Going, but the Rebellion Carries On

Older mothers are becoming more common all over the world, but they have yet to be accepted into the realms of yummy glamour. To still be hell-in-a-wrap-dress at a preschool PTA meeting well over thirty-five takes some application. When you become a mum and turn forty at the same time, you face two roadblocks to sensuality and style: "mom" dressing *and* older woman dressing, which are famous for their unspoken laws of restraint. *Tasteful* and *practical* are the first words that spring to mind. Oh, and *sturdy* too. In my playground, if you wear a miniskirt, lipstick, or a push-up bra, most other mothers assume you are the nanny or the second wife/step mama. I love being called the nanny. I am forty-two.

The older moms in my neighborhood form a heavily educated, heavily mortgaged clique. They don't wear makeup, cowboy boots, or dangly earrings. No time to shop. They don't gossip in that chirpy way that really young mothers do. No reason. They are self-possessed and very stretched; many have packed in a twenty-year career before starting a family, and some of them are still maintaining one. Their plain, no-nonsense almost Puritan look (tight chignon, Timberlands, Black-Berry in hand) is a little forbidding to a less composed or simply much younger woman, to a woman who has never read *The New Yorker,* to a woman who might still chew gum. By a stroke of inverse snobbery, I almost always gravitate to the gum chewers, to the mothers who are twenty years younger and raw to the job, or to the odd grandmother with a wild look in her eye. Wisdom often skips a generation in either direction, and I am allergic to my own demographic. Hated tight-knit groups at high school, hate them now.

Drifting to the *other* side of the playground, I have to keep up with the girls whose crashing estrogen doesn't mess with their knee joints and who can chase a toddler and not draw breath. I love it so much when they tell me they're bone tired. God bless! My girlfriend Paulina is thirty-one, a mother of a toddler and a one-year-old, and the healthiest female on the planet. She drinks liquid chlorophyll and noni juice for breakfast. And yes, she gets tired. But the beauty of her complaining is that she never puts it down to age, simply the nature of the job. Mothering is exhausting, hard on your body, and testing to your spirit. My mother had her first baby very young, and she still tells me how the lack of sleep just killed her. As an older mother, that's an incredible comfort, but facts are facts: Sometimes my skeleton feels like it is going to collapse like a deck of cards. Sometimes when I'm on my knees under the crib at two in the morning groping around for a pacifier, I grumble (half joking), "This is no job for an old lady!" Yet I swear that the energy of new children is in fact the secret fountain of youth. Goofing off, daydreaming, and sitting around making stuff are profoundly beautifying, as restful as meditation, but sweeter. Sniffing my son's chestnut wisps makes my skin flush like a rose. Seeing myself through his eyes, I find no cracks, no fragility, no decay. And yet I'm sure in five years he will turn to me as my girlfriend Nicky's daughter did and pronounce very loudly, "Mummy, you're so-ooo old." He'll be right, but then everybody looks ancient when you're five.

Any mother over the age of thirty-five facing the conception drama head-on will ask herself if she should or could have started younger. Fertility is possibility. Young mothers grow up side by side with their daughters almost like sisters, and they can wear the same jeans. Later on, these girl-mothers may choose to start the cycle all over again and have one last baby. A final gift. I had my chance years ago. At twenty-eight my eggs were ripe gold, and my body was like a lightning rod, but my mind was a dispersing cloud. Chasing this boy and that band, traveling in single-engine planes to remote islands, surviving by waitressing, I lived for tenuous pleasures. Perhaps a baby would have matured me, but perhaps that baby would have been sleeping in a field at a rock festival next to a man who wasn't his dad.

In life, as in movies, the heroine rarely gets a chance to shake free of her inevitable duty to mature and slow down. The wildness is followed by the steadiness, and those who try to steal back youth look ludicrous: less like *Thelma & Louise,* more like *The Banger Sisters.* Yet mothers of all ages have a moment where they wonder about the world outside their house and the other lives they might be living. My mother says she didn't swing in the sixties, she made stew. Responsibility can be the fence that blocks the view of the frontier, and almost any grass looks greener beyond your own gate. Next month I'm taking my son on a little journey up the coast. We're going to sleep on couches and dance under the stars. He's just small enough to hang in a backpack. He loves blues. It will be a stress and stretch, but I want to show him what freedom tastes like. Before he has to go to school and do homework. Before he has to worry what other kids think. Before he gets embarrassed of what Mummy is wearing to the PTA meeting. Before he gets old.

25. ECO MAMA

Walk Tall and Leave a Tiny Carbon Footprint

My grandmother did the laundry by hand and hung it in the sun, whisked cakes from scratch, boiled the coffee on a gas stove, and rode a bicycle to work. She had one good perfume, Tweed, and one very smart suit, and had her hair done every second Friday, setting it in pin curls and air-drying it the rest of the time. She simply couldn't afford doodads.

Sixty years later, by informed choice, I want to live very much as she did. My grandmother loved fashion but lived in an era when thrift was respected even more. Like her, I want to live with fewer and better things, to be decisive about the one good coat, the perfect silk scarf, and the signature scent that replaces a forest of bottles. And yes, that perfume might just be a dab of pure rose oil. I look for ways to do things around the house very simply, trying to replace the work of

appliances with my hands, and, when I can, substituting mechanized distractions and comforts with quality time for my son. We sometimes lock our television in the china cupboard and wheel it out for movie night. We share a car with another family. We grow herbs on the windowsill and shop at a food co-op for bulk grains and seasonal produce shared among a small group of mothers who get together fortnightly for big cook-ups, where we make batches of bread, casseroles, soups, cookies, and cakes to freeze and stretch out through the month.

In many ways, I try to live like a farmer's wife in the middle of the city. My favorite household books are almanacs, written by women in their eighties, which are full of very basic, natural, and cheap household tips. Marjorie Bligh, a self-published Tasmanian domestic guru, wrote a book called *Homely Hints on Everything.* In it, she suggests making pillowcases for the nursery out of old floral cotton dresses. The intent is to recycle, but the result looks cool—like a kid's room designed by Marni. Fashionably or not, I aim to find a million funky ways to waste less.

Eco mothering just takes a little more thought, a little more love, and a lot more elbow grease. The governing principle is to save here to spend there. If hand sewing a quilt takes time, then I simply steal that time from watching TV or using the Internet. Not watching television (day or night) can give you up to thirty-five free hours a week; more than a whole day. To some, my ideas might sound like they're straight out of the seventies—and a fantasy. The vision of life before the washing machine is terrifying to many modern women. We marvel at the Amish for their slow labor and meticulous ways. But the truth is, the Amish have been conserving their carbon footprint—the individual measure of carbon emissions generated by one person—for centuries, and we are just waking up to the real cost of global warming generated by our insane energy consumption. As huge nations such as China and India grow more affluent, the carbon footprint of each man, woman, and child is increasing, and the results are catastrophic: ozone depletion, pollution, climate change—in whole, an ailing planet.

Domestically speaking, it's time to get unplugged and go acoustic. Personally, I think it's an exciting challenge to know as a woman and a mother what a tremendous difference you can make in every small daily choice. Mothers have huge consumer power. If we really wanted genetically modified foods off our supermarket shelves, less sugar in our cereal, or less plastic wrapping on our toys, we could vote with our feet and simply stop shopping for the wrong stuff, therefore creating a gap in the market for the right stuff. And when you become a conscious shopper, an energy conserver, and a recycler, you immediately create your own small but intensely powerful environment-friendly lifestyle. Something as simple as changing your brand of lightbulbs makes a difference, and from there each small choice rooted in energy conservation (and thrift) has a magical way of leading to a far richer quality of life.

Simplicity fosters creativity, and creativity makes everyone feel competent and happy. Take a look at a child who has baked something or decorated a wall in her room herself. Compare these joys with the deep disconnect created by screen-based recreation. The more you use handmade children's toys, the less you watch TV; the more time spent outdoors, the better your family's health and emotional connection; the fresher the food you eat, the more energy you have for . . . making puppets out of socks and kites out of hand-painted newspaper, among a million other things. At first, this outlook takes a bit of effort, a bit like running a summer camp from home, but if this is what it takes to save the planet and make a childhood richer, I say bake those apples and keep those kids out of McNasty's, build that cubby house and throw away the handheld computer toys. Make a game from recycling, and lead the little ones out of the malls and toy stores and back into the woods and gardens. The only way to really love the earth is to roll in it from time to time. (PS: Please skip along to my website www.yummy mummymanifesto.com for eco-housekeeping, recipes, links, and ideas.)

26. MESS

Martha, Mania, and the Middle Road

The ideal 1950s house was fanatically sparse. As clean as a mental asylum, the midcentury domestic dream was a static display unit for new appliances, scrubbed surfaces, and small self-consciously artistic touches: an Italian ceramic bowl here, a seashell there. Objects floated on divider shelves with a decisive, and well-dusted, flourish. Gentle pastel colors such as mint green and lilac prevailed, with splashes of lemon yellow and fire engine red to jog the retina. Clutter, like dust, was taboo. To maintain a home that looked as spiffy as a furniture showroom took rigorous planning, a large sacrifice of time, and repetitious action that bludgeoned personal creativity.

Feminists argued that their mothers' souls had been literally sucked up into the bag of a vacuum cleaner, and responded with a minimalist and deliberately ambivalent attitude to housework. In her refreshingly glib 1978 self-help bible *Superwoman*, Shirley Conran espoused domestic shortcuts that would make Martha Stewart wince: wash-and-wear duvet covers flung over unmade beds, fast and furious Crock-Pot casseroles, and a frankly revolting antihousekeeping stance. To deal with an old-fashioned mother-in-law, Conran blithely suggested: "Never mind scrubbing and polishing. Just fill a huge vase with flowers and push a strong gin and tonic into her hand." Love that.

My mother belonged to *that* generation, the un-ironed sisterhood who agreed that life was indeed too short to stuff a mushroom, plump a pillow, or dust a damn lampshade. I don't believe we *owned* lampshades, just Noguchi paper lanterns from Chinatown, and clip-on lamps from the hardware store. "Furniture," my mother always said, "makes me feel so heavy, so tired. And furniture that matches is the living end." Hideous. So instead we sat on the floor, Moroccan-style.

Our very seventies communal cleaning routine involved the fast and furious filling of garbage bags, the secret cosseting of empty closets, and any leftover miscellanea being stuffed under the bed. In our quest for speedy cleaning, we were almost feral, and yet there were always fresh flowers and mountains of cheap fruit such as lemons or hard green apples on the dining room table and an amazing Balinese sarong slung over the windows where curtains had been. "Aesthetics," my father said through a plume of Marlboro cigarette smoke, "are more important than good taste; aesthetics mean you have a point of view." From an early age, I realized that "aesthetics" provided the distractions that concealed our obvious but very inventive poverty: A rustic kilim covered bare boards and the ripped patch of Depression-era linoleum; a poster of Matisse's red studio covered a door with a great big crack down the middle; a massive fern dominated the kitchen and detracted from the fact that the ceiling was no more than a wooden lattice and a sagging panel of plasterboard. We had moved to Australian suburbia in 1977 to soften the edges of seven hard years spent in the urban heart of New York City, and we were the shame of the neighborhood. The side of the house that we rented was painted half Indian red and half chocolate brown. No one in the family can remember if we ran out of paint, or if my mother decided she hated the neighbors sufficiently to halt all works. Our poor, put-upon, next-door neighbors.

On Saturday mornings, when our entire family slept till well after ten o'clock, we could hear the grinding choke of the lawn mower, the squeak of sponges and newspaper on glass windows, and the dull moan of a vacuum cleaner scudding across dustless polyester carpets. Emerging from their immaculate interior dressed all in white, the elderly couple next door would walk to their bowling club past our wild hip-deep weedy lawn, visibly shuddering with revulsion. When I first left home at nineteen, I recall a similar scenario of lying on a mattress on the floor with my first love, laughing out loud as the Portuguese landlady rammed the nozzle of her vacuum cleaner against our front door and swore in her native tongue.

I was raised to believe that compulsive cleanliness was a mild form of mental illness. How could people relax, think, or possibly create if they were perpetually wiping down the counter or straightening the drapes? The houses of very clean people still strike me as airless and tense, less for the methodical routines of their watchful occupants than for the sheer potential for havoc: a fallen lipstick, a tumbling claret bottle, or a child with a fistful of crayons. A neat freak with a child has a double burden, as kids are all about damage and traces. They are rolling smudges in human form, like Pigpen from *Peanuts* with an octopus reach. Perhaps in response to this fact, my mother designated specific areas for intense levels of mess, which meant freedom and bliss for us kids. On the old wooden wall by the telephone were scrawled dinosaurs, poems, phone numbers, children's heights, telephone doodles, and many, many grubby fingerprints. For my family, there seemed to be little shame in the personal: why reserve the fridge door for children's drawings when you could use a whole wall? Guests were whisked past this strange, grimy edifice into the heavily "aesthetic" living room festooned with carved masks, native flowers, modern paintings, and dim candlelight. And no one ever seemed to notice that we had graffiti inside our home instead of outside.

In today's context of pin-neat Pottery Barn catalogs, stacked *Real*

Simple storage systems, and Martha's helpful suggestions about how to arrange a linen cupboard (no speedily stuffed garbage bags, please), the idea of deliberate mess seems archaic, crass . . . faintly heretical. Feng shui made cleaning the house a spiritual pursuit. Then Nigella Lawson (the domestic goddess), with her spotless kitchen full of muffins, made it sexy. Bizarre reality shows depicting SWAT teams pouncing on houses to clear clutter and disinfect sinks would not have rated thirty years ago but, weirdly, have become compulsive viewing now. Alice Munro, in her moving feminist novel *Lives of Girls and Women*, described in an acid tone two fifties teenagers earnestly discussing methods of scrubbing bra straps with toothbrushes. Today whole websites are devoted to subjects such as cleansing with a Swiffer or methods of hand washing cashmere. Cleaning has become a rite of purification and an expression of personal control in an uncertain and hazardous world. Women—and specifically, mothers—are invited by many, many aspirational TV shows, websites, and magazines to create a sanctuary very similar to the gleaming houses their grandmothers aspired to: with mud rooms and pies on sills and little aprons hanging on mint green pegs. How does one rationalize this?

Caitlin Flanagan, a skilled apologist for all things fifties (pot roast, lipstick, monogamy, and so on), argues that Martha Stewart's mystique dwells in her perverse appeal to time-poor women. Stewart's squeaky realm is appealing, she explains, by virtue of its impossibility. In the book *To Hell with All That: Loving and Loathing Our Inner Housewife*, Flanagan defends her passion for Martha as involving "a certain level of fantasy and wish fulfillment, having to do with old dreams of wealth and elegance but also with a new one of time." Sometimes I confess to my own dreams of waking up between ironed bedsheets in an immaculately sterile sage green room, but only for the briefest dose of emotional neutrality. The seduction of Martha's world is that of a suburban zendo, rooms scrubbed so bare of personality that one can safely forget both herself and all the tangled obligations, stains, relics, and compressed chores that make up a real life. If only

life could be sorted in gingham-lined boxes and sealed inside color-coded Ziploc bags!

My contemporary, Maggie Alderson, a pithy fashion columnist, mother, and novelist based in rural England, was onto the "domestic fantasy" trend some years ago when she developed an irrational desire to polish silver on her weekends and spray lavender water onto her ironed pillowcases. Clearly this was a retro-housewife utopia viewed through a misty lens distorted by her decades of ten-hour workdays cooped up in an office cubicle very far from a country kitchen or a tray of warm scones. It's hardly an irony that the women who are pressing us all to scamper home and attack the window ledges with a fluffy duster are *not* actual housewives at all but well-heeled peddlers of domestic nostalgia. Such high-profile working women can get steamed up over sticking rose sachets in wallpapered closets and cleaning the fridge with vanilla essence, but they rarely wax lyrical about cleaning the loo.

The real grunt work of keeping a house clean—the mind-numbing and very unaesthetic aspects of habitual tidiness—are outside the realms of the housewife revival and the domestic diva industry. And this is for the simple fact that everyday cleaning is and always has been incredibly boring. It is not spiritually uplifting, godly, romantic, or relaxing. It is dull as dishwater. Soul-crushingly bland. And all too often delegated to the woman of the house, no matter what her professional or personal obligations may be.

When children arrive, the mother lode of cleaning chores lands in a woman's hands no matter what her ideological stance. Hard-core seventies feminists declared housework unpaid labor and demanded retrospective compensation for all women who had been slaving in the home for shoe money. It does seem rather sad that for all the gains of the feminist revolution, most cleaning websites, product advertising, and related media continue to focus on the woman of the house. There is a lingering and very pernicious confusion between the role of mother and the job of house cleaner, and it seems that no amount of chore rosters scrawled on kitchen whiteboards helps alter this imbalance. Vacuuming is not an act of instinct like breast-feeding or breathing, but men will continue to swindle women with their fantasies of the nurturer who cleans. Like Mama and Grandmama before her. Once, when I was scrubbing a flight of stairs in a slip dress, my husband declared he had never seen anything more sexy. The flattery got him nowhere. I feel no perverse delight in donning an apron or scouring the tub on all fours, especially after a thirteen-hour day with an eleven-month-old baby. Who does?

And yes, I do feel oppressed by the constant needs of my house, but the simple fact is my son will suck hardened banana off the floor if I don't get to it first. Cleanliness is a health issue for families, and clutter simply compounds the daily confusion. Mothers need simple systems to make their homes work, and while I refuse to swallow the commercial fantasy that cleaning and fastidious organization are a balm for the soul, few of us can function free of the task. Every mother will face her IKEA moment, the mess crisis that pushes her to accept a better garbage bin or contemplate the correct shape for a paper-towel dispenser. The banality of running a household continues to horrify me, but on some levels I am forced to submit: I can no longer store my contact lenses in a wineglass or use a hatbox as a receipt file, and dresses either get hung up or are trampled by small, sweaty feet. Call it progress.

So, in answer to the fact that mothers in America have come full circle from the gleaming fifties ideal to liberated Bohemian/feminist backlash and back to the gleaming ideal, I offer pause, compromise, and even the odd garbage bag. For though I once believed that owning many, many shocking-pink storage boxes would make my home a restful sanctuary, I have since realized that the only way to have a clean home is to actually clean it. Some wives and freakishly rare husbands are born with that imperative (singing "The Sound of Music" as they iron), and many, many more millions are not.

27. MUMMY'S ROOM
How to Build a Sanctuary

There will come a day in your motherhood when you will be unable to gaze upon bright primary colors without getting an anxious, trapped feeling in the pit of your stomach. Red, yellow, and blue symbolize play, and can trigger a secret habitual boredom in Mama's heart. For as much as we cherish our children, a certain ambivalence comes with the constant sight of toys and quirky, perky kid's stuff . . . everywhere.

Looking through the wreckage of the living room, the chaos of the kitchen, and beyond, we see the spread of ketchup-colored kid stuff leaking into every corner. There are crayons in our suit pockets, the Chanel No. 5 is hidden on the top shelf of the fridge wedged in with the farmhouse cheddar, and tribes of *Dora the Explorer* DVDs sit where your Milan Kundera novels once lived.

Damn, we need our space! Yet it is not always easy to seize room, cultivate it, and protect it. One of the oddities of motherhood is the ongoing sacrifice of style on the altar of practicality. And the more children we have, the less we seem to claim the right to owning objects that are simply beautiful or impractical, or both. Forget the pyramid of Mexican glass balls. Good taste is immediately suspect, implying something breakable, expensive, or vulnerable to stains. Auntie Mame doesn't live here anymore: Velvet doesn't wipe clean. Tassels seem a hassle.

Flying in the face of such a dreary reality, we need one place in the house that is liberated from function and is simply one's own. A purposely posh place with a big, pristine white bed, a crazy Venetian glass vase, or a wildly inappropriate erotic etching. Is this so decadent, really? The corporate mother has her office, an excellent place to be someone else. Here her aggression, her accomplishment, her less saccharine side, can be as bold as an Andy Warhol lithograph, and no one mutters "Selfish!" under his breath. Also, an office can be deliciously impersonal, when back at home every surface is crowded with talismans of bond and duty. Those forests of framed family snaps that clutter every flat surface can feel so suffocating. A woman cannot live in a self-created museum of family life. What about her inner life?

Space provides that visual respite to be completely individual, to retain and reveal all the elements that ignite your personality. Many women don't claim this right even a day out of college. The to-do list replaces the mood board, and, slowly, little pieces of the self are cast further and further adrift. Revealingly, everything really intimate about a woman with children is usually crushed onto her dressing table or literally swept up into the bedroom closet. This simply isn't enough space for a human creative soul to breathe, and for this reason, you need an entire room (even a nook), a huge display-style bookshelf, or a massive velvet daybed that is simply *yours*. The purpose of a Mummy space is ritualistic. Like an altar, it's a good place to go and reflect, but it is also an aesthetic stand against Toyland eating you alive.

Who could honestly make love or drink cold white wine in a crèche after hours? Once you know you don't want Play-Doh martians on top of your jewelry box, it's high time to create an energizing micro-decor that lets your kids know who you are. And you are not . . . Elmo.

CREATING MUMMY'S ROOM

Clear the Way

Though clearing clutter is critical to the creation of a fresh space, space for a mother is not to be confused with mere tidiness. Sometimes cleaning is a form of personal excavation. Look around your home and identify the zones that are purely personal to you. Then locate the areas that are perpetually blocked with clutter. Usually there will be a direct correlation between personal and emotional areas you are neglecting and the rooms and spaces with which they correspond. Before you can allocate personal space to yourself, you need to ruthlessly reorganize room by room, balancing emotional needs against functional realities. If a bedroom, for example, is stuffed to the rafters with books, clothes, and toys that leak from the nursery, it is no longer restful and very far from a boudoir. If a dining room is clean and empty in almost overreactive contrast to the rest of your home, how much of you resides there? The most livable houses flow from one space and one task to the next.

Karen Kingston's excellent site, Space Clearing (www.spaceclearing.com), will help you empty and purify your rooms. Read the excerpt "The Problem with Clutter" to spur you on. Expanding on the principles of feng shui, Kathryn Robyn's interesting theories on spiritual housecleaning, at Emotional House (www.emotionalhouse.com), will help you think about where you're stuck and why. This might sound like a lot of homework, but it's cheaper and swifter than hiring a personal organizer to get you sorted. And only rooms that function well are ready to be decorated.

Create Space within Space

If you don't have an entire room to designate as your own (and most aspiring decor divas don't), then it makes perfect sense to claim a corner, a wall, a series of shelves, or a partitioned space. Most women micro-organize a small space like a pantry, so apply the same logic to a living room corner.

Mark Your Territory

Even if you live in a small apartment, you can claim and designate a zone of your own. Rooms of common use after a certain hour can revert to being mother temples with a few small changes. In my bathroom, I keep my sensuality kit, which consists of a lace shower cap, a cane tray that sits across the tub, a locked drawer full of exotic toiletries and scented French candles, a CD player, and a stack of Italian fashion magazines, and my beloved D. H. Lawrence. Come nine at night, I imagine I am in a marble spa in the heart of Rome, and for one hour, this plain, small room is a citadel of Venus. After my soak, I put my son's yellow ducks and safety mat back on the rim of the bath.

With the help of large, lidded container baskets, the living room can return to being an adult (and restful) space by clearing away all toys and books, casting hand-embroidered quilts or throws across the couches, lighting several large lantern-style candles, and placing a large vase of fresh flowers on a low table surrounded by tea lights. Lighting is the major source of magic and mystery in every room; make a rule to ban all overhead lighting after 8:00 p.m., to soothe the senses and heighten a sense of intimacy.

Altar the View

The kitchen might have heavy traffic, but there is plenty of wall space for an altar. I bought an old Javanese field altar in Bali (a simple plinth

will do as well) and placed it high on the kitchen wall above the sink. During banal tasks, I gaze at a postcard of Tina Modotti, a beautiful pearl shell, a miniature Buddha, and a single stem of fresh freesia. Your own sacred objects and household gods might be even more esoteric. Change them weekly and cast your spells all around them.

Create Focus with Blocks of Color

To make the dining room a more personal space, I cluster all my favorite white and cream objects at one end of the main table and create monochrome tableaux with them. Jugs, candelabra, and vases are clustered with shells, stones, white flowers, and candles of all different sizes so that on entering the room, all eyes travel to the table. At night I set up the table with white linen and white bone-handled vintage cutlery and create special mummy and daddy dinners with no anxiety about candles crashing down. The food is usually simple, but the sense of occasion creates respite and romance. The same table is ideal for drawing, reading, and crafts, yet with the high chair hidden away and all my personal things displayed, the simple expanse is transformed into a private atelier. The same effect would be created with all-silver, all-glass, or all-blue-and-white themes. For a sense of abundance, drama, and privacy, spread two inexpensive bunches of same-colored flowers across three vases of different heights, and pop five individual blooms in bud vases or empty bottles along the sills. Suddenly you're Donna Karan deep in creative thought in your imaginary monochromatic loft.

Deck the Walls

Transitional spaces such as landings, wide halls, and window boxes can all serve as private places if made visually special. Install a small bookshelf in any of these spots and line them only with your own books—a nice temptation for rainy nights or the odd solitary morning hour.

Your Cup of Tea

Forget the mug with a message, Mama! Reserve one plate, one fine china cup, one special teapot, one Bohemian crystal champagne glass, and a lacquered tray just for private use in your mummy zone, or two if you feel like sharing. So much will shatter in years to come. Possibly your whole wedding service. So keep a little Spode up your sleeve and the sort of tea that takes its sweet time to brew. Arabi by Mariage frères or Twinings Lady Grey are both excellent teas for solitude and reflection.

Time Is Space

If members of your family commandeer the TV each night, the house shrinks as sound fills the space. It's useless to allocate space to yourself if you are not given adequate peace to use it. Request the complete use of one major room—dining room, living room, or study—at least two nights a week and plan constructively for that time. I keep project baskets handy to stop myself from falling into TV or Internet limbo-land.

Make the Home Office Intimate

Paying bills, tracking medical records, running the mortgage, and Internet shopping all happen in one spot, so this place should be the most orderly and calming of all. Paint the main wall of your office a deeply pacific shade of aqua or peony pink. Think about lining the drawers with vintage wallpaper. Invest in a beautiful wastepaper basket and the best folders and matching storage boxes you can afford. If this is your sole space in the house, beautify it, and don't be afraid to go to extremes. Go to *domino* magazine's website (www.dominomagazine.com) for tips on organization, vintage wallpaper, color schemes, and more. Diana Vreeland painted her office jungle red and rolled out a zebra skin, and no one was in doubt as to who the boss was.

Paradise in the Bedroom

Of all rooms in the house, this is the one that can most reflect your dreams and experimental visions. Clear the room of all unnecessary conventional furniture: bookshelves, chests, armchairs, framed photos, and drawers. And focus all your creative energy on the bed. An ordinary queen-size bed can be transformed by the bedding you choose, and the "dressing" created above the mattress, on the wall behind, and in the spaces flanking both sides (rich, heavy colors; wild, funky wallpapers; bold artwork; and even multicolors in the lush fashion of *Pattern* by Tricia Guild) make this room stand out from the "pleasant" conventions of a nursery or a kitchen.

Be a Mistress of Illusion

Veils, bamboo blinds, standing screens, carved folding panels, divider bookshelves, and even a brightly upholstered chintz wingback chair can create enclosed sanctuary within a larger space. My artist friend Wendy Frost divides her loft with several clever space cleavers: hand-painted screens, an old Singer sewing machine covered in ferns and amaryllis, the back of a large standing chest of drawers decorated with small cameos, and hanging Indian silver. For each object, the eye stops and rests, and behind each there is a lone cushioned chair, a light cane daybed, or a small writing desk. Wives need to hide from husbands, and mothers need to retreat from children. And locking the toilet door, *People* magazine in hand, is not enough.

Add Sensual Touches

A $40 French candle can actually last a year if used only on special occasions. Send smoke signs to Daddy with your exquisite scented flame, or chill with a delicate room fragrance, oil burner, or everyday candle for a few minutes each day. I use sandalwood incense to draw a

smoky line between night and day, baby time and grown-up time. Night is your secret pleasure—a time for sexy scents, evocative lighting, and big, beautiful, old-fashioned lampshades that cast long, dancing shadows. Make sure one room in the house has mood light. Otherwise you'll never get in the mood!

Bring Yourself Flowers

A small bouquet by the bed has the power to transport you far from your own madding crowd. To be thrifty, buy flowering bulbs such as paperwhites or hyacinths and enjoy a month of ambrosial nectar. Flowers make a woman feel cherished and in turn help her to nurture.

Change with the Seasons

In Scandinavia, white and arctic blue are used as year-round decor to stretch out the pale winter light. In America, the seasons are much more distinct and responsive to both shifts in light and particular customs and pleasures. It costs very little to change textiles such as pillowcases and table coverings with seasonal colors, prints, and textures. Try tartan one month and Swiss voile the next, because, let's face it, half the seasonal clothes and shoes we buy never have the same impact or the same heavy use as what we use in the living room and in the boudoir.

28. WHAT ABOUT THE BAD DAYS?

Mantras of the Survivalist Mother

Until I finally joined the ranks, I hated every homily I heard about the lifestyle, commitment, and knotty conundrums of motherhood. The cynicism, the bleeding martyrdom, the knowing exasperation, and ceaseless self-deprecation all struck me as hopelessly negative. I vowed to never, ever become wry like Erma Bombeck. Then just yesterday morning I found myself in a modernized version of her world: inexplicably, exasperated to the point of absurdity. At ten o'clock, the pest control man arrived to find a half-eaten chicken carcass on the kitchen counter and the bin overflowing with watermelon rinds and diapers. I suppose he was early. The pest man looked Italian. His face made my son cry because he looked like Daddy. "The man! The man! Daddy? The man!" my baby wailed as I tried to ex-

plain why Daddy was away working for two more months. But not forever. The pest man finished up swiftly, then came into the living room looking pale. "It's best if you remove old boxes and cartons from the top closets," he said, and passed me an unopened box containing a rubber inflatable doll that boasted in bright red letters "SEXTEEN—Three holes!" At that moment, the phone rang. "Sorry Mum, I can't talk now, I have a hysterically bereft toddler clinging to one leg, a half-eaten chicken on the sideboard, a rubber sex doll in one hand, and the fumigator's invoice in the other. Can I call you back in five?"

Mothers don't sweat the small stuff. Clearly. Looking at the unpleasant object in my hands, all I could think of in that moment was, Which recycling bin does this thing go in? Paper or plastic?

A sort of rolling triage-style pragmatism takes over when you're a mother, and the really dreadful events seem less dramatic if they are averted in a timely manner. There's no time for what-ifs. You remove a disposable razor from your tot's mouth, and when you don't find blood, you move directly to the kitchen and wordlessly check every babyproof danger zone in the room. Action is more useful than remorse; humor makes the stress bearable. The physical challenge of keeping a child in one piece gives life the dimension of an action movie. Still, we have bad days. Days when it just isn't funny anymore. Days when there is no anecdotal merit to the pain and the stress. Days when you simply want to be rescued or, more simply, disappear.

The day that followed the carcass/infant depression/sex doll episode was even worse. Many stupid little inconsequential incidents began to compound until they culminated in the ridiculous spectacle of mother and child running through a rainstorm to buy a pacifier. A temporary single mother for just three months, I now saw in agonizing detail how small and poor choices can swiftly transform into major parenting disasters. When you're stressed and rushing, you rarely notice the clouds gathering overhead. Mothers too tired to think ahead often fall under the wheels. Running through the rain, I wanted very badly to cry. But I rarely ever let a tear leak out, as I imagine some other mother out there has it tougher, with more kids or less time. To weep would be to admit defeat, and I am never quite ready for the self-pity that goes with that. Motherhood is hardening by necessity; it's the ultimate feminine art, but, in fact, it's a very macho job. Every ounce of excess emotion is fed back into the survival of the species: No tears on Noah's Ark; single file and straight onto that boat.

Finally home and out of the torrent, a rush of warm air greets us from the dim glow of the hall. The scent from the nursery is sweet and enveloping. A hushed house with the promise of sleep washes away the panic and pain of a tired child crying. I sit holding my son for a very long time, feeling his heart beating and his limbs growing heavier and heavier. I think hard about what it is that guides a mother through the very worst days (and nights) and paints a weak smile on her weary face each new morning.

Perhaps built in with the duty comes a sort of amnesia. A pain threshold that grows in proportion to the love we receive. And perhaps we also receive a sense of the absolute absurd complexity of life presented in parable form. Bad days in mothering happen when we fail to get our ducks in a row, or when we can't get to the third item on a list of twenty things to do, or even when the failings are much more subtle: when everybody in the house wants to cry and scream and run away all at the same time—and they just can't. Few would dispute that mothering is an existential riddle, not just a practical hurdle. Yet we always blame the worst days on physical facts—time, money, or a missing pacifier—when really it's every raw, unpredictable emotional pulse in between that trips us up. Erma Bombeck carried on about domestic angst and housewife hell with a dry, endless cackle, but now I realize she was a Buddha of suburbia. Only a Zen master could sail through all this smiling, and monks don't mother. They meditate.

29. PANCAKES FOR DINNER AND FLYING RAISINS

The Kitchen as Playground

When I was a kid, there was a familiar feeding routine in our house. Shopping day, Thursday, was also gorge day, a culinary Garden of Eden where the homey smell of brown supermarket bags promised great feasting. This was the night the kitchen got stocked with all the fresh fruit, whole wheat cookies, raspberry jam, and this weird, almost wartime delicacy we insisted on having: canned rice pudding. By Monday night the pantry was stripped as if by locusts, and my mother would challenge us to make the best of the bottom of the fridge. This led to art contests for who could make the most abstract two-dimensional sculpture from Kraft cheese slices or who could build the tallest peanut butter and cucumber sandwich. There was never a question of supply and demand in our house, or too many stringent rules on snacking in the middle of the night. If it was left standing, we could eat it. By consequence of thrift and kid greed, there was very little waste of food. Even asparagus looked good by the time Hungry Wednesday came around, and we were taught many years before college how to concoct real meals out of exotic and ordinary scraps. Spaghetti can really be delicious with olive oil, garlic, fresh parsley, two lemons, and a can of sardines—as we often found out on Resourceful Tuesday, when we were down to dry foods only.

The playfulness my mother brought to the kitchen was probably the result of having come from an Irish family of seven in postwar London, hardly an environment for fussy eaters or food issues. Dad came from seven too. My parents inherited the Darwinian spirit of the honest-to-God battle for the last piece of raisin toast and the bittersweet sound of the butter knife scraping the dregs of the honey from the bottom of the jar. My brother and I always felt silently grateful for the five absent siblings who couldn't get at our scrumptious 79-cent canned rice pudding. And, like any seventies mum, our mother mixed nutritious "hippie food" with occasionally trashy treats. When she got thoroughly bored with her revolving menus, she'd let us eat pancakes and bananas for dinner, or hero sandwiches, or, on very decadent occasions, a frozen pizza and Coca-Cola ice-cream floats.

While cooking, we were always expected to help prepare some small aspect of the meal, but even then there was room for radical improvisation. The kid with the best aim was allowed to throw raisins into the mixing bowl from across the room, a cheap diversion. Whoever whipped the cream could lick the bowl, and whoever grated the cheese could gobble the last chunk for themselves. Maybe modern kids are too jaded for such simple delights as flinging raisins across a pinewood table, but making the kitchen a sensual, fairly free place where everyone lends a hand, improvises a dish, or takes responsibility for diminishing supplies of the "good stuff" sets the template for inventive eating for life. My mother showed me six ways to cook eggs, told me that melted cheese on toast cures the blues, and that fresh flowers make a salad smile. Sniffing, washing, slicing, and stirring food from a very tender age deepens your emotional connection to it and kills the problem of kids becoming whining customers at Mom's Café.

While it's true that some nights the fare you plunk down on the table might not be especially yummy, stylish, or even remotely sensuous, a dose of humor and a dash of invention always sweeten the routine. If you burn the cake, find a clever way to slice off the damage, ice the rest, and call dessert a fire sale. The packet cake I baked for my son's second birthday sagged deep enough in the middle to hold two small baskets of blueberries. He ate them all. One by one. If you overcook the carrots, mash them with ginger and a pat of butter and pepper. If the kids scorch the rice (I spent fifteen years burning rice!), why not let them salvage the best of it and boil it up with butter, milk, sugar, and cinnamon for a lumpy but lovable rice pudding? Prepare for off nights with dinners that are deliberately dumbed down but embellished in some personal, wholesome way. I love to add fresh herbs, penne pasta, or chopped arugula to a canned soup, and the same principle applies to preprepared pasta sauces, frozen casseroles, and pizza, and conventional cake mixes where almonds and tiny sultanas spruce things up. The best lesson for a baby chef is that there is no such thing as a real recipe, and everything in the world tastes better with something fresh and green, dry and sweet, or heartfelt and original dropped into the mix.

PS:

Here's something I never had the heart to tell my wonderfully inventive father: Honey and peanut butter rarely improve any dish, except a seven-grain sandwich.

30. STILLNESS AT WARP SPEED
Stay-at-home Survival Tactics

The moniker "stay-at-home mom" has a soporific ring to it. Say these words very slowly, and your mouth will stretch to the size of a yawn. It's simply a phrase that summons several unfortunate images: the specter of a woman pushing a vacuum cleaner across a silent room, the image of a mother shackled to her house with a child attached to each leg, or the taunting line "Stay at home, Sunday girl," sung with worldly pity by Blondie. Change the wording slightly, and the vocation becomes an order: Stay at home, Mama—and don't move!

Just as the working mother has been made into a caricature of non-stop frenetic action, the domestic mother has an indelible image of inertia clinging to her skirts, and being labeled a stay-at-home mom just doesn't help. SAHM (pronounced *psalm?*) is a badge of pride for the

women who have chosen to leave the workforce or simply carry on a more traditional model of homemaking made less fashionable in the wake of seventies feminism. After two generations of women who swore they would never wear an apron again, the notion of full-time motherhood is chic at all social levels and for all different reasons. Flick open a British *Vogue* or a society page from *W*, and many very fancy, well-dressed women will describe themselves simply as . . . mothers. One supposes the stay-at-home bit is a given. Yet for the few that vaunt full-time mothering as a status symbol (replete with FreshDirect—bespoke Internet grocery shopping—and cashmere Agnes b), there are just as many who see it as a form of humble destiny. Or a stroke of incredible fortune. It just feels right.

More the pity, then, that the idea of staying home to raise children is seized upon as a return to traditional values and gender roles. My own mother played Howlin' Wolf full blast, hand-sewed velvet dresses, fairy tutus, and vast Indian-looking pillows. She stayed up all night experimenting with dense, yellowed Asian cookbooks with Dad and danced in the kitchen to the radio after school. She had a horror of the 1957 British film called *Woman in a Dressing Gown* and always had her kohl eyeliner on by breakfast. We never stopped to think she was staying at home to be solely with us, and we never stopped to think of all the places she might have preferred to be. We wouldn't have dreamed of calling her a housewife.

Housewife is a word so dreary and so thoroughly out of date that it now has a retro appeal. Perhaps that's the reductive and seductive drawing card of the 2005 book *Happy Housewives* by Darla Shine, whose main claim to fame is embracing all things domestic: from the Swiss cheese soufflé to the Swiffer. It's kitsch to run a dishwasher, bake a tuna fish casserole, iron, and sing to the radio with rollers in your hair and pink slippers on your feet. It's cute and corny and bland, but it's also real life for millions of women, including a die-hard henna-soaked Bohemian like me. On the many days I am home with my son, I am that woman with a vacuum cleaner who probably looks like an Edward Hopper painting if viewed from outside the house, a shaft of

light settling on the ratty corner of a once-white sofa. And I am that woman sitting at the kitchen table on a Sunday night working out three ways to cook spinach, recycle a lamb roast, and reduce the mortgage.

If I stay home long enough, I find myself making weird plans to rip down all our antiquated Pottery Barn drapes and dye them purple so I can change the view. On quiet, snowy mornings with my son, I find myself mouthing the words to *Thomas the Tank Engine* and *Postman Pat,* and laughing at the little whimsies—only to look up and find that the toddler has left the room, and the mother is engrossed in fictional British village life. There's no escaping the banality of simply running a house, looking after a small child, scrimping on one income, and endlessly planning and preparing meals. The food porn of glossy recipe books and cooking shows doesn't really add sheen to veggie chopping, and all of the essays in the world about the art of mothering and the joy of deep cleaning cannot mitigate against the patches of boredom, isolation, confusion, and ambivalence that come with steering the helm of the battleship we call home. I swing like a pendulum between the sacred role as nurturer and the abject reality of servitude.

For example, I swore that I would never do the nagging-housewife *Who's Afraid of Virginia Woolf?* thing until my husband came home at four in the morning two nights in a row. Yet, as if primally driven by seven generations of mad mothers, I reached for the biggest wooden spoon I could find and chased him round the kitchen like a shrew. "You think I'm a couch!" I shrieked. "I have *become* furniture, be-cause you know I'll be here when you leave, and you know I'll still be here when you get home—at bloody dawn!" Since that night, I have re-fused to sit on, lean on, or acknowledge the presence of the big, stolid, shabby couch in our home. I love only chairs with thin, elegant legs that look like they can run away.

That feeling of being stuck comes and goes for the woman who ded-icates a slice of her life to concentrating fully on the needs of the fam-ily. One aspect about the job is that it is a terrible power trip. The matriarch chooses what is eaten, what is worn, what is said, and what goes on in her Queendom from bathroom to mudroom. But then, without a paycheck to validate the work, or coworkers to cheer her on, she can feel equally powerless. A frequent complaint of the woman who runs the seemingly seamless house is that the job is endless and unwitnessed, and mind-numbingly inevitable. "I'm losing it," I hear my friends moan at a weekly playgroup. "My daughter told me what day it was to get here today." So deeply invested in the needs of others, it's pretty obvious that many at-home mothers fall into a state of free fall. The signs of self-neglect and loss of soul are subtle: a liking for the same outfit for many months running, a vague feeling of having forgotten something, an inability to converse about world events, a habit of talking too loudly or overlapping sentences like a child, a tendency to repeat the same anecdotes with gradually less conviction about their meaning, an occasional short temper. Tears.

Unbeknownst to many critics and even cynics, full-time mothering at home is searingly intense and involving. Time is both stretched out till it is ragged, and strangely padded and compressed. It is stillness at warp speed. The greatest challenge for many women is making their day as interesting for themselves as it is for their child. My son has a magnificent time from seven in the morning till midday. He munches oatmeal in front of a DVD, draws all over the walls in pale chalk, dances to Motown, puts feathers down the toilet, smashes wooden trains together, throws my manuscript on the floor, and then starts singing in Italian. That takes us up to seven-thirty. The morning hours from seven till ten have my soul screaming for rescue, for more sleep, for Sting to pull up in front of my house with a magnum of Perrier-Jouët and a nanny. After ten, the adventure of the day kicks in and the knowledge that a two-hour nap for both of us is on offer. It is this nectar, the scent of my own pillowcase, that lures me on, scraping tahini off upholstery, laughing and singing and grateful.

In summer, the afternoon slides by spent almost always outdoors, pestering strangers to love and entertain us. We go to museums and pinch the marble bottoms of Roman statues, we eat mangoes with our hands on a blanket in the park, we have a bad time at Target trying on trousers that never fit, we flirt with young men in romantic bookstores, and visit Marcello's harem of toddler girlfriends. The more time we spend rambling, the quicker the day goes, and the more I feel the child is immersed in the flow of life rather than the mire of boredom.

And it's all very lovely until the deadly turnaround between five o'clock and seven o'clock, when said Smurf has to be fed, bathed, storied, and dragged screaming to bed. By eight, when I have been with my son for eleven hours straight, I go to the toilet in peace, face a caked and filthy kitchen floor, a half written chapter sitting stale on a laptop, and a husband who says mockingly, "I wish I could be home all day." *"Oh no you do not!"* I seethe, falling into the trap of resentment for a day that I usually love but which is always just a few moments too long.

You see, the trouble with the endless hours of stay-at-homing is that to everyone else—working mothers, in-laws, single girlfriends, husbands—they look aimless. Comfortable. Relaxed. Fun, even. Time spent with children, if a mother is very patient and clever, can be pleasurable. But many more of the hours drag on and on and on, encasing the intricacies of teaching, relating, and simply patiently tolerating. Look closely at the mother alone with her children, locked in small struggles of will, great screaming fights, imperceptible acts of discipline, and the draining flow of empathy and intuitive caring. There's all that, plus the avalanche of just basic housework to keep a home habitable and functioning. Not even sparkly.

It's a passion and it's a job, and just because it needs to be done, it shouldn't obliterate the identity and importance of the woman doing it. The worst part of a woman mothering well is that she doesn't look like she's doing anything at all. A seven-year-old quiet by her mother's side in a boutique draws no attention. No one slaps Mama on the back, saying excellent job, all is well. Only when the system breaks down does the "job" of mothering come up for review. And it's invariably negative. Now, this conundrum faces all mothers: working, free-

lancing, or fully at-home. Yet it seems to plague the full-time domestic working mother the most because it is her sole job. How she lives *is* what she does for a living. The pressure this brings to bear is not subtle at all, but huge. It can result in competitive mothering: the cake wars that begin the novel *I Don't Know How She Does It* (Allison Pearson) or the terrible, bitchy Olympian consumerism of the wives of Wisteria Lane.

Many mothers I know describe a feeling of disappearance, a sort of nameless obscurity that comes from constantly smoothing out everyone else's rough edges. Just tonight, sitting at a street café feeding my son lasagna, I watched young women leaping from taxis in short skirts and men rushing to meet lovers with cold bottles of wine and quick steps. I watched these people like a ghost while my son's eyes burned into me, gleaming with connection. One of the weirdest things about mothering without a break is that you become so vivid to your child and so irrelevant to everyone else. It's both glorious and utterly ego crushing. The deeper your language grows with your kid, sometimes the less everyone else can understand what you struggle to say.

Of course, this state of suspended animation and agitated inward focus does not last. Without doubt, the most intense years at home are the first three. Before the baby fully becomes a child. Before the mother finds her way back fully to being a woman. Some days I feel an enormous relief at the way children make time stand still, at the patience they demand of us to study tiny things and make everything look like a miracle and a ticker tape parade. Showing life to a child is a little like spooling your own existence backward in real time. Other days, I envy the respite of a cool office to escape to or a sophisticated lunch with "clients"—or anyone who can speak in full sentences.

The extremes of being home are rich in comedy, profundity, and incident that seem to slide from the mind when people who do not mother full-time ask that dreadful question "And what do you do?" How do you tell someone that you do many, many things and nothing in a very detailed way? How do you say "mother" or "housewife" or "stay-at-home mom" without mechanically putting the prefix "just a" first? Pilloried for being smug if we enjoy being home or spoiled if we do not, the modern face of an ancient art looks abstract to the outside eye.

Coming up on my son's third birthday, I can say that I stayed home almost every day mothering and struggled to write almost every night. Averaging five hours of sleep a night. I despaired over that crazy imbalance but persisted because I wanted to share this time with him. I rarely bake, I run out the door in all weather to stop the walls caving in on us, and every day I take off my hat and bow to the women who do this unpartnered, below the poverty line, in their teens, with multiples, with children with special needs, or who simply start their day earlier than six o'clock. Twelve hours in anyone's house, in anyone's language, is a long day.

31. WORKING MAMA

Striking the Balance for a Life Split in Two

DOUBLE BINDS AND DOUBLE DUTY

Nobody mothers by degree. Once a baby is born, that little body and soul claim their mother for every second of her waking life. Once you have a child, your child has you, on the deepest level. This potent connection is the same for all mothers, but for working mothers it is like an invisible force field. We might not always *be with* our babies, but our babies are always with us. Maybe that is the magic that makes being a working mother possible: Love moves mountains. And American mothers who work are definitely placed between a rock and a hard place.

Choosing to return to work after having a baby will make your life possibly richer—and a lot more complicated. And despite your greatest efforts it might not actually bring you the financial rewards and career advancement you had envisioned before you started a family. In lots of ways, working mums just can't compete like we used to. Single, childless women can work inhuman hours. They can put in overtime and take on projects that vault them forward. Working mothers have less time. Period. Not less talent, not less conviction or ambition, but less physical time. And for this reason alone, everything in their lives becomes an act of balance, bargaining, and compromise.

You might choose (or have little choice) to jump straight back into full-time work after a baby, or you might edge back into freelance or part-time work very slowly. No matter what, the transition between home and the working world—Crayolas to computers—can be a challenging adjustment. My oldest friend, Karen, returned to her teaching job when her son was six months old. She spent the first week doing what many new working mothers do: crying in the bathroom and calling her day-care center several times throughout the day. I don't see this as a failing or even as a tragedy. Rent emotions and a divided sense of obligation and self are central to the life of a mother who works. We leave our kids in order to care for them, and in that process make both an advance for our own independence/survival and a substantial sacrifice of time.

One night Karen called me to talk about her work and her son. At one year old, Joseph is cheerful at day care but suffers heavy colds from the constant contact with other babies. Karen works every second day to ensure the continuity of her own time with her son, and, as a divorced single mother on a fairly low income, she says she's happy. "After I pay for child care and my mortgage, I don't have much left for indulgences, but that was never the point. I help the kids I teach. I love the son I have, and I have resigned myself to not looking in shop windows. Joseph doesn't care what I'm wearing as long as I'm smiling."

Such a graceful and grateful perspective is typical of many working mothers. "Wow," my freelance friend Hilary sighs, "it's just great to earn *something,* for a change." But, of course, generating an income and striking a personal balance are not a matter of sheer luck for a mother who works. Instead, they are the fruits of quick thinking, compromise, hard choices, and the peculiar genius that comes from being a woman split in two.

THE PARADOX OF TIME AND MONEY

If you measure hours away from your child against money earned, you might just fail to motivate yourself to become a working mother. Only a minority earn huge salaries, an injustice on many levels. One would think that if a woman gave up time being with her baby, she would at least be compensated for this sacrifice with the security of having more money. The bittersweet truth is that she might actually wind up with less. If we factor in the dip in income experienced by mothers and the high cost of quality child care, every woman who wants to work must be ruthless in her choices for how, where, and why she is doing it. Some mothers invest time in slow-burn careers, some need to stay involved in their chosen industry for fear of losing footing, many mothers hold down jobs that are merely stopgaps to cover food and shelter, and some mothers get so fed up with their limited options that they commence a new endeavor or career altogether when their babies arrive. I was enormously inspired by the women I spoke to for this book who made creative opportunities for themselves out of the skills and needs that mothering brought. With the proliferation of webzines, sponsored blogs, telecommuting, and a booming baby marketplace, it's a very good time to think outside the box.

Websites for working mothers range from the perfunctory to the profound, but even if a site is a sea of bullet points and weird stock images of eighties office moms and their toddlers, I log on anyway. The best place for information about money, balance, survival, and business smarts is often quite outside of your own experience or even perceived demographic. So forget your search for fancy fonts or bloggers "just like you," a working mother is a survivalist mother, drawing wisdom from every sort of well. Here is my pick from a diverse range of online blog sites and magazines for working mothers:

- www.momsrefuge.com features many brief articles packed with clever how-tos and extended threads on our obsessive themes. Housework features heavily!

- www.singlemom.com is an excellent source of support for issues you *don't* find in mainstream mothering sites and features brilliant financial advice that is both comprehensive and intelligent.

- www.mommytoo.com is written by and for mothers of color but is a source of inspiration to all, with quality blogs and an intense focus on mompreneurs, starting a business from home, and generating ideas and investment for home business.

- www.bluesuitmom.com offers an online job search and detailed information about money management and financial planning. The emphasis is corporate, but the smarts can be applied to many fields.

- I like the communal professional blog www.workitmom.com because of the eclectic content. These are mothers who show you how they make everything work from a pot roast to a start-up business.

- When I want something short and sweet pertaining to balancing homemaking and business, I sometimes pop into www.solutionsforbusymoms.com. Often the simple nuggets of advice make the most difference!

- www.workoptions.com is a website that focuses entirely on flexible, at-home, and telecommuting work. It has incisive and comforting strategies for women who want to change the structure and location of their work without compromising their careers.

DESPERATION IS THE MOTHER OF INVENTION

The conventional industrial model of working more hours for more pay doesn't work for mothers. And the idea that the father must become a workaholic for his wife to mother isn't working either. Perhaps one of the most confronting challenges of raising kids and earning money is finding the job that actually makes the work worth it. Many mothers speak of the "mommy wall," a surface just as hard as the glass ceiling that we butt up against when employers discriminate against us for being mothers or underestimate our ability to contribute or advance. If your field is refusing the flexibility needed to mother well, you must give serious attention to every alternative you can find.

In suggesting that becoming a mother might force you to switch careers or seek training for a more appropriate job, I am not telling you to go fly a kite or reinvent the wheel. Instead, I am trying to point out that children force compromise with one hand and inspire creativity with the other. Once my son came, I had more ideas than ever before and less time to execute them. I had to temper ambition with patience, and opportunity with cunning. This double bind created a discipline I lacked before I was stone broke with a baby on my knee, a perverse new work ethic based on fewer resources but more will. Ask any mother studying a new language, getting seed money for a business, or shifting course by sculpting a new résumé. They don't sleep much. But at least they're not losing sleep to worry. My son is both my muse and catalyst. If I go too fast, I miss the details. If I don't call back a contact, I'm wasting a rare chance at new avenues of work. I no longer dawdle. Few working mothers do. In downtime I simple enjoy my son and try not to sweat the career moves I'm blowing. Ideas still come. And every single one of my best ideas came when I was doing something dreamy, dull, or detail oriented, with him.

MAKING WORK . . . WORK BETTER

Connecting Online

The weird upside-down life of night nursing and long daytime naps is an excellent time to work out what the heck you're doing for work online. The chat rooms, bulletin boards, and postings on www.workingmother.com and the constantly diversifying lists of the hundred best companies (for increasing niche groups of mothers) serve as an optimistic reminder that big companies want mums on board and that millions of mothers are looking to connect professionally.

Career surfing and seemingly aimless domain searches can be very fruitful. One good example is the motherhood websites themselves. Can't find a site for mothers you can relate to? Can't find a product or service? Maybe what you have found is your very own gap in the market.

Networking for Nervous Nellies

I remember the exact moment when I tried to crash back into the working world and kick-start my career. I was invited to a networking dinner in Manhattan on very short notice. Someone had put my name on the list, ignorant to the fact that I had been missing in action inside my manuscript and my mothering for almost two years and had not written for a fashion magazine for many moons. No matter; I seized the chance to feel professional again.

Then I took a look at myself in the mirror. I had not plucked my eyebrows for eighteen months, silvery roots framed an old dye job, I was wearing glorified pajamas, and my lingerie was an old maternity bra I'd grown fond of. I looked a little like a favorite comfortable chair with a long plait trailing down its back. I felt sick. In a panic, I visited another mother with a much better wardrobe. She had to lend me everything, right down to the chocolate brown fishnet tights and the discreet perfume. Sitting on the floor of my son's nursery, trying to breast-feed him to sleep and not crease my dress, I was already an hour late. I walked into the flashy big-city event uncertain in my heels. The shoes, as well as the breezy smile, were borrowed and half a size too big. Seated between a childless, stick-thin actress and a mile-a-minute publicist, I struggled for something to say, some witty anecdote to dredge up from a life spent essentially nursing, writing, cooking, and cleaning. Halfway through the dinner, I noticed the hosts had no mustard. Without even thinking, I sprang across the street to the corner deli and bought two jars of Grey Poupon. Plunking them in the middle of the table, I finally felt relaxed. "Yes," I said, laughing out loud, "I'm a mother now, and it doesn't stop when I leave the house."

Somehow that broke the ice, and I found my way among the small talk and the flying business cards. But there is always that first time, when you walk into a boardroom or a cocktail lounge or a movie screening, and everyone looks slicker and more focused than you. And it's because they are.

The trick, I found, to integrating passionate mothering and occasional schmoozing/job interviews/networking is to not overplay or underplay your hand. Do talk about your family, but not more so than your listener wants to share. Do explain that you've been off the market for a while, but never apologize for it. Do accept a compliment for your outfit, but don't blurt out (as I did) "vintage/begged/borrowed . . . stolen." The terrible truth about reentering the working world is that few people can understand where you've been and what you're going through, and many genuinely do not care. Find your allies. Those wise women who've nursed a sick child all night and managed a meeting the next day. And forgive the ignorant hordes. OK, so your shirt is missing two buttons, your hair is a touch frizzy, and your shoes are Aerosoles and not Marc Jacobs. You're the one with the gorgeous child waiting on an angel cloud at home. You win! Don't explain. Don't gripe. Take that business card and keep moving.

Organization and Confidence

Many mothers feel the universe is in place if they have breakfast and lunch sorted out the night before—oh, and enough diapers for a week. But in truth, most working or job-searching mothers need much more planned in advance. If you are caring for a small baby and doing a round of job interviews, it pays to have up to four pressed outfits hanging in your closet, complete with accessories, and a manicure set by your bed for quick repair.

Because life is not presently run by clocks or even adult free will anymore, you must cushion yourself with almost OCD levels of organization. I enjoy the regular survival tips and organization strategies on the website www.mommytrackd.com and also found some good ideas in *This Is How We Do It: The Working Mother Manifesto* by Carol Evans, CEO and publisher of *Working Mother* magazine.

No matter how naturally footloose or poetic you might have been before your baby, now is the time to radically overcompensate by being extra neat, punctual, and list driven. Life for the first year of working and mothering might feel like one big memo. That's okay. The brain fog and despair of exhaustion will not last forever—give yourself an hour more than you need for almost everything and keep going. No one is looking at you as hard or as closely as you are judging yourself.

HOW IT FEELS FOR A MUM

Working mothers are conditioned not to complain. My agent, who has three children under ten, rarely breaks a sweat when a family crisis hits. Or, if she does feel the strain, she doesn't show it at work. Years in the cutthroat publishing industry have taught her to cover her back by preserving her front. She is a loving, feeling woman with bulletproof boundaries. It is as if the onus to appear professional is doubled by familial ties, not loosened.

I sense this very strongly in the blunt style of many working mother websites. Heavy, really complex issues, such as guilt or grieving over a death, are often addressed in breezy, dismissive bullet points. Deflect the guilt (about working long hours), one website suggested, by knowing you can afford "violin lessons and summer camp" for your kids. "Feel proud in your choices rather than pain in your losses," another urges. The strong aspect of denial that informs such a cavalier approach is reflected in the structure of the sites themselves. Online, everything is compartmentalized into neat boxes: *career, family, quality time, self,* and so on. I can see how this is comforting for women (I love my lists!), but ultimately frustrating and unreal. For in truth, all of those watertight categories are bleeding and bashing into one another at any given moment. When I work at home, I will stop many times a day and run a ragged line from my desk to the kitchen sink, the changing table, the fridge, the phone, the nursery, and back to the kitchen sink, all the while trying to hold on to some tenuous train of thought, some thread of a broken hour. I am here so I can be closer to my son, but many times wish I was a million miles away, if only for some time to do one thing well rather than two things messily.

I stand by my choices; I do my best. I use my old gifts and skills while growing totally new ones with my son. I'd say that's enormous personal progress, but I won't accept advice in bullet form about any aspect of my working and loving day. By the time any of us has mastered one balancing act, a whole new set of obstacles will turn up to trash our peace. I admit that now I have to put work second—it's just not something I share with the people for whom I work.

Instead, I, like so many others, am locked in an unseen Saint Vitus dance between family care and frantic professional compensation. If, at the end of the day, my son is settled, clean, well fed, and sleeping sweetly, I return to work with joy, and push through to the early hours. If, by contrast, the writing is going well but my son is ill, I might use the energy of a creative success to nourish his needs. And if the balance is off, my kid's needs always take priority. The days when work and mothering feed each other are a rare triumph but possibly the point of

it all. Please let there be more books and websites that allow working mothers to show their frailties. Corporate jargon doesn't wash, and we all need more than the spin cycle.

PUTTING THE GUILT BACK WHERE IT BELONGS

Sixty-five percent of American mothers with children under eighteen work, many return to work in the first months of their babies' lives, and many commit extra hours to commuting, overtime, and business travel. We all know that means sacrifice of not just time but connection. The bind of being a working mother dwells in the fact that work is a right, a privilege, a vision, a vocation, but also a necessity. The paradoxes of the modern working mother's life make my head and heart ache: She works to afford a family and sees less of them. She pays for child care at such a high cost that her earnings become marginal. In some low-profit careers, she feels she is actually "paying to work." She earns less than male and childless female coworkers. And, if she works only part-time, she loses access to health care, social security, and retirement fund benefits.

Mothering and continuing to work should not be such a sacrifice. Economically, working moms contribute to society in two substantial ways: the first, by raising citizens and future workers; the second, by providing their own skills often at a bargain price. Many of us have been too busy getting on with loving, living, and surviving to stop and question the status quo. Many of us decide to take maternity leave without pay and have to plan before the baby is due. Many mothers I know feel so lucky to be working that they simply take the money and run. I certainly don't stop to ask what a male freelance writer or a single woman who can pull more overtime is earning for the job I'm about to take; I'm too busy working out how to pay my nanny. That, and feeling guilty for the days I'll need away from my son to do my work well in the first place.

Guilt is like a Medusa head for working moms. It is the one thing that freezes us from demanding better conditions, more flexible hours, or even just a raise. It is the emotion that erodes our best efforts on both fronts: home and workplace. And it is probably the one thing that has kept the so-called Mommy Wars in the media for so long. If mothers are all fighting among themselves and within their own psyche, it is doubtful they will take the time to write to Congress, lobby their local city hall, or take to the streets to demand universal child care and better pay. The Mommy Wars and the guilt trip laid on working mothers are a pretty cheap smoke screen for a much deeper social failing. But, at last, the air is clearing.

In 2006 Joan Blades and Kristin Rowe-Finkbeiner started Moms Rising (www.momsrising.org), a grassroots online awareness campaign and do-it-yourself activist's kit advocating mother/working mother/family rights. Their book, *The Motherhood Manifesto,* spells out in detail the immediate needs of American families and the means to change. Mothers and writers before them had paved the way. Ann Crittenden's revolutionary book *The Price of Motherhood* also asserted that working moms and stay-at-home moms were not just undervalued but undercut. As she put it—

> *Social policy does little to ensure these risks or reward mothers for their economic contribution. Nannies earn Social Security credits; mothers do not. They earn a zero for every year they spend caring for family members. This means that motherhood is the single biggest risk factor for poverty in old age.*
>
> *This treatment of mothers is an anachronism. We need to stop sentimentalizing mothers and other caregivers and start according their work the respect and material recognition that it deserves—and earns. I believe that this is the big unfinished business of the women's movement."*

The unfinished work of feminism will always be equality, but for mothers it is doubly urgent. We simply can't be stretched any further.

If guilt is a cocktail of anger and regret turned inward, I suggest that every mother put that particular social- and media-generated gift in an envelope marked *"Return to Sender."* No one needs to feel heavy for a system she didn't create and is actively trying to survive in or maybe even change. The issue of working mothers lacking support on so many fronts brings out the militant in me, and that's OK. It's high time we became as uppity as a bluestocking; we're asking for human rights, not special-interest perks. What do you want to see changed in your working life, and what are you doing about it? That's what needs to be discussed by the water cooler or at your next Mommy and Me Saturday morning yoga class. Never mind the baby weight—what gains can be made in your maternity leave, income, benefits, rights to nurse or pump, and access to child care and health care?

When it comes to being a working mother, it's not enough that we serve as role models for our young. What the next generation demands is nothing short of revolution. Consider throwing a working mother baby shower to equip an expectant mother with more than just diapers. Mobilize a local chapter of Moms Rising among your own mothers group, or form a loose networking group online based on your industry or skills. Use social occasions as an arena for discussion of hot issues.

If the crucible of nineteenth-century feminism was the right for a woman to work, the issue of the twenty-first century should be the right to live *and* work. If technology can't give mothers the ability to have more time with their children and more flexibility, then machines surely are not so intelligent after all.

32. CRAFTS
For Women Who Hate Them

There are people who can make a patchwork quilt while taking a conference call and rocking a papasan with one foot, and then there are the rest of us. I drool madly over the French do-it-yourself bible *Marie Claire Idées* (and the fantastic website www .marieclaire.dees.com where you can download the magazine online), but there is no way I will be up at midnight hand stitching seashells onto a linen drawstring bag. No way. Yet there is a difference between craft projects designed to impress and intimidate other adults (glue guns are often involved), and the clumsy, quick, fun kinds that very small children enjoy. Making things with your kids makes time melt. I especially like to get out the art materials in the dragging hours that are usually clogged with television (midmorning/late afternoon) and on days when the weather creates cabin fever.

Sure, kids' crafts can be a little bit . . . ugly. Tots will come home proudly displaying dream catchers that look like Chewbacca's armpit, and one will quietly shudder and then display them in the kitchen—some distance from the food. But if we jump in and help create crafts at home, they can include more tasteful and groovy materials, and they become beautiful, for the process involved as much as for the end result. Art bleeds into every corner of life, from arranging the teddy bear collection to bunching wild flowers or tossing a salad. Stressing that art is integral to life rather than a special talent, a privilege, or a segregated activity is the best approach of all. I make a habit of carrying chalk in my pockets all through the summer so that we leave a trail of drawings all over the city; asphalt is an excellent canvas. By making, recycling, and inventing "stuff," we infuse a spirit of creative confidence and sensory excitement into each day, giving the power of transformation and discovery to our child's own chubby little hands.

STAGES FOR AGES

Most crafts that involve scissors can be preprepared (with ready-cut shapes) for toddlers, to stop them from fussing over the forbidden. Judge each activity based on the dexterity (most kids under two love to use their whole hands!), attention span, and basic interest of little Picasso. Quick crafts such as paper dyeing, roller prints, foam prints, and window painting give very small children the confidence to want to make more. Don't be defeated if you set up an amazing array of materials, and little Frida only wants to play with a bowl of ribbons. A blot painting or simple scratch of pencil is plenty for a first-timer.

ARTS AND CRAFTS BASICS

STICKING MATERIALS

- Roll of wide adhesive tape, stick glue, homemade craft paste (safer than clear craft glue and easy to make; please see recipes at chapter's end).

Projects

- Make a paper collage on a dramatic background such as black, shiny card stock.

- Make a collage by sticking colored paper on clear plastic sheets (this looks lovely stuck to the nursery window).

- Make a four-window frame by folding thick black paper into eighths and cutting a square in the center. Prepare the "stained glass" by gluing cellophane pieces onto a sheet of wax paper, allowing for overlap. When the glue is dry, tape the wax paper to the frame and place on the brightest window in the house: *Voila! Chartres!*

- Make a garden out of homemade collage flowers, pieces of floral fabric, pictures of grass and plants from magazines and green shiny paper cut into strips. Dreamy!

DRAWING MATERIALS

- Chunky crayons and pencils 1½ inches in diameter for best grip; nontoxic markers; Crayola oil pastels; large, soft-colored chalks (stored in a Ziploc bag to protect your diaper bag/pockets).

Projects

- Cover an entire page with ink pen rainbow colors. Cover half the page with a thick black crayon and then scratch a drawing into the black to reveal the colors beneath.

- Draw around Mummy's hand and then decorate with hand-drawn jewels or plastic glue-on beads.

- Let Mummy draw a house or a handbag and let the child fill it in with what he'd like to find there.

- Draw faces without features, fish without scales, and birds without wings or beaks and fill in the gaps together, inventing as you go.

- Play with different sorts of lines—swirly, curly, jagged, diagonal, and crosshatched. See what each pattern reminds you of.

PAINTING MATERIALS

- Long brushes, ideally with six-inch handles (if used regularly, designate a brush for each color). For very young children, start with homemade paints (see recipes) and then proceed to nontoxic water-based paints for toddlers three and up. Lay down an old sheet for floor painting, set up easels in the yard, and use old plastic pots for paints and brushes. Dress the kids in their shaggiest pajamas and biggest aprons. Make a communal bath part of the ritual after painting and make sure all the brushes get rinsed.

Projects

- The wildest and best project to start with has to be finger painting. Pour contrasting colors on top of one another; lime on hot pink, or yellow on purple, and then squish and splat it all over. Be careful when pushing hair out of your eyes!

- Fold a piece of paper in the center and dot thick globs of paint along the center crease line. Squash the facing pages together and open. I see a butterfly—no, maybe it's a moose in the mist!

- Make a hands-and-feet mural with a long roll of paper and little toes and fingers sponged with color or dipped in the paint. Full-on Yves Klein–style body printing could get messy, so save this project for older kids in their bathing suits.

- For kids over two, fill up pump packs with thin water-based paint, set up very wide printing paper on an outside wall or garage door, cover the ground or floor with plastic or old tarp, and get spraying. Add interesting shapes by sticking leaves and objects onto the paper, to be removed after the paint dries.

- For kids over three, mix paint into deep bowls full of warm water and add a small amount of dishwashing liquid. Blow air into the bowls with a plastic straw (best if Mum does this because of the temptation to drink this stuff!). When the bubbles rise up into a brightly colored cloud, pass paper gently over them to get the impressions of color and shape. Pass one sheet over several different bubble bowls to create your own marbled paper.

PRINTING MATERIALS

- Household sponges; foam rollers; kitchen gizmos such as old spatulas, whisks, and ice-cube trays; potato slices; leaves; flowers; and even large plastic buttons make beautiful prints when dipped in paint or food dye and pressed to the paper. Choose thick, super-absorbent paper for works you want to keep. The best way to make a print pad is to soak a thin household sponge in the desired color in a shallow tray (a shoe box lid sealed with masking tape is perfect!).

Projects

- Anything that makes a pattern is your printing tool. Mix man-made objects with natural ones (a big button and a cut potato, a leaf and a foam roller) or let smaller children concentrate on one material at a time.

- Make a sponge landscape—sponge clouds, sponge trees, sponge people—using different sized sponges dipped in different colors.

COLLAGE MATERIALS

- Absolutely anything that can be torn and stuck is the stuff of a toddler collage. Work highly contrasting materials together such as foil, shiny wrapping paper, fabric, and newsprint to give a sense of texture. Cut out shapes (circles, squares, triangles) and glue them in boxes of the same shape. Use glue that brushes or rolls on easily, and for fast, clean results, use adhesive tape.

Projects

- Collect diverse stickers and striking images cut from magazines to make your own collage books. Here are some sample themes: *The Book of Smiles, The Book of Everything Blue, Kid's Faces, Food We Love, Things That Grow, Flowers, Cats and Dogs.*

SCULPTING MATERIALS

- Play-Doh; beads; large, flat beans; glitter (place in a coarse-salt shaker); feathers; wooden dowels

Projects

- Honestly, this should just be a free-for-all of squashing and molding and making sure no one eats the art!

- Make potato heads, Mummy's breasts(!), sunflowers, cups, and saucers.

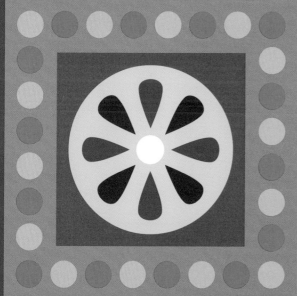

SUPERMARKET ART MATERIALS

- Colored foil, paper cups, cake pans, crepe paper streamers, shaped pasta (fusilli, penne, spiral, farfalle), aluminum foil, string, waxed paper, straws, bottle tops, cotton wool, empty matchboxes, plastic spray bottles, food coloring.

STUDIO TIP: Keep materials that are food based (beans, pasta, and so forth) in sealed containers, and use empty take-out containers to store each item separately. Make cleanup and studio care part of the fun each day. A small tabletop, an easel, and a double bookshelf are all you need for a tiny atelier. Clear jars with labels are also very useful for remembering which materials you have and for inspiring new projects.

Projects

- For a Japanese garden mobile, choose harmoniously colored paper cups that look like paper lanterns. Thread them onto a long string of wool with knots in between, and add other elements that tie on easily, such as feathers, lightweight beads, silk or fabric flowers, or patches of fabrics cut into funny shapes. The longer the string, the more ways to decorate with it. Hang in deep loops from a colored coat hanger or drape high above a crib or doorway.

WORKING WITH FELT MATERIALS

- Brightly colored felt is easy to cut, glue, and sew. It's also really cheap. The only limitation of this material is that it is not colorfast and tends to shrink when washed. Use it for collage projects on a board, for family holiday ornaments, and for dolls and puppets that don't require laundering. For decorative use on clothing, consider soaking it in warm water first to preshrink, and then launder using a product like Shout ColorCatcher. Dry wool felt in a dryer with a fabric-softener sheet until slightly damp. Dry similar colors together, as they may rub off on one another in the dryer (although this is a fun way to get slightly marbled colors!). Depending on fiber content, temperature of water and dryer, and length of time washed and dried, you can expect wool felt to shrink anywhere from three to five inches in length and two to four inches in width.

To get the outlines you need for your cutouts, trace shapes onto the smooth side of freezer paper. Cut loosely around the traced pattern. Iron onto wool felt. The wax side of the freezer paper will stick temporarily to the wool but will not leave a residue. Cut out shapes on traced lines. Remove freezer paper. I do not recommend using an iron-on adhesive; it will often make the pieces too stiff to stitch through.

Position shapes as desired on background, using a small drop of craft glue. For decorative cutouts appliquéd to clothing, use blanket or primitive stitch around shapes with Pearl Cotton or embroidery thread. Any felt being used for clothes definitely needs preparation, but for handbags, dolls, and other fun decorative objects, feel free to use felt straight from the bolt.

Projects

I love felt because once you've cut it, it's almost done. The first children's dolls were made of felt by simply cutting out the outline of a small body and stitching it together. You can make a movable doll by making a skeleton from pipe cleaners and sewing the felt figure on top. The projects I have illustrated are even simpler. Basic geometric shapes such as circles, squares, hearts, and small scallop-shaped petals can build up to make very pretty decorative panels for the side of a diaper bag. I use craft glue for these projects and suggest hand stitching for fashion items. Kids may not be able to cut and sew the pieces, but they

can suggest colors and help you lay out the designs. Begin by cutting uniform squares and work up your small collages on each. For templates of the felt patterns I have illustrated, please go to the crafts page on my website: www.yummymummymanifesto.com.

WONDERFUL RECYCLED HOUSEHOLD STUFF

- Socks, large buttons, panty hose, shoelaces, string, ribbons, fabric squares and shapes, cardboard rolls (from loo paper and paper towels), gift-wrapping paper, magazines, newsprint, egg cartons, fancy paper shopping bags, gift boxes, paper plates, skeins of wool, potatoes (for printing), flour and water (for homemade paint and glue), large cardboard boxes.

Projects

- Use socks and tights to make hand puppets. For hair, pull a few loops of wool through the toes and knot on the inside. Sew or glue on button eyes. The younger the baby, the less fussy the execution. Puppets are excellent for voice play and, believe it or not, potty training and mealtime.

- Make masks from paper plates, cardboard paper-towel rolls, and egg cartons. Plain painted masks are fine for little ones, while older kids will enjoy sculpting ears and noses from shaped paper, cardboard, and cellophane.

- Make a funky car from a cardboard box. Cut a large circular hole in the top, make "headlights" by gluing two small foil pie tins to the front of the box, attach a steering wheel made from a paper party plate with glued-on ice-cream sticks or plastic spoons, attach four large picnic plates (two on each side) for the wheels, and paint a big number (your child's age?) on the side. Small children can sit and play in their car, and older ones can attach string or sturdy ribbon straps to their shoulders to wear the box and run around in it, yelling "Vroom, vroom!" (PS: This project will need help from you with a stapler, masking tape, scissors, and a chunky needle to thread and attach the strings.)

Recipes for Homemade Paint and Glue

COLLAGE GLUE

Mix together a half cup of flour, a half cup of water, a drop of food coloring, and a drop of peppermint oil to preserve (halve quantities for less-used colors).

BASIC PAINT

Mix together one cup of cornstarch, three cups of water, one tablespoon of glycerin (for gloss), and food coloring. Boil up the water in a saucepan and let it cool. Dissolve the cornstarch in a little cold water and add to the hot water, stirring swiftly to avoid lumpy bits. Boil until thick and clear, then add color for desired shade.

NOTE: All homemade art materials are best stored in the fridge in a sealed jar!

33. HOW TO DRESS A CHILD

The Pleasures of Little Red Buttons, Magic Capes, and Unmatched Socks

BABY LOVE

For a brief wink in time, your baby is . . . babyish. Soft and plump and cute as a kitten painted on velvet. This is the moment to dress your infant in ice-cream colors, lace trims, sailor collars, old-fashioned hand knits, Peter Rabbit velvet onesies, winsome hats with big pom-poms, and emerald green corduroy overalls embroidered with baby carrots. Quickly, quickly! Indulge these whimsies now before you bat an eye and have a three-year-old fashionista standing before you in Wellington boots, a My Pretty Pony T-shirt, denim minidress, and a tiara, giving you terrible cheek about clothes. The joy of having a tiny body about is the privilege of laying out their dainty

little outfits on the changing table, never mind their inevitable ruin from spittle and poo.

Dressing children is delightful, and it does not have to be fussy or costly. Just as you plan your own wardrobe, a bargain must be struck between showy investments and everyday basics. I call pricey baby clothes the photo-op outfits, of which you only really need about four per year: a funny hat, a zip-up reindeer suit or holiday novelty outfit, a very smart coat for church and family visits, and a favorite hand-knitted jacket or sweater. Christening dresses are more a keepsake for the mother than a joy for the baby, and shoes for infants are just cruel. Set those tiny toes free!

Babies grow shockingly fast. Hesitate over an outfit, and the chance to wear it will be gone in a matter of weeks. On choosing any item, always look for generous necklines, minimum fastenings, no detachable trims or buttons, safe, natural fibers, plenty of stretch, and internal labels that can be easily removed for comfort.

0 TO 3 MONTHS
Onesies, singlets, tiny cardigans, little beanies, and tights form the core of a newborn's wardrobe. Stockpile these from friends, and ask for stretchy socks instead of booties, which are fussy and never stay on. Taste tip: Please resist the urge to pose the baby in little decorated headbands; they make all infants look like featherweight boxers.

3 TO 6 MONTHS
As babies spend so much time on their backs and tummies, avoid items with appliqués, ribbon ties, back buttons, or decorative doodads that hinder comfort. Choose sleeves and necklines with plenty of ease. Indulge in one fussy, precious outfit just for the cameras, as they will seriously never be this tiny or compliant again.

6 TO 9 MONTHS
At this stage, sweaters and cardigans are still superior to vests, waist-coats, or zip-up parkas. Remember that tiny fingers get stuck. Boys

and girls at this age benefit from tights, as they contain the diaper well and protect the knees for early crawlers.

9 TO 12 MONTHS

Choose baby's birthday outfit early, as the day will arrive, and you will find yourself crying over a hamper of dirty T-shirts. Have plenty of size 1 clothes at hand from friends and relatives, but ask for eighteen-month items as birthday gifts, as the growth spurt of the next six months is the most radical.

12 TO 18 MONTHS

When walking begins, pay special attention to shoes. Soft-bottomed slipper-style shoes are best for the first months of mobility and cruising. Hard-bottomed shoes need to have plenty of give. The next shoe for a baby or toddler has strong support from the heel all the way up through the ankle and a sole that moves with the foot, so do bend them in your hand before choosing. Also buy double sets of affordable shoes and socks, as many naughty imps toss shoes from the stroller.

24 MONTHS AND BEYOND

Finally you can relax about the constant shift in size, as many babies stabilize in growth between two and three and can mix and match plenty of bigger items from older siblings: hand-me-downs. This is the age when outerwear needs to be sturdy and practical, and hats and gloves need to have drawstrings, snaps, or ties. For the sake of style, avoid *total looks* for toddlers or mini-me matching ensembles à la those spooky American Girl dolls. Individual fashion and flair start early but only if encouraged. The kid can matchy match in her fifties at the golf course, but until then, work stripes and flowers and polka dots. All at once, just for fun.

NOTE: Protection is an important element of kids' clothing. All babies have a sensitive response to the sun, climate, and the seasons, and need pieces that can layer simply, to cool down or warm up fast. Invest in a

cashmere beanie for winter, and there will be fewer complaints about it being too hot or scratchy. Also select sun protection swimwear with longer sleeves and a range of floppy, UV-protected sun hats.

TYRANTS AND TODDLERISTAS

Mobility and durability are the big demands of choosing clothes for a toddler. Gear that doesn't bend or stretch with the body can be potentially dangerous, and clothes with fussy fastenings will be met with tempestuous resistance. Getting the kid dressed needs to be fun and fast, as toddlers can require up to three changes a day if they're playing hard and wild. Tune into their natural sense of drama and fantasy and allow them one dreamy or playful item per outfit. It could be as simple as a pirate's belt or as madcap as a velvet Snow White cape. Diana Vreeland suggested dressing a little girl as a Velázquez infanta. The pannier skirt might be a bit of a tough call getting in and out of a Chevy Suburban, but the spirit is perfect. A huge part of the pleasure of dressing is playing dress-up, and anything that inspires a quick change is a good thing.

Supernanny Jo Frost suggests not giving small children a large range of choices when dressing them so that the process is swift, but one choice that is simple and changes often (socks or tights Monday, sweater or cardigan Tuesday, and so forth) gives the child a sense of autonomy. The big drama with toddlers is often related to shoes. Girls especially have a tendency to fixate on unseasonal or unsuitable shoes. Trick them into wearing their Clarks by trimming them with real satin ribbons or little stickers that they can apply themselves.

Trend or Tradition?

The way children are dressed often says much more about their parents' aspirations than their own budding personalities. Hit the Upper East Side in Manhattan, and you will see flocks of mini-aristos in

Ralph Lauren cashmere pullovers, button-down shirts, and chinos. Then visit Brooklyn's Williamsburg to find tiny grunge rockers in message T-shirts, hand-painted Converse sneakers, and baby Diesel jeans. The extremes of traditional or trendy fashion can rob children in different ways. If they are made to look too crisp, groomed, and overly mature, their little spirits seem inhibited by a sense of pompous display. (Who wouldn't be prissy and tense in a $400 Italian Viyella party dress with a starched voile collar?) And, if they are strutting around in an Iggy Pop T-shirt and camouflage combat pants, they seem to be copping an attitude that is a little too cool for school. Far more winsome is the joy of letting kids wear the clothes utterly specific to childhood: Mary Janes, stripy leggings, pom-pom ponchos, ballet skirts, loud polka dots, rickrack trim, *broderie anglaise,* sailor suits, dungarees, hats with propellers on top. *No* hot pants with *Angel* written across the rump, please. One has the rest of life to look sophisticated, sexy, rich, or rebellious, but there is only early childhood to be sweet and soft and willfully silly.

The Gender Ghettos

Shopping for tots can feel oddly lopsided. The boys get all the rough-and-tumble practical play gear, and the girls get all the great colors, cool sleeve and trouser cuts, and groovy prints. I resent the ways boys' clothes are routinely decorated with trucks, cars, trains, hardware, and machinery, while girls get the natural world, from fish and flowers to butterflies and rainbows. For this reason, I have always let my son cross-dress: He gets girls' coats in winter because they have fur collars and funky linings, and socks with ladybugs and love hearts. He loves girls' shoes in bright orange, purple, and red. To make him bully proof, I usually team psychedelic or cutesy items with tough denims and butch checks. For girls, I feel the mind-set of being able to do anything, move anywhere, and keep up with the boys is fostered by letting them roll around in very active and tough playwear. Boys' overalls are perfect. The creeping passivity of girlhood begins with clothes that make them feel more delicate, precious, or fancy than they need to. Tell your little girl that a real princess is prepared to let her plastic tiara go flying and rescue it from the dust all by herself! Head-to-toe pink might be demanded, but if a girl looks like a marshmallow or a fragile fairy, she will be treated like one. Fight for her spirit and let her wear fire-engine red or feisty emerald green.

Vintage Victory

My son is dressed in 80 percent vintage. His threads come from friends, consignment stores, and eBay. This way he gets to wear designer labels, amazing older items such as hand knits and handmade shirts, trendy nonessential items (like mini-tuxedo pants and black silk neckties for birthday parties), and a more diverse array of basics at a price that leaves me adequate money for toys and books. My tips for the best secondhand baby shopping are very simple:

- If a baby consignment store doesn't exist in your area, set up a monthly clothes swap among your friends, mothers group, or church. Some moms label all their clothes and only loan them out, but this can be a major pain for tiny or matching items. Share your used clothes in the full spirit of letting go, and you'll be amazed what will arrive in their place.

- Search eBay and craigslist for job lot baby clothes rather than buying individual items (who has the time?). Make sure the pieces are from a smoke-free and pet-free home.

- Scour vintage stores for adult clothes that make for good dress-ups. A perfectly hideous, glitzy, frilly eighties prom dress can convert nicely to a toddler ball gown with some cutting down, and all children love hats and capes of all kinds. The evening capelets and shrugs that were so trendy in past seasons make great magic capes for tots.

PS:

- Vintage kids' clothes of the most enduring value are hand knits in natural fibers; well-tailored, lined overcoats; hand-embroidered party dresses; antique lace occasion pieces; and velveteen snowsuits in good condition. I keep very delicate items: Victorian bonnets, midcentury knits, and lace booties, and frame them for the nursery.

- Keep a budget in mind and balance it against the realistic cost of new clothes. For example, good T-shirts can be found cheaper new at Target, so spend vintage dollars on more complex, rare, or designer items. I would spend more than $25 on an item only for a special occasion or an heirloom piece.

- The least satisfying used items are always shoes and socks. Invest in new ones for hygiene and comfort. Secondhand chic need never feel down at the heel.

34. WHEN MAMA RECLAIMS THE NIGHT

An Invitation to Walk on the Wild Side

There will come a time late in the second year of your first baby's life when you will look at the moon and simply want to howl. When you will walk outside to put out the trash and want to keep walking . . . until you reach music. Do not stop to add up how many nights you have spent crib-side, guarding the baby like a she-wolf. Don't think about how the time has passed like the hours inside the walls of a convent: in the form of one long, starlit sigh.

Now, suddenly the air in the nursery strikes you as stifling rather than sweet, and you want to run. Just run and leave the wild weight of perpetual caring behind. All the socially condoned releases from the house that involve family or shopping or dinner dates or church don't

appeal in this moment. Frankly, woman, you've got to let your hair down—and shake it.

This is about the time that you get an itch to buy a dark perfume, a backless evening dress, some heels, and hammer the stereo with the White Stripes. You feel a weird primal restlessness at the sight of an open freezer door or a tangle of unwashed laundry. Mama needs a break; she needs to taste her freedom and simply transgress from the well-oiled routine in some small way. I am not saying that we want to forget we are mothers; how would that be possible? Rather, we want to know we can let go, if just for a few crazy hours, and not return to a house in flames. Father or grandmother or sister needs to seize the reins and be deeply trusted with the honor of holding down the fort.

Risk. It's not a word closely associated with mothering, and yet we conduct calculated acts of daring every day. We watch a toddler climb to the precipice of a sofa, without moving, just trusting and perhaps praying until the little body gains its balance and its pride. We nonchalantly sit in front of a mountain of bills or a jaded supervisor at work. We face some sort of impossible emotional or domestic calamity each day and act like a pro despite a total lack of sleep or experience or courage or money—or all four. Is it any wonder that after almost two years of intensive mothering we need to find our heart's desire somewhere outside of the house? I did. I still do.

At twenty months postpartum I had the crazy urges for anonymity, secrecy, and glamour that French writers, spies, and actresses seem to have. To walk into a beautiful, dimly lit bistro and silently drink a tall glass of champagne without a sign blinking over my head announcing "Runaway Mother." To dance in perfect time to a song I've never heard. To stand safe and purely solitary under a grove of moonlit trees like a heroine from a D. H. Lawrence novel. To go to a hotel room just to read a book, as Julianne Moore did so furtively in *The Hours*.

One might presume that all this burning need is the prelude to an affair. The smoldering buildup to the postman knocking twice, three times, and then pounding down the door. But truly, this is not the sort of transgression I have in mind. Freedom, for all mothers and many,

many wives, is rarely just a matter of sex. Fidelity, like motherhood, is a job with security and benefits. Trust is like a wish that we live into being. But expression, the really deep kind that bubbles up in times of rare silence, is rarely satisfied by a flitting romance. The 1950s really are another century ago.

Inside the newfound passion of mothering, millions of women find a reservoir of buried emotion and distilled courage of limitless potential. Put simply, we find our feet and our guts at the same time. And in this discovery, we get the urge to venture out into a subtly expanded horizon or commit a major radical act. A little tango class here, a little grassroots activism there. I don't think it is a coincidence that the major revolutionaries of history were mothers or that the most erotic, spirited, and shocking free thinkers had children before they became famous. Children provide that strange contradictory mix of total wildness and a total need for security. We love them savagely, and at the same time shelter them within tight boundaries and benign routines. Yet within this ordered new realm, once the boundaries are in place and the lunches planned, we find some quiet pocket in the night when the stillness outside starts to call us back to our dreams. And we catch ourselves wondering just how much we can be: both outside and within our mothering life.

For the five-hundred nights you spend quietly observing every breath inside the house and every footfall on the street, there will be that first night when you know the world has not abandoned you, and there is a seat in a café with your name on it, or a book in a store window beckoning you to come collect its mysteries. I say listen to the call of restlessness, especially at night. At night, all of the habits of day are silenced, and your soul, so long buried under the performance of loving and serving, finally gets a chance to speak. Turn off the television, the radio, and all the lights. Light a chain of candles and listen closely . . .

If the moon asks you to come dancing, don't ignore her. Put on your new dress and go.

35. TWENTY SELFISH LITTLE PLEASURES

That Are Not So Selfish After All

1. *One set of bra and knickers that match,* with lace, ribbons, embroidery, an Italian or French accent, and many other needless, breathlessly erotic features.

2. *A monthly crush* that brings color to your cheeks: The Saturday morning barista who foams the milk on your son's baby-cino is perfect fodder. But be sure to rotate regularly. Infatuation is enlivening, but obsession is maddening. And dangerous.

3. *Chocolate-covered almonds* in the glove box, smoky Russian Caravan tea in a special tin at the office, your favorite scent in your

handbag (parfum rather than eau de toilette) and an extra emergency Chanel lipstick kept in the cutlery drawer. Small ammunition to fend off the banality of existence.

4. *Four really grown-up hot novels* right next to your bed and a dab of ylang-ylang oil on the crown of the bedside lamp lightbulb to read them by.

5. *A flower box* on your bedroom sill that hangs with the most fragrant seasonal bulbs you can find—homegrown or store bought. Never wake up without seeing and smelling something alive other than one's husband.

6. *A pair of very high-heel shoes* that you can barely walk in and don't need to—they never leave the bedroom.

7. *Cashmere-lined gloves,* a soft hand-crocheted hat, and a lace-trimmed, long-sleeved silk jersey to brighten the dead heart of winter.

8. *A magic floaty dress* worn only for dancing with children. Yes, you can also wear your daughter's angel wings when no one is home or when you're making phone calls that require magic protection.

9. *A pair of very elaborate Wellington boots* worn only for standing stark naked in the rain—and matching umbrella for clothed voyages elsewhere.

10. *A cache of DVDs* organized into the following categories: Laughing, Crying, Dreaming, Believing, and . . . Prelude to Lust. Sometimes you need a little help in every one of these areas, especially permission to weep.

11. *Something stashed in the fridge* that is homemade, healthy, and soul nurturing at all times: almond butter and banana bread, stewed apples and rhubarb, crème fraîche and wild honey, local pears, fresh mint for tea, wafer-thin organic chocolate biscuits—and for everyday emergencies and spontaneous celebrations, a bottle of ice-cold French champagne.

12. *One set of exquisite cotton bedding* in its original packaging, tied up with sprigs of lavender and gray satin ribbons, to be placed on the bed when the world feels completely stale.

13. *A dress that really suits you in three sizes:* thin, ordinary, and tired/emotional (premenstrual/postnatal). A well-designed wrap dress can span all three body states, so invest in two.

14. *A private CD player* hidden high up inside your dressing room or on your bedroom wall that plays morning magic music to lift you way, way up. There is plenty of music that children don't like, but that does not mean that the Wiggles should supplant Wolfmother on your iPod. Use the time you have alone to blast music that is complex, silly, or clearly a bad example to the young. One day they will slam the door and play AC/DC's "Highway to Hell" full blast; before that day comes, it is actually your turn to be surly and misunderstood. At least once in a blue moon.

15. *A generous gift voucher* for a day spa, favorite shoe shop, art supply store, or favorite bookstore bought by you for you—when the mood strikes.

16. *One credit card* with a nice conservative limit that is just for . . . shoes. Now, that's what I call shoe money.

17. *A beautiful, very personal piece of jewelry* to commemorate the birth of each child. Semiprecious stones, from moonstones to garnet and amber, cost little but resonate through the years with enormous heart warmth.

18. *A simple raincoat* lined with an outrageous fabric such as shantung, moiré, taffeta, or chintz. Why the hell not?

19. *A slipper chair* upholstered with a fabric you absolutely love but can't afford or can't risk for the rest of the house.

20. *Ten minutes a day* doing something personal very, *very* slowly and in complete privacy, from shaving your legs to eating a peach. Lock the door if needed—I said *slooooowly.*

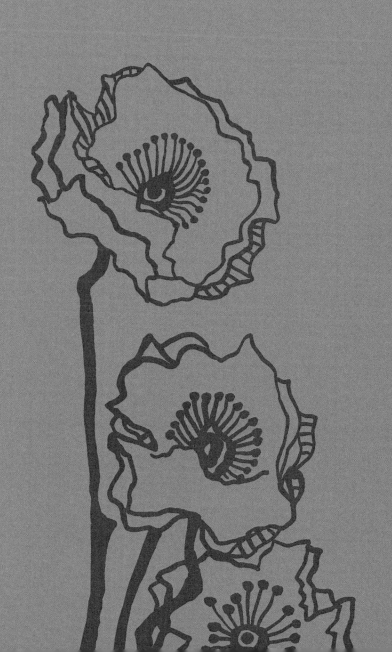

Acknowledgments

This book was a collaboration that enmeshed many souls. It began with a baby. Three cheers, Marcello, for being my muse, and profound thanks to *il mio marito bello*, Matteo De Cosmo, for making me a mother on a rainy and unpromising day and for guiding our family with love, warmth, and sweet humor.

And then, crazy applause for my agent, Sally Wofford Girand, for putting the spark of a great book idea into action and designing the best baby shower cake ever. Sheer amazement at the cool head and soft but firm sculpting hand of my bright and lovely editor, Laura Ford, whose perceptions, patience, and persistence made this book a healthy home birth. Thanks, babe. My deep appreciation for and great joy in working with Maree Oaten, who forged the design vision for the book and spent more than two years hammering out layout, color, and crazy wallpaper concepts at all hours, giving this project her very best, even with a new baby in tow. Take a deep bow, Blondie! I would also like to thank George Epaminondas, for picking up the phone at all hours, Karin Calt for her long-standing good sense and wit, and Jessica Adams for her godmotherly and editorial insights. Appreciation to everyone at Ballantine: Dana Leigh Blanchette, Laurie Kahn, Robbin Schiff, Victoria Allen, Alexandra Rudd, Shona McCarthy, Brian McLendon, Jane von Mehren, Cindy Murray, Sanyu Dillon, and Philip Bashe for copyediting. And last but definitely not least, a heartfelt thank-you to the very special people who really helped me out, day in, day out, with mothering and working. Bringing their rare gifts, energy, and calm to our home: Margot and Michael Johnson, Jasmine Johnson, Naomi Edison, Anna Urbanski, Alicia Richardson, Karen Markham, and lovely Lisa Babli. *Tanti baci!*

The following people made very special personal, professional, creative, and inspirational contributions to this project. Please know that every page of this book is here because of each of you:

Renee Adair of Birth Central Sydney; Jessica Adams; Kristina Ammitzboll and family; Guy Benfield; Donna May Bolinger and Benton; Robin Bowden; Pam Bradbury; Melinda Brown; Kim Butler; Laurel Axen Carroll; Aaron Clendenning; Claudio, Katt, and Quetzal; Alexandra "Ally" Collier; Yameek Cooley; Emma Cooper; Anna, Lucia, Michele, Nicola, and Erica De Cosmo; Giovanni D'Ercole of *Love and Hatred;* Jillian D'Ercole and family; Diana and Holly Yee; Kevin Doyle; Warren Ellis; Patricia Field; Thomas Fisher; The Flying Squirrel (Brooklyn, NY)—especially Kate and Judith; Amy Fodor; Wendy Frost and Victor Vasquez; Edwige Geminel; Gimili and Elliot Glavin; Richard Goodwin and Dr. Annie Murray and family; Steven Gorndley; Harriet Griffey; Lulu Guinness; Robert and Helen Harrison and family; Kristyna Higgins and family; Ruth Howard and Harry Sir Barry Humphries; Carmen Indovino; Jessica Iverson; Stephanie Day Iverson; Marta Jaremko; the Jefferson Market Public Library; Jeremy and Jewell Johnson; Michael, Margot, Matthew, Remy, and Helga Groves Johnson; Zorka Kavacevic; Gordon Kindlon and Reynaldo Hernandez; Charlotte, Gordan, and Morgan Kipping; Samantha Lang;

Frederique and Jeremy; Annette Larkin; Steve Leder; John "L" Lindsay; Tina Lowe; Karen Markham and Joseph Diego; Tina Matthews and family; Barney and Jen McAll and Elias; Catherine Malandrino; the Reverend Clinton M. Miller and the beautiful congregation of the Brown Memorial Baptist Church (Brooklyn, NY); Igor Vander and the staff of Moschino and Aeffe; Lorca, Salvador, and Guillermo; Paulina Nissenblatt; Peggy O'Mara and *Mothering* magazine's editorial staff; Karen Pakula; Esther Perel; Playgroups NSW, and the very special mothers at the Lilyfield Playgroup; Delores Richardson and her family, the heart of Clermont Avenue; Hilary Robertson and Gus; Ruth Roche at Rare Hair Salon; Marina Rozenman; Luca Scalisi; Wendy Schelah; Smooch Café (Brooklyn, NY); Sabino and Stephania Ernesto Solo; Anna Sui; Urban Spring Café (Brooklyn, NY); Jillian Veran, director of makeup artistry, Prescriptives; Michael Wagstaff and the Bratz Brigade; Pumpkin Wentzel; Miss Lillian and Miss Inez Woods and the Woods family; Elizabeth Wynn, Tara Wynne, and Pippa Masson at Curtis Brown (London).

Index

Born in England and raised in London, New York, and Sydney, ANNA JOHNSON has been writing and drawing for twenty-four years, mothering for going on three, and baking lumpy pineapple carrot cake for six months. She is the author of *Three Black Skirts: All You Need to Survive* and *Handbags: The Power of the Purse.* Anna has written for V*ogue, Vanity Fair, InStyle, Elle, The Guardian,* and *Condé Nast Traveler.* While writing this book, she thought of many tangents, ideas, and recipes that could not be contained within its pages, so please go to www.yummymanifesto.com for further madness and inspiration. Anna lives in Brooklyn with her husband, son, four vintage teapots, one pair of Wellington boots, and not a single pet.